DAILY LIVES OF

Civilians in Wartime Europe, 1618–1900

Recent Titles in the
Greenwood Press "Daily Life through History" Series

Science and Technology in Medieval European Life
Jeffrey R. Wigelsworth

Civilians in Wartime Africa: From Slavery Days to the
Rwandan Genocide
John Laband, editor

Christians in Ancient Rome
James W. Ermatinger

The Army in Transformation, 1790–1860
James M. McCaffrey

The Korean War
Paul M. Edwards

World War I
Jennifer D. Keene

Civilians in Wartime Early America: From the Colonial
Era to the Civil War
David S. Heidler and Jeanne T. Heidler, editors

Civilians in Wartime Modern America: From the
Indian Wars to the Vietnam War
David S. Heidler and Jeanne T. Heidler, editors

Civilians in Wartime Asia: From the Taiping Rebellion
to the Vietnam War
Stewart Lone, editor

The French Revolution
James M. Anderson

Stuart England
Jeffrey Forgeng

The Revolutionary War
Charles P. Neimeyer

DAILY LIVES OF

Civilians in Wartime Europe, 1618–1900

Edited by Linda S. Frey and Marsha L. Frey

The Greenwood Press "Daily Life through History" Series

Daily Life of Civilians during Wartime
David S. Heidler and Jeanne T. Heidler, Series Editors

GREENWOOD PRESS
Westport, Connecticut • London

Library of Congress Cataloging-in-Publication Data

Daily lives of civilians in wartime Europe, 1618–1900 / edited by Linda S. Frey and Marsha L. Frey.
    p. cm. — (The Greenwood Press daily life through history series, ISSN 1080–4749)
    Includes index.
    ISBN-13: 978–0–313–33566–2 (alk. paper)
    ISBN-10: 0–313–33566–4 (alk. paper)
    1. Europe—History—17th century.   2. Europe—History—18th century.
3. Europe—History—1789–1900.   4. Europe—Social life and customs—
History.   5. Europe—Social conditions—History.   6. War and society—
Europe—History.   I. Frey, Linda.   II. Frey, Marsha.
    D247.D35   2007
    940.2—dc22   2007014329

British Library Cataloguing in Publication Data is available.

Library of Congress Catalog Card Number: 2007014329
ISBN-13: 978–0–313–33566–2
ISSN: 1080–4749

First published in 2007

Greenwood Press, 88 Post Road West, Westport, CT 06881
An imprint of Greenwood Publishing Group, Inc.
www.greenwood.com

Printed in the United States of America

The paper used in this book complies with the
Permanent Paper Standard issued by the National
Information Standards Organization (Z39.48–1984).

10 9 8 7 6 5 4 3 2 1

To our parents, Dolores A. and Henry H. Frey, Jr.,
who live on in our memories.

Contents

Series Foreword

Few scenes are as poignant as that of civilian refugees torn from their homes and put to plodding flight along dusty roads, carrying their possessions in crude bundles and makeshift carts. We have all seen the images. Before photography, paintings and crude drawings told the story, but despite the media, the same sense of the awful emerges from these striking portrayals: the pace of the flight is agonizingly slow; the numbers are sobering and usually arrayed in single file along the edges of byways that stretch to the horizon. The men appear hunched and beaten, the women haggard, the children strangely old, and usually the wide-eyed look of fear has been replaced by one of bone-grinding weariness. They likely stagger through country redolent of the odor of smoke and death as heavy guns mutter in the distance. It always seems to be raining on these people, or snowing, and it is either brutally cold or oppressively hot. In the past, clattering hooves would send them skittering away from the path of cavalry; more recently, whirring engines of motorized convoys push them from the road. Aside from becoming casualties, civilians who become refugees experience the most devastating impact of war, for they truly become orphans of the storm, lacking the barest necessities of food and clothing except for what they can carry and eventually what they can steal.

The volumes in this series seek to illuminate that extreme example of the civilian experience in wartime and more, for those on distant home fronts also can make remarkable sacrifices, whether through their labors to support the war effort or by enduring the absence of loved ones far from home and in great peril. And war can impinge on indigenous populations in eccentric ways. Stories of a medieval world in which a farmer fearful about his crops could prevail on armies to fight elsewhere are possibly exaggerated, the product of nostalgia for a chivalric code that most likely did not hold much sway during a coarse and vicious time. In any period and at any place, the fundamental reality of war is that organized violence is no less brutal for its being structured by strategy and tactics. The advent of total war might have been signaled by the famous *levée en masse* of the French Revolution, but that development was more a culmination of a trend than an innovation away from more pacific times. In short, all wars have assailed and will assail civilians in one way or another to a greater or lesser degree. The Thirty Years' War displaced populations just as the American Revolution saw settlements preyed upon, houses razed, and farms pillaged. Modern codes of conduct adopted by both international consent and embraced by the armies of the civilized world have heightened awareness about the sanctity of civilians and have improved vigilance about violations of that sanctity, but in the end such codes will never guarantee immunity from the rage of battle or the rigors of war.

In this series, accomplished scholars have recruited prescient colleagues to write essays that reveal both the universal civilian experience in wartime and aspects of it made unique by time and place. Readers will discover in these pages the other side of warfare, one that is never placid, even if far removed from the scenes of fighting. As these talented authors show, the shifting expectations of governments markedly transformed the civilian wartime experience from virtual non-involvement in early modern times to the twentieth century's expectation of sacrifice, exertion, and contribution. Finally, as the Western powers have come full circle by asking virtually no sacrifice from civilians at all, they have stumbled upon the peculiar result that diminishing deprivation during a war can increase civilian dissent against it.

Moreover, the geographical and chronological span of these books is broad and encompassing to reveal the unique perspectives of how war affects people whether they are separated by hemispheres or centuries, people who are distinct by way of different cultures yet similar because of their common humanity. As readers will see, days on a home front far from battle usually become a surreal routine of the ordinary existing in tandem with the extraordinary, a situation in which hours of waiting and expectation become blurred against the backdrop of normal tasks and everyday events. That situation is a constant, whether for a village in Asia or Africa, or Europe or the Americas.

Consequently, these books confirm that the human condition always produces the similar as well the singular, a paradox that war tends to amplify. Every war is much like another, but no war is really the same as any other. All places are much alike, but no place is wholly separable from its matchless identity. The civilian experience in war mirrors these verities. We are certain that readers will find in these books a vivid illumination of those truths.

David S. Heidler and Jeanne T. Heidler
Series Editors

Acknowledgments

This book would not have been possible without the knowledge, dedication, and unswerving patience of our colleagues and friends—in particular, our colleagues, especially Brigadier General (Ret.) Robert A. Doughty and Jeremy Black; our selfless series editors, David S. and Jeanne T. Heidler; our ever cheerful and supportive editor at Greenwood Press, Michael Hermann; and our knowledgeable contributors, Michael Broers, Michael Neiberg, Michael Rowe, Dennis Showalter, Paul Sonnino, and Tryntje Helfferich. Our indefatigable secretaries and assistants, Diane Rapp, Andrew De Cock, Susan Hanefeld, and Elisabeth Fong, and the ever supportive librarians at the New York Public Library, the U.S. Military Academy Library, the Library of Congress, The Ohio State University Libraries, the Kansas State University Libraries, and the Mansfield Library at the University of Montana provided technical and cheerful expertise. In particular, we would like to acknowledge the gracious support and encouragement of James Holland, Jr.; Alan C. Aimone, Senior Special Collections Librarian, U.S. Military Academy; and Suzanne M. Christoff, Associate Director for Special Collections and Archives, U.S. Military Academy. We would also like to thank the Earhart Foundation, the Boone Endowment for Faculty Development, and the Institute for Military History and Twentieth Century Studies for funding this research. Last, but never least, we need to thank our ever patient sister, Debbie Bellisari, and our always less than patient canine crew.

Chronology of Principal Events

1735–1739	Austro-Russian-Turkish War
1739	Peace of Belgrade
1740–1742, 1744–1745	Silesian Wars
1740–1748	War of the Austrian Succession
1748	Treaty of Aix-la-Chapelle
1741–1743	Russo-Swedish War
1756	Diplomatic Revolution: Habsburg-Bourbon Alliance
1756–1763	Seven Years' War
1757	Battle of Rossbach
1763	Treaties of Paris and Hubertusburg
1768–1774	Russo-Turkish War
1774	Treaty of Kuchuk Kainarji
1772	First Partition of Poland
1780–1784	Anglo-Dutch War
1776–1783	War of American Independence
1778–1779	War of the Bavarian Succession
1787–1790	Russo-Swedish War
1787–1792	Russo-Austro-Turkish War
1792	Russo-Polish War
1793	Second Partition of Poland
1795	Third Partition of Poland
1792–1815	Revolutionary and Napoleonic Wars
1792–1797	War of the First Coalition
1792	Battle of Valmy, Battle of Jemappes
1794	Battle of Fleurus
1795	Peace of Basel
1797	Battle of Rivoli
1797	Treaty of Campo Formio
1798–1801	War of the Second Coalition
1800	Battle of Marengo, Battle of Hohenlinden
1801	Treaty of Lunéville
1802	Treaty of Amiens

1805	War of the Third Coalition
1805	Battle of Trafalgar; Battle of Austerlitz (Battle of the Three Emperors)
1806	End of the Holy Roman Empire
1806–1807	War of the Fourth Coalition
1806	Battle of Jena, Battle of Auerstadt
1807	Battle of Eylau, Battle of Friedland
1808–1814	Napoleon's Spanish Campaign
1809	War of the Fifth Coalition
1809	Battle of Aspern-Essling, Battle of Wagram
1812–1814	War of the Sixth Coalition
1812	Napoleon's invasion of Russia
1813	Battle of Leipzig
1814–1815	Congress of Vienna
1814	Restoration of Bourbons
1815	Hundred Days
1815	Waterloo
1806–1812	Russo-Turkish War
1828–1829	Russo-Turkish War
1848–1849	Austro-Sardinian War
1852–1853	Montenegrin War with Turkey
1853–1856	Crimean War
1859	Austrian War with France and Piedmont
1861–1862	Montenegrin War with Turkey
1864	War over Schleswig Holstein
1866	Seven Weeks' War
1870–1871	Franco-Prussian War
1871	Capitulation of Paris
1876–1878	Turkish War with Serbia and Montenegro
1877–1878	Russo-Turkish War
1885–1886	Serbo-Bulgarian War

ONE

Introduction

Linda S. Frey and Marsha L. Frey

> In peacetime, after all, cases were looked on at their merits, but, when war was closing in, innocent and guilty alike fell side by side.
>
> —Tacitus, *Annals* 1.48.2–3

The insightful Roman historian Tacitus tell us in his *Annals* that, when Germanicus gathered an army and warned that he would soon arrive and resort to "indiscriminate slaughter," Caecina is said to have remarked that "in peacetime, after all, cases were looked on at their merits, but, when war was closing in, innocent and guilty, alike fell side by side."[1] Caecina was analyzing the effects of civil war, but his perceptive remark holds equally true for wars throughout the ages. Wars do not spare the innocent.

In the period from 1648 to 1900, wars varied in their impact on noncombatants. Some conflicts have been notoriously destructive: the Thirty Years' War, Louis XIV's destruction of the Palatinate, and the Russian campaign, among others. Jacob Walter, a soldier in the allied contingent who fought with Napoleon in Russia, vividly described the area around Smolensk: "the war displayed its horrible work of destruction: all the roads, fields and woods lay as though sown with people, horses, wagons, burned villages and cities; everything looked like the complete ruin of all that lived."[2] Armies were pitiless in their exactions, decimating the areas through which they passed.[3] His comments echoed those of Simplicissimus, Grimmelshausen's protagonist, who lamented the "horrifying and quite unheard of cruelties perpetrated" in the Thirty Years' War[4] and described soldiers "in short nothing but hurting and harming and being in their turn, hurt and harmed, this was their sole purpose and existence. From this nothing could divert them—not winter or summer, snow or ice, heat or cold, wind or rain."[5] In the early modern era, the "Military Revolution" meant a dramatic growth in the size of armies and a corresponding and dramatic increase in the impact of warfare on society through conscription, taxes, contributions, and so on.[6] The hostile relationship between soldiers and civilians in this period, according to Jeremy Black, was engendered not only because of a "brutal competition for resources" but also because of the "differentiation of soldiers as a social group." Soldiers, he contends, "protected and enforced their status and honour by a harsh treatment of others." The high mortality rates in battle "habituated soldiers to killing."[7] Nonetheless, the endless complaints about mistreatment indicate, as Redlich has pointed out, that there was a prevailing and higher standard. The number of marriages recorded between soldiers quartered in the area and local women also proves that some combatants behaved decently.[8]

Geoffrey Parker has underscored that the laws of war in Early Modern Europe rested on five foundations: prescriptive texts such as the Bible, canon law, and Roman law; the principles stipulated by the Peace of God and the Truce of God; articles of war laid down by the armies themselves; customs or precedents established; and, last, what he terms "a contractual etiquette of belligerence" that provided the belligerents with a sense of the other's expectations.[9] The fragmentation of Christendom triggered by the Reformation destroyed some of the traditional restraints. For example, pilgrims and clerics, spared in the past, were increasingly inviolate only if they belonged to the same creed as the victor.[10] Certain rules were understood. For example, after the walls in a town were breached, if the town did not surrender, the besieged had no right to quarter. Shakespeare enunciated just that in Henry V's speech to the citizens of Harfleur:

> If I begin the batt'ry once again,
> I will not leave the half-achieved Harfleur
> Till in her ashes she lie buried.
> The gates of mercy shall be all shut up. . . .
> With conscience wide as well, mowing like grass
> Your fresh fair virgins and your flow'ring infants.[11]

The widely cited sacking of Magdeburg during the Thirty Years' War followed the rules of Shakespeare's "impious war," for the city had resisted.[12] It was generally accepted that should towns surrender, they would not be sacked. As the noted theorist Alberico Gentili pithily phrased it: "Cities are sacked when taken; they are not sacked when surrendered."[13] It was also accepted that unarmed camp followers should not be killed. Again, to quote Shakespeare, Henry IV on such bloodshed: "'Tis expressly against the law of arms; 'tis as arrant a piece of knavery mark you now, as can be offert."[14] Some widely understood conventions governed the conduct of war.

This volume begins with the Thirty Years' War, one of the most destructive in European history. The marching of troops rapidly turned an area into a "wasteland" as armies resorted to plundering to survive.[15] The war ruined both peasants and burghers and provided, in Weigley's words, evidence of a "long night of barbarism."[16] The raping and pillaging, murdering and devastation, famine and plague that characterized the war horrified contemporaries. The advice given to one of the more inept protagonists, the elector of the Palatinate, to pursue the conflict with "sword, fire, spoile, slaughter, till the streets be full" seemed all too typical. [17] Even the staunchly Protestant Gustavus Adolphus's determination to wage war in a Christian manner had to be abandoned. As Weigley has so graphically phrased it: "these lofty aims . . . founder[ed] on the grubby reality of logistics."[18] The Swedish troops acted pretty much like other troops. Because armies had to live off the countryside, plundering was essential. It was equally essential to destroy any land that an enemy might occupy, along with its resources. As Michael Roberts has phrased it, "frightfulness became a logical necessity."[19] These horrors prompted contemporaries such as the poet Andreas Gryphius to write poems such as "Tears of the Fatherland," which describes the devastation.[20] Others spoke of the peace of Westphalia, which ended the conflict, as one that was "dearly bought"[21] and increasingly raised and debated the question of *ius in bello*, the just conduct of war, especially the treatment of civilians.

Nonetheless, a number of historians make clear that the old view that European wars after the Thirty Years' War (1618–1648) were less destructive needs to be reexamined. The treatment of noncombatants did improve—but this happened over centuries, and any improvement was gradual and sporadic. As Russell Weigley has pointed out, this amelioration "rested on the thin reed of expediency."[22] Both Weigley and Jeremy Black stress that even after 1648, war was often unlimited rather than limited.[23] Gunther Rothenberg would concur. He underscores that commanders of the old regime had been just "as ruthless as their successors and abandoned restraints when military necessity required it."[24] Some theorists have pointed out that historians have mislabeled the eighteenth century a time of limited warfare only in contrast to the appalling suffering of the civilian population during the Thirty Years' War and the horrors of twentieth-century warfare. Although soldiers were more disciplined and more organized in the eighteenth century, wars were still destructive[25] and the aim of the belligerents often unlimited. During most of the eighteenth century, Europe was at war.

The emergence of more efficient logistical systems was more critical than "moralistic or legalistic restraints" in lessening the destructiveness of war.[26] The governments of Early Modern Europe increasingly relied on depots and convoys to supply their troops because it gave them more control over the soldiers. Discipline was better, morale higher. As Richelieu pointed out, "history knows more armies ruined by want and disorder than by the efforts of their enemies."[27] The increasing availability of supplies also lessened the danger of mutinies by unpaid and hungry soldiers, a perennial problem in the Early Modern period. Mutinies caused even greater devastation than plundering. The sack of Rome in 1527, the mutinies of the Spanish army in Flanders, the sack of Antwerp (1576), and the revolt of the Swedish army in 1633 are but a few examples. For ministers, such as Louvois, depots had the advantage of making the army more mobile and literally giving them a march on their opponents. The growing reliance on such magazines also made it possible to expand the size of the army to a scale not even visualized by ruthless generals, such as Wallenstein, during the Thirty Years' War. As John Lynn has pointed out, the almost sixfold increase in the size of the French army between the 1630s and the reign of Louis XIV demanded more resources than the state had available. Armies still had to requisition goods, to require contributions from the surrounding areas, to "live at the expense of the enemy,"[28] and to rely on pillaging, "the tax of violence." "War fed war." Troops committed both "minor abuses" and "major barbarities," extorting money, food, goods, and sex.[29] Still, Parker argues that, in general, war became less frightful because of the growth of deconfessionalization, a growing revulsion toward the excesses of war, and the spread of reciprocity. [30]

Those very shifts made the conscious adoption of terror by some armies more shocking. In the l670s, Louis XIV strove to ruin the area around Cologne because the elector had allied against him.[31] From 1688 to 1689, French armies thoroughly devastated the Palatinate, with the goal of creating "an artificial desert" along the eastern periphery of France.[32] Louis XIV ordered his soldiers in the Palatinate to destroy every significant town, including Mannheim, Worms, and Speyer. Instead of deterring his foes, Louis's actions galvanized them into uniting against him. As a contemporary noted: "There is no amount of time that can abolish, nor torrential rain that can wash away, nor fire than can efface, nor gilt and paint that can make beautiful the memory that King Louis left there, in causing to flow the blood and tears of thousands of oppressed and innocent people." [33] That could also be said of the Basse-Meuse area. There, Louvois and his troops did more damage than had troops during the Thirty Years' War.[34] During the War of the Spanish Succession, the allies deliberately ravaged Bavaria in 1704 to force the elector out of the war.[35] Later, during the War of the Austrian Succession (1740–1748), Frederick II adopted a ruthless policy in Silesia, arguing that fear was "the great tranquilizer."[36] His policy of destroying strategic towns, levying harsh taxes, and forcing Silesians into the army turned the people into "sworn enemies."[37] The Austrians also made no attempt to control the troops they let loose in Bavaria, where the Croats and the guards previously stationed along the Turkish border could not "be confined like monks in cloisters."[38] This plundering, looting, and burning ignited an armed response from the peasants just as even more destructive Prussian actions in Moravia had. Nor were these isolated instances. Austrian troops behaved in a similarly inhumane fashion when they took Genoa: castrating priests, killing, destroying. Conversely, Charles Albert of Bavaria, who controlled Prague and half of Bohemia, won over many by insisting that his troops behave humanely and abstain from the typical depredations.[39] Charles's policies were clearly the exception. Reed Browning has estimated that the War of the Austrian Succession killed about half a million people; of those, 100,000 were soldiers and the rest noncombatants.[40] Such brutality prompted this scathing observation: "Not since the Goths has war been waged in this fashion."[41] The brutality of the Seven Years' War (1756–1763) has prompted some historians to compare it to the Thirty Years' War.[42] Later, in 1790, the sack of Ismail, in Bessarabia, by troops under Suvorov seemed to many a replay of some of the worst horrors of the Thirty Years' War. During the Peninsular Wars, one observer thought that the taking of San Sebastián made the "horrors" at Magdeburg look like "child's play," so horrific were the actions of the soldiers and the devastation of the town.[43] Even countries that had declared neutrality often suffered. During the Seven Years' War, Saxony, and Dresden in particular, suffered from both Prussian and Austrian depredations as the city changed hands. The Prussians conscripted Saxons into the army, requisitioned anything valuable, and razed houses to the ground, impoverishing many civilians. When the Prussians besieged the city, they fired not only cannonballs but also oil-filled incendiary devices, setting streets ablaze—an eerie precedent for what would happen in the twentieth century. During the eighteenth century, the population of Dresden plummeted from 62,000 to 36,000. Goethe sorrowfully noted the ruin of the city and the destruction of its most beautiful parts, as well as the impoverishment of its citizens.[44]

During the Revolutionary Wars, although the French had boasted that they would carry "wars to the *châteaux* and peace to the cottages," both suffered alike. These "armed missionaries" often wrecked havoc and created enemies, not converts. Peasants "with tears of despair in their eyes" confided to one soldier "that they preferred the *ancien régime* a thousand times more than our Constitution since at least no one then carried off their property."[45] The city council of Zweibrücken complained that "Our people have been attacked and robbed. . . . Cellar doors have been smashed and the barrels stove in; what the soldiers could not drink, they allowed to gush away on the ground. They have forced their way into homes and stolen money. The hovels of the poor have been spared no more than the homes of the well off."[46] In September 1795, an artillery captain wrestled with a moral dilemma often endemic in war: "the measures we take are cruel, and . . . repugnant to humanity, but I hardly know how to balance the interests of my country with a conquered land."[47] Others were even more disenchanted. A French lieutenant complained that what upset him the most was the conduct of his compatriots: "They are laying the country waste, they are looting, they are stealing—everywhere there is devastation."[48] Yet another noted that his fellow soldiers were "thieves." For him, the pillaging "was even more inexcusable because his unit never lacked supplies."[49] Too few soldiers, however, grappled with such principles. Looting, levying, requisitioning, raping, and pillaging brought the brutality of the French to the lives of those who could not or would not flee. In the winter of 1793–94, the town council of Speyer complained of the "pitiless commissars" who seized "all the public and private property in town . . . arranged for the emptying of cellars, all granaries, and the seizing of basic foodstuffs." The council then went on to list some of the items taken: "horses, livestock in general, goods lodged at the customs house, and from the shops: cloth, linen, groceries, leather, bedsteads, tin, copper, brass, tools of every kind, furniture, clothing." The town council then complained that "The windows of the all the churches were broken . . . the interiors were vandalized; the organs dismantled, the lead from the steeples, the slates from the roofs, the wrought-iron work from the windows, doors, and staircases—it was all torn out and taken away."[50]

On December 15, 1792, the French enacted into law what had up to then been only practice; they decreed that the occupied were to pay the costs of the war.[51] In Guiomar's words, the defeated were "forced to contribute financially to their liberation." It was the "beginning of organized pillage of the conquered lands."[52] Carnot acknowledged this reality when he wrote on March 31, 1794, to representatives with the *armée du Nord:* "It is necessary to live at the expense of the enemy or perish."[53] Supply commissars were often called "birds of prey."[54] As Michael Rowe has pointed out, feeding the two French armies in the Sambre-Meuse region and the one between the Rhine and the Moselle, approximately 136,000 to 187,000 troops, was a "colossal burden" for a population of 1.6 million.[55] The French extended such treatment even to their allies, the Swiss, prompting Talleyrand to protest that it was "unjust and dangerous to treat an independent and allied country as a conquered and enemy country."[56] Some historians contend that the depredations of revolutionary troops were worse even than those of Louis XIV's armies.[57] Such practices prompted one of Marshal Ney's aides de camp to complain that "This is no longer a campaign . . . it is rather a devastation by bandits in uniform."[58] Yet the enemy, the British, during the Peninsular Wars also left behind them "a trail of arson, theft, rape and murder."[59] Remarking on the British seizure of mules, oxen, artillery, and munitions and the senseless destruction of property, one contemporary concluded that the French could not have found agents "better calculated to whip up hatred of the British army" than the British themselves.[60]

In the nineteenth century, some armies, but not the French, were more disciplined. During the Franco-Prussian War, the army behaved as armies had for centuries: soldiers looted and drank. The *francs-tireurs* acquired an even worse image of rapacity and indiscipline, just as the *miqueletes* had during the Peninsular Wars. The German army, however, was as "disciplined, moderate and sober" as any Europe had seen.[61] The Prussians had ensured that their army was well and regularly supplied and strictly disciplined. In that conflict, there was no large-scale execution of civilians or razing of French towns. At the outset of the war, Prussia's King Wilhelm I had warned the soldiers that they were not "waging war against the peaceful inhabitants of the country" and that it was their duty "to spare private property."[62] There were exceptions, especially as the war dragged on and as the lines between soldiers and civilians became blurred. The conflict with guerrillas was fanned by the French authorities such as Gambetta, who urged the French to adopt a *"guerre à outrance,"* a war that would involve the entire nation. Frenchmen were not only to destroy bridges and railways but also to "wage partisan war, to harass the enemy's detachments without pause or relaxation . . . disturb him day and night, always and everywhere." The *francs-tireurs* killed more than 1,000 Germans. Yet another French official urged his countrymen to hang the enemy from trees—but only after mutilating them. He even urged the deployment of 20,000 Kabyle tribesmen from Africa in Germany to "burn, pillage, and rape all they can find on their way."[63] Those who had advocated such policies did not pay the heavy price in lives and property that such actions entailed. Others did. Such actions invited reprisals and inevitably changed the nature of the conflict. As Crown Prince Friedrich of Prussia noted in his diary: "Individual shots are fired everywhere at patrols, mostly in a treacherous cowardly manner, so that we have no choice but to resort to counter measures of setting fire to houses where the shots come from. . . . It is ghastly, but necessary to prevent worse."[64] The *francs-tireurs* were treated as murderers; they had no rights as belligerents and were to be summarily shot. If the snipers could not be located, the house was to be destroyed and if necessary, the entire village. As the conflict dragged on, one German officer complained that the war was "gradually acquiring a hideous character. Murder and burning is now the order of the day on both sides and one cannot sufficiently beg Almighty God finally to make an end of it."[65] When Jules Favre pointed out to Bismarck that the Germans had waged a guerrilla war during the revolutionary conflicts, Bismarck riposted: "This is quite true; but our trees still bear the marks where your general hanged our people."[66] The Prussians had found themselves in the impossible position of adopting the same stance the French had toward the *somaténes* and the *miqueletes* during the peninsular campaign. Such retaliatory actions over time reduced the level of partisan activity, as did the populace's increasing disaffection with such resistance.

Earlier, during the Thirty Years' War, no clear line distinguished combatant from noncombatant. This problem was worsened when some military commanders thought it clever to disguise soldiers as peasants.[67] In towns, burghers, often both men and women, were expected to defend the town. Throughout the conflict, princes often called on their peasants to attack the enemy, as the elector of Bavaria did against the Swedes. When Tilly marched into Lower Saxony, peasants attacked his troops. Peasants were also ordered to destroy key bridges and roads, as they did in the Black Forest. In some cases, peasants acted on their own and undertook organized defensive maneuvers to prevent the billeting of troops and deter the excesses of soldiers. Undoubtedly, some peasants were embittered by the destruction of their villages and livelihoods. The mass production of broadsheets such as *The Lord's Prayer of Common Peasants against the Merciless Soldiers* reflected the suffering of the peasantry.[68] In a contemporary novel of the Thirty Years' War, a peasant says tellingly to the soldier: "none of us knows who is friend and who is foe."[69] Later, in 1658, peasants attacked the invaders in Courland, just as they did in the 1700s in Piedmont, Dauphiné, Spain, and Poland.[70] The numerous cases of noncombatants in besieged towns or in the countryside attacking armies compellingly refutes the often reiterated thesis that the conflicts before the Revolutionary Wars were "cabinet wars," fought only by professional armies.

The locale of civilians also influenced their treatment. In Eastern Europe, the different civilizations, cultures, and religions, coupled with the long traditions of hostility, translated into crueler wars and often more violent population displacement. In the seventeenth century, during the Austro-Turkish wars, when the Turks seized Perchtoldsdorf, they massacred the garrison, which had surrendered, murdered noncombatants, and set fire to the church and its tower, which were filled with women and children.[71] When the Habsburg armies seized Buda from the Turks in 1686, they slaughtered most of the inhabitants. An eyewitness to the carnage described it thus: "Not even the child in the mother's body was spared. . . . Naked children of one or two years of age were spitted and flung over the city walls. I was amazed by what was done and to see that mankind shows itself far crueler to its own than the beasts."[72] When Prince Eugene of Savoy invaded Eastern Europe in the 1680s and 1690s, he destroyed all the Turkish cities and either killed or enslaved the inhabitants.[73] During the Austro-Turkish wars, approximately 200,000 orthodox Christians fled into Habsburg territory; conversely, in 1699, approximately 130,000 Muslims fled to Ottoman Bosnia.[74] Because Balkan fortresses were rarely surrendered even after the walls had been breached, the inhabitants were allowed no quarter, and a frightful carnage took place.[75] Still later, when Ochakov was stormed in 1788, more than 10,000 Turks died, and, in 1790, as many as 30,000 may have perished when Ismail was taken. During the Austro-Turkish wars in the late seventeenth century, the loss of approximately 100,000 civilians either enslaved or killed in southern Austria forced the government to resettle the area.[76]

Ideology also conditioned the attitude of soldiers toward civilians. During the Revolutionary Wars, the French tended to regard those they conquered as unfit to be free. As Robespierre told the Convention in May 1794: "The French people seemed to have outstripped the rest of the human race by two thousand years."[77] The French attitude toward Italians was indicative. As a French commissar wrote back to Paris: "In Italy there is nothing but hatred for France. Lombardy regards us with abhorrence. Genoa likes us no better, Rome loathes us; the common people are decadent and degenerate."[78] Others dismissed those in the Austrian Netherlands as "imbecilic and fanatical idiots."[79]

Armies often resorted to starvation to force an enemy to surrender. Those who lived in towns under siege suffered not only from the effects of bombardment but also from hunger and deprivation. Some sieges, such as those of Koblenz (1688) and Liège (1691), were especially destructive. Outside towns, soldiers often not only confiscated all the food and forage they could find but also destroyed trees and crops and killed animals. As a curé of Emael wrote of the soldiers' pillaging in 1634: "they behaved worse than barbarously; they destroyed everything; they cut trees, completely demolished many houses and trampled whatever grain they could not steal, not even leaving enough to appease the hunger of the poor."[80] Even if troops did not destroy the crops, they requisitioned them, thus reducing the food supply and forcing prices higher. Famine was often accompanied by something just as deadly: disease. *The Chronicle of Moldavia* gives a wrenching description of the country after it had been destroyed by invading troops: "After the occupation, a great famine occurred. . . . Many souls died, many others fled abroad. After the famine came the plague . . . fterwards the cattle were struck with disease."[81] Those who escaped from the advancing troops often fared no better. A contemporary described the condition of those who fled during the Thirty Years' War: "During this flight many animals and horses died of hunger. The people also suffered from great hunger [and after their return] all became sick, so that almost no one healthy was left in the village."[82] The same situation recurred during the Peninsular campaigns. One contemporary left a vivid portrayal of the Portuguese refugees: "In the course of the winter the number of Portuguese who died of want was quite dreadful. It was not unusual to see hordes of these poor wretches, old and young, male and female in rags, the very picture of death, round a miserable fire . . . the emaciated faces were sufficient to touch the hearts of the most callous and unfeeling."[83] Yet another tells us that animals as well "fell dead either from fatigue or hunger."[84]

Armies were still using hunger as a weapon in the modern period. When the Prussians completely encircled Paris on September 19, 1870, the city was threatened with starvation and cold. Although it was a harsh winter, the populace could neither light their streets nor heat their homes. In addition, they were running out of food. The populace ate not only rats and dogs but also zoo animals.[85] The discovery that the capital had only two days of flour left prompted Moltke to remark that "Civil war was a few yards away . . . Famine a few hours."[86] Moltke had even argued that the Prussians should wait for hunger to force the Parisians to surrender.[87] Shortages especially affected the very young and the very old, who died of intestinal and respiratory diseases. During the siege, 42,000 more citizens died than had in the corresponding months of the preceding year.[88] In Metz, also under siege, flour, sugar, coffee, rice, and salt were unavailable. Citizens perished from dysentery and diarrhea, as well as from hunger. [89]

Soldiers also carried diseases that spread to the local populace: typhus, typhoid fever, dysentery, malaria, bubonic plague, smallpox, and venereal diseases. These killers were more lethal than the soldiers. Tilly's troops in the 1620s carried not only the plague but also dysentery. In 1629, the French and Austrian armies carried the plague into Italy. During the Thirty Years' War, those who had fled to safety inside Nuremberg's city walls found there an even deadlier enemy: the plague.[90] The Netherlands suffered from epidemics of dysentery carried by soldiers in the 1670s and 1690s. The plague of 1708 in the Baltic was spread by Russian and Swedish soldiers and killed between one-third and one-half of the population of Danzig.[91] In the wars between 1735 and 1739, Bucharest lost 33,300 residents in three years; Transylvania lost more than 41,000.[92] As late as 1747, when Austrian troops devastated the area around the Ligurian coast, 24,000 perished, most from disease and hunger.[93] The War of 1787–1792 left a trail of death. The troops brought the plague, which decimated first the cities and then the countryside. An estimated 10,000 died in Bucharest alone.[94] In Eastern Europe, during the eighteenth century, many fled to avoid the plague as Russian, Ottoman, or Austrian troops advanced. During the Napoleonic wars, many fled to Zaragoza, creating problems of overcrowding. When the city eventually surrendered to the French, 24,000 of the garrison had perished, along with 30,000 civilians, many of whom had died from the typhus epidemic that had swept through the city.[95] During these wars, French troops carried a typhus epidemic into Mainz.[96] Soldiers also brought with them animals that spread diseases, compounding the hardship. When Russian troops withdrew from Moldavia in 1740, not only was the countryside laid waste, but also cattle and sheep were dying from disease.[97] Governmental attempts to limit the spread of disease, however, had repercussions. When Austria imposed rigorous but ineffectual quarantines on Romania, the restrictions seriously disrupted trading patterns.[98]

On the whole, war retarded economic development and destroyed resources—houses, towns, crops, animals, and, most important, human lives. Armies often demanded contributions from the local populace, payments in money and in kind extorted by threats. For example, Nuremberg paid out large sums in the 1620s to the various armies. During the Thirty Years' War, the local lords and the occupying forces reached an agreement, a *salva guardia*, that guaranteed the local villages protection against abuses by the troops in exchange for aid.[99] The difficulty was not only the "relative inflexibility of the local economy" but also the marginal subsistence of many inhabitants even before the outbreak of war and the difficulty of maintaining discipline over the troops.[100] Such difficulties led, as even Tilly recognized, to the "distress and poverty of the currently completely exhausted and worn down lands."[101] During Louis XIV's wars in the Netherlands (1673–1678), Louis established bureaus of contribution to impose taxes on the Spanish Netherlands. The intendants used these taxes to supply French garrisons. French subjects who lived near the war zone also had to pay special excise taxes on wine and beer and fuel.[102] As one of Louis's diplomats remarked in a letter of April 1697: "Meanwhile, the people suffer, the people cry, and the people pay."[103] The French, in short, were attempting to appropriate enemy, neutral, and domestic resources to finance wars.[104] Similarly, Prussia impoverished Saxony during the Seven Years' War. Frederick callously compared Saxony to a sack of flour and said that no matter how hard or how often you hit it, a puff of flour would come out. One recent historian has estimated that Saxon sacrifices financed approximately one-third of the Prussian war effort.[105]

Wars impoverished populations that had to provide not only food and fodder and shelter but also farm animals and money. In addition, armies, whether stationary or passing through, caused a great deal of physical destruction; they disrupted trading patterns and often destroyed industry and agriculture. Soldiers who were demobilized for the winter often caused a great deal of destruction.[106] Because farmers often found it impossible to sow their fields, not only one year's harvest was lost but also the next. Desperation drove the alienated and embittered peasants to attack defeated armies, as happened to Tilly's forces after Breitenfeld and to the Swedes in 1632. Towns suffered when the countryside, which had provided food, was ravaged. For example, Berlin had a population of 12,000 in 1618; two years later, its residents numbered only 7,500.[107] One French duchess provided money in her will to compensate the villages through which her son and his troops had passed to appease "the wrath of God, which she feared so much cruelty and so many extortions might attract."[108] In the seventeenth century, a small village, Zembroth, was so efficiently plundered by numerous armies that a chronicler tells us that "as we had nothing more, no one sought much from us. They left us in misery."[109] When Augsburg was "liberated" by the Swedes during the Thirty Years' War, its citizens had to support the four to five regiments stationed in the city, ultimately bankrupting the city. It was ultimately plundered by its "liberators,"[110] proving the truth of the contemporary view of the three plagues: the occupying force, the invading force, and the plague.[111] During the Revolutionary and Napoleonic wars, the army forcibly requisitioned needed goods such as draft animals and livestock or resorted to forced loans, often causing severe deprivation. One historian has estimated that in year 11 (1802–1803), the Convention requisitioned 40,000 cavalry horses.[112] Workers in key industries were conscripted: gunsmiths, metalworkers, saddlers, tailors, and locksmiths.[113] The French armies also conscripted locals to do forced labor on fortifications and roads and to perform a variety of menial tasks.[114]

Yet another consequence of war was demographic. During the Thirty Years' War, parts of Central Europe lost between 30 and 40 percent of their population. Certain parts of Lorraine and the Franche-Comté lost between two-thirds and three-quarters of their populations, creating what Colin Jones has aptly termed a "profound caesura" in the development of the area.[115] Although it is difficult to differentiate between population movements, which were often temporary, and population losses, undoubtedly some areas suffered terribly during the wars. The loss of men in the wars impacted population growth, as did the movements of troops, which often forced food prices higher and in turn translated into delayed marriage. In the Habsburg lands, recovery was possible only after the end of the wars with the Turks and the French. In a petition to the imperial diet of 1721, one town noted that it had lost half its population and that most of the town still lay in ruins.[116] In Eastern Europe, the same scenario was replayed. Many historians blamed Romania's lagging development in the eighteenth century on the continual warfare that ravaged the country. A contemporary described his country as being "turned into a wasteland by war, scoured by retreating troops, and overrun with tears."[117]

War often had other economic repercussions. In the Early Modern period, war generally reduced or shifted seaborne trade. The Spanish embargo of the Dutch towns meant economic opportunity for the Hanse towns. On the seas, corsairs armed with letters of marque attacked many trading ships. During the War of the Spanish Succession, the pirates at Dunkirk seized more than 4,000 prizes and ransomed more than 2,000 others.[118] On the continent, armies often disrupted transportation and blocked vital waterways. Historians concur that the Peninsular Wars were a disaster for both Spain and Portugal. Their industry and trade were decimated and the vital trading link with South American frayed; both towns and countryside were ravaged by army after army.[119] During the Revolutionary and Napoleonic wars, when the French occupied an area, they often abolished the guilds, destroying the livelihoods of some and enriching others. War also increased the demand for uniforms, guns, ammunition, food, and camp followers. During the Thirty Years' War, Hamburg's population increased by about 50 percent, while that of Augsburg declined by about 60 percent.[120] Smelters, tailors, cobblers, manufacturers of small arms, and iron producers benefited. In Eastern Europe, the influx of troops did stimulate grain production; the sheer number of troops meant there were more consumers.[121] The Prussian armament industry clearly benefited from the Franco-Prussian War.[122]

Even areas that were not occupied, besieged, or in the path of the troops had to pay additional taxes and supply recruits for the army. Though Strasbourg successfully avoided military involvement during the Thirty

Years' War, an impressive feat, its citizens nonetheless suffered because they had to pay higher and higher taxes to support the city's own militia and to strengthen its fortifications.[123] Levels of taxation in many areas of Europe not only increased rapidly but became onerous. Gutmann has estimated that, in the Early Modern period, war doubled or tripled the normal tax burden[124]—and this often in countries where the population was not significantly increasing, as Jeremy Black has pointed out.[125] In Russia, by 1680, 60 percent of the budget was spent on the army. Michael Duffy points out that some states that saw an enormous growth in their armed forces in the Early Modern period were ultimately destroyed by that very growth. In France, in 1788, 26.3 percent of state expenditure went to the army, and 49.3 percent went to pay off debts incurred in previous wars.[126] Most obviously, war diverted manpower to unproductive uses. Armies took men away from their fields, their professions. By the beginning of the Revolution in France, the government had emerged as the single largest purchaser of food, ammunition, and clothing. Armies not only destroyed but also built; soldiers constructed roads and bridges.

Conscription increasingly affected more and more of the population. By the midseventeenth century, in sparsely populated states such as Prussia and Sweden, as many as 1 out of 13 or 14 citizens were soldiers. In the Early Modern period, governments often had to rely on brute force to meet their quotas—in France, *la presse*, and, in the German lands, *Zwangswerbung*. Conscription, however, impeded economic development, often caused mass flight, and precipitated unproductive economic decisions, such as the transfer of businesses or property or early marriage.[127] In Poland, the *szlachta* were not only reluctant to arm their serfs but also reluctant to lose their labor.[128] In *ancien régime* France, the burden of conscription fell on the unprivileged rural people, but the burden of conscription altered during the Revolutionary and Napoleonic wars, falling on ever larger portions of the population. As Woloch points out, the very survival of the Napoleonic state depended on the implementation of conscription. About one-third of potential conscripts could escape the draft legally because of short stature or infirmities or deformities. The system was also known to be corrupt and fraudulent. The implementation of conscription often set off riots, for example, in the Vendée and in the Nord and in the countries annexed to France, because it constituted a real hardship; families were often deprived of one of their main sources of labor. For a general such as Napoleon, who was said to have remarked to Metternich that "A man like me troubles himself little about the lives of a million men," the need for such men was unquenchable[129] and his demands unprecedented.[130] Napoleon's introduction of a yearly conscription in his satellite states triggered widespread opposition. When the French government annexed Piacenza and demanded not only new taxes but also recruits for the army, revolts broke out.[131] During the Napoleonic wars, the British mobilized about 2.5 percent of the population, Russia about 2 percent (800,000 men) for the 1812 campaign, Prussia in 1813 about 5.6 percent (279,000 men), and Austria between .9 and 1.6 percent (between 250,000 and 425,000 men).[132] Little wonder that an Italian priest labeled conscription "a punishment from God."[133]

War often meant significant social change. As M. S. Anderson has so evocatively pointed out, war damaged the "fabric of society."[134] In one village in Sweden, 230 were recruited for the army, and, of those, 215 died.[135] In Bohemia, during the Thirty Years' War, the position of peasants and townsmen was permanently eroded to the advantage of the nobles and the king. One of the significant effects of the Thirty Years' War in general was a shift in the ownership of property. In the Low Countries, peasant ownership of land decreased. Poland enjoyed only seven years of peace between 1648 and 1716. The population declined by about one third, many towns were completely leveled, the condition of the peasants deteriorated, and the power of the great magnates grew.[136] The high percentage of men who were in the military in some states also meant that the army took over what had been civilian duties, such as tax collection. States also increasingly intervened in education, founding, for example, military academies for sons of the nobility and establishing medical schools to train surgeons for the army.[137] The psychological effects of warfare, though difficult to measure, were often just as severe. Many of the chroniclers during the Thirty Years' War often spoke yearningly about the desperate need for peace. The departure of men for the war was traumatic and had a long-term impact on the men themselves and on their families, creating a significant shift of responsibility within the family and within villages.

Yet another collateral effect of war was an increase in criminality caused by former soldiers and deserters and those who fled to avoid conscription. After the Habsburgs captured Hungary from the Turks at the end of the seventeenth century, they discharged a number of soldiers who had served in the extensive fortifications along the border. These soldiers gathered together in gangs, especially in the Great Hungarian Plain between the Danube and the Tisza rivers.[138] In the Netherlands, in the seventeenth century, renegade soldiers and deserters also turned to crime to survive.[139] Sometimes the number of deserters was quite high. As Jeremy Black has pointed out, 42 percent of the Saxon infantry between 1717 and 1728 deserted.[140] Richard Cobb has stressed that those who avoided conscription constituted a significant element in the breakdown of law and order. Deserters were often marginal and rootless. But both groups—deserters and those who dodged conscription—often turned to crime.[141] During the French Revolutionary Wars, especially early in the conflict, the army witnessed mass desertion. Men, lacking goods or supplies, increasingly turned to pillage and fled home.[142] In Napoleonic Italy, between June 1803 and February 1804, 4,199 soldiers deserted; between 1806 and 1810, 17,750 did so; and from October 1711 to December 1812, 7,339 left.[143] During the Franco-Prussian War, the collective French desertions, which morphed into a virtual dissolution of the armies, reflect the psychological trauma and the increasingly realization that any sacrifice the troops made would be a useless one.[144] The French revolutionary government also allowed volunteers to leave when the troops went into winter quarters. This homeward migration also encouraged plundering. During the Peninsular Wars, Wellington complained that British troops behaved terribly and described them as no better than "a rabble."[145] One British officer openly worried about returning such men to Britain because they were daily "more ferocious and less fit to return to the duties of citizens." He feared that when the soldiers returned home, Britain would be overrun with "pilferers and marauders of every description."[146]

A corollary effect of the Revolutionary and Napoleonic wars was the destruction or appropriation of the traditional sources of charity. Churches and monasteries, which in the past had taken care of the destitute, were closed, hurting the poor the most and impacting poverty relief and public health. Historians estimate that, by 1795, between 20,000 and 30,000 of the 60,000 inhabitants of Brussels and 16,000 of the 55,000 residents of Ghent were destitute. At Verviers, 3,000 out of 9,000 inhabitants died from hypothermia or malnutrition.[147] The French also attacked traditional cultural values; they banned processions and festivals and abolished religious education, in addition to arresting and deporting more than 8,000 priests in the Austrian Netherlands.[148]

War also entailed significant cultural losses. In the period covered by this book (1618–1900), probably the two best examples are the Thirty Years' War and the Revolutionary and Napoleonic wars. During the Thirty Years' War, libraries and archives were destroyed and cultural treasures were seized and never returned. Duke Maximilian of Bavaria seized the Biblioteca Palatina and presented it to the pope. The Swedes, however, were far more predatory; they seized the books and precious objects of monasteries and cathedrals in Riga, Courland, Prussia, Marienburg, and Würzberg. Their most infamous loot came from Rudolph I's collection at Prague. There they took 3,000 paintings by Lucas Cranach the Elder, Da Vinci, Michelangelo, and Titian, as well as rare Gothic manuscripts. Many treasures did not survive the war. Duke Christian of Brunswick was noted for melting down precious statues and artifacts. Some universities, such as the one at Heidelberg, were closed for a while; others, such as Leiden, flourished because students fled there. Painters and musicians, as well, fled abroad. One historian has even estimated that because of the war, book production in the Holy Roman Empire did not return to its 1620 level until 1765.[149]

During the Revolutionary and Napoleonic wars, the French became legendary for their destruction or plundering of priceless artifacts. In June 1794, the Committee for Public Education ordered that experts be attached to the army to identify objects worth appropriating. From Aachen the French took numerous priceless books and manuscripts; from Cologne they seized more than 25 boxes of manuscripts, books, engravings, and artifacts, as well as paintings by Dürer and Rubens. This pattern repeated itself throughout Europe.[150] Napoleon, for example, seized 20 master-pieces from the duchy of Parma. During the Italian campaigns, the French haul was extensive: the Apollo Belvedere, the Medici Venus, the Dying Gladiator and more than 60 other pieces, in addition to nine paintings by Raphael, two Correggios, works by Titian and Tintoretto, animals from the zoos, and incunabula from Rome. The French often seized literally monumental pieces of art, such as the four bronze horses from St. Mark's in Venice.[151] The French were sometimes discriminate in their looting. In the Germanies, they removed the marble pillars in one of the chapels at Aachen. They also took stained glass and a number of priceless manu-scripts and incunabula, as well as most of the remarkable library of the duke of Brunswick.[152] In Prussia, the French took the quadriga (a two-wheeled chariot drawn by horses) down from the Brandenburg gate and sent it to Paris for the Arc de Triomphe, then under construction. In some cases, the French just destroyed. For example, Napoleon razed the column in Saxony that celebrated the victory of Rossbach against the French and melted down precious tiaras and works of gold and silver. Some treasures were lost to posterity. For example, the French seized the sword lying on the coffin of Frederick II at Potsdam and placed it in the Tuileries and, later, in the Invalides. When the allies advanced on Paris in 1814, the sword was lost, presumably tossed in the Seine with other war trophies.[153] The French attempted to justify their actions by arguing that the works of art had been "soiled too long by slavery" and even demanded that the losers pay the costs of transporting their treasures to France.[154] This specious justification did not appease the people who saw their priceless treasures being hauled off by the French, and riots broke out, for example, in Rome, Milan, and Parma. After Napoleon's defeat, the French predictably were unwilling to disgorge their booty. Many items were never returned or were lost or damaged. The winged lion from St. Mark's, for example, shattered when workers attempted to remove it from the Invalides, and many other works of art were damaged during their journeys to and from Paris. Nothing could be done about the treasures that had been sold, for example, to the tsar or given to others or melted down.[155] The French also closed universi-ties at Bonn, Cologne, Triers, and Mainz in 1798.[156] In short, the artistic and cultural losses from the Revolutionary and Napoleonic wars were incal-culable.

War can, however, have positive cultural consequences. When troops from the West invaded Eastern Europe, they brought with them new ideas. Warfare also meant urban renewal; the building, extension, or destruction of fortifications changed the look of towns. For example, when the Turks approached Vienna, the Austrians destroyed all the buildings outside the fortifications. After the Revolutionary and Napoleonic wars, the Viennese tore down the old fortifications, realizing that, although the walls had protected them against the Tartars and the Turks, they had not done so against Napoleon, who had easily twice seized the city. They built instead a wide boulevard, the Ringstrasse, which transformed the metropolis.

Wars and the demands of war from 1618 to 1900 transformed Europe and drew the attention of artists such as Rubens, Callot, Velasquez, Brueghel, and Goya, to name but a few. These artists often depicted war as a devouring beast, as a minatory Mars dominating the landscape, or as a threatening darkness. Just as they have provided us with new insights, so have our contributors to this volume: Paul Sonnino, Trintje Hellferich, Dennis Showalter, Michael Rowe, Michael Broers, and Michael Neiberg.

NOTES

1. Tacitus, *The Annals,* translated by A. J. Woodman (Indianapolis: Hackett Publishing Co., 2004), 26.

2. Jacob Walter, *The Diary of a Napoleonic Soldier* (New York: Penguin Books, 1991), 52.

3. See also John H. Gill, ed., *A Soldier for Napoleon: The Campaigns of Lieutenant Franz Joseph Hausmann, 7th Bavarian Infantry,* translated by Cynthia Joy Hausmann (London: Greenhill Books, 1998), 93.

4. Jans Jacob Christoffel von Grimmelshausen, *The Adventures of a Simpleton (Simplicius Simplicissimus)* (New York: Frederick Ungar Publishing Co., 1963), 7.

5. Ibid., 27.

6. Michael Roberts, "The Military Revolution, 1560–1660," in *The Military Revolution Debate: Readings on the Military Transformation of Early Modern Europe,* edited by Clifford Rogers (Boulder, CO: Westview Press, 1995).

7. Jeremy Black, "Civilians in Warfare, 1500–1789," unpublished paper, 1.

8. Fritz Redlich, *The German Military Enterpriser and His Work Force, A Study in European Economic and Social History* (Wiesbaden: Franz Steiner Verlag, 1964), 1: 523. See also 531–532.

9. Geoffrey Parker, "The Etiquette of Atrocity: The Laws of War in Early Modern Europe," in ed. Geoffrey Parker, *Success Is Never Final: Empire, War, and Faith in Early Modern Europe* (New York: Basic Books. 2002), 144–147.

10. Ibid., 151–152.

11. Ibid., 155.

12. Ibid., 158.

13. Ibid., 159.

14. Ibid., 167

15. Russell Weigley, *The Age of Battles, the Quest for Decisive Warfare from Breitenfeld to Waterloo* (Bloomington: Indiana University Press, 1991), 28.

16. Ibid., 46.

17. Barbara Donagan, "Codes and Conducts in the English Civil War," *Past and Present* no. 1118 (February 1988): 65–95.

18. Weigley, *The Age of Battles,* 27.

19. Michael Roberts, "The Military Revolution, 1560–1660," 27.

20. Andreas Gryphius, *Werke in einem Band* (Berlin: Aufbau Verlag, 1966), 3–4.

21. Georges Pagès, *The Thirty Years' War, 1618–1648* (New York: Harper and Row, 1939), 247.

22. Weigley, *The Age of Battles*, 84.

23. Weigley, *The Age of Battles*, 84, and Jeremy Black, *A Military Revolution? Military Change and European Society, 1550–1800* (New York: Macmillan, 1991), 45.

24. Gunther Rothenberg, "The Age of Napoleon," in *The Laws of War: Constraints on Warfare in the Western World*, edited by Michael Howard, George P. Andreopoulos, and Mark R. Schulman (New Haven, CT: Yale University Press, 1994), 87

25. Roger Chickering, "'Total War': The Use and Abuse of a Concept," in *Anticipating Total War The German and American Experiences, 1871–1914*, edited by Manfred F. Boemeke, Roger Chickering, and Stig Förster (Cambridge: Cambridge University Press, 1999), 21–23.

26. Weigley, *The Age of Battles*, 71.

27. Quoted in Colin Jones, "The Military Revolution and the Professionalisation of the French Army during the Ancien Regime," in Rogers, *The Military Revolution Debate*, 155. See also Guy Rowlands, *The Dynastic State and the Army under Louis XIV: Royal Service and Private Interest, 1661–1701* (Cambridge: Cambridge University Press, 2002), 256.

28. Jones, "The Military Revolution and the Professionalisation of the French Army," 159.

29. John Lynn, "How War Fed War: The Tax of Violence and Contributions during the Grand Siècle," *Journal of Modern History* 65, no. 2 (June 1993): 286–288, 291.

30. Parker, "The Etiquette of Atrocity," 161–165.

31. George Satterfield, *Princes, Posts and Partisans, The Army of Louis XIV and Partisan Warfare in the Netherlands (1673–1678)* (Boston: Brill, 2003) 175.

32. John Lynn, "A Brutal Necessity? The Devastation of the Palatinate, 1688–1689," in *Civilians in the Path of War*, edited by Mark Grimsley and Clifford J. Rogers (Lincoln: University of Nebraska Press, 2002), xix.

33. Ibid., 102.

34. Myron Gutmann, *War and Rural Life in the Early Modern Low Countries* (Princeton: Princeton University Press, 1980), 202.

35. Weigley, *The Age of Battles*, 84.

36. Reed Browning, *The War of the Austrian Succession* (New York: St. Martin's Press, 1993), 44.

37. Ibid., 44.

38. Ibid., 92.

39. Ibid., 82–83.

40. Ibid., 377.

41. Ibid., 376.

42. Peter H. Wilson, *German Armies: War and German Politics, 1648–1806* (London: UCL Press, 1998), 277.

43. Charles Esdaile, *The Peninsular War, A New History* (London: Allen Lane, 2002), 469.

44. Frederick Taylor, *Dresden: Tuesday, February 13, 1945* (New York: HarperCollins, 2004), 27–28.

45. John Lynn, *The Bayonets of the Republic: Motivation and Tactics in the Army of Revolutionary France, 1791–94* (Urbana: University of Illinois Press, 1984), 113.

46. Quoted in T.C.W. Blanning, "Liberation or Occupation? Theory and Practice in the French Revolutionaries' Treatment of Civilians outside France," in

Civilians in the Path of War, edited by Mark Grimsley and Clifford J. Rogers (Lincoln: University of Nebraska Press, 2002), 118.

47. Peter Wetzler, *War and Subsistence: The Sambre and Meuse Army in 1794* (New York: Peter Lang, 1985), xxi.

48. Quoted in Blanning, "Liberation or Occupation? Theory and Practice in the French Revolutionaries' Treatment of Civilians outside France," 118. See also Geoffrey Wawro, *Warfare and Society in Europe, 1792–1914* (London: Routledge, 2000), 5.

49. Quoted in Blanning, "Liberation or Occupation? Theory and Practice in the French Revolutionaries' Treatment of Civilians outside France," 118.

50. T.C.W. Blanning, *The French Revolution in Germany: Occupation and Resistance in the Rhineland, 1792–1802* (Oxford: Clarendon Press, 1983), 117.

51. Linda Frey and Marsha Frey, *The French Revolution* (Westport, CT: Greenwood Press, 2004), 151.

52. Jean-Yves Guiomar, *L'Invention de la guerre totale: XVIIIe–XXXe siècle* (Paris: Kiron, 2004), 68.

53. Ibid., 72.

54. Wetzler, *War and Subsistence,* 208.

55. Michael Rowe, *From Reich to State, The Rhineland in the Revolutionary Age, 1780–1830* (New York: Cambridge University Press, 2003), 55.

56. Talleyrand, letter of 18 Brumaire, year vii, in Emile Dunant, ed., *Les Relations diplomatiques de la France et de la République Helvétique 1798–1803: Recueil des documents tirés des archives de Paris* (Basel: Verlag der Basler Buch-und Antiquariatshandlung, 1901), 129.

57. *Civilians in the Path of War,* edited by Mark Grimsley and Clifford J. Rogers (Lincoln: University of Nebraska Press, 2002), xix.

58. Esdaile, *The Peninsular War,* 170.

59. Ibid., 151.

60. Ibid., 153.

61. Michael Howard, *The Franco-Prussian War, The German Invasion of France, 1870–1871* (New York: Methuen, 1979), 378.

62. Mark R. Stoneman, "The Bavarian Army and French Civilians in the War of 1870–1871: A Cultural Interpretation," *War in History* 8, no. 3 (2001): 272–273.

63. David Stone, *"First Reich," Inside the German Army during the War with France, 1870–71* (London: Brassey's, 2002), 157, 184.

64. Stoneman, "The Bavarian Army and French Civilians in the War of 1870–1871," 274.

65. Howard, *The Franco-Prussian War,* 379.

66. Ibid., 251. For the Napoleonic wars see, for example, Gill, ed., *A Soldier for Napoleon,* 75.

67. Redlich, *The German Military Enterpriser,* 1: 520.

68. Andrew Cunningham and Ole Peter Grell, *The Four Horsemen of the Apocalypse: Religion, War, Famine and Death in Reformation Europe* (Cambridge: Cambridge University Press, 2000), 175.

69. Moscherosch quoted in Redlich, *The German Military Enterpriser,* 1: 523. See also 515–523.

70. Jeremy Black, "Civilians in Warfare, 1500–1789," 8–9.

71. Christon Archer et al., *World History of Warfare* (Lincoln: University of Nebraska Press, 2002), 30.

72. Wilson, *German Armies,* 84.

73. Ibid., 85.

74. Ibid.

75. Ibid., 84.

76. Michael Hochedlinger, *Austria's Wars of Emergence, War, State, and Society in the Habsburg Monarchy* (New York: Longman, 2003), 157. See also Wilson, *German Armies*, 85.

77. Quoted in Blanning, "Liberation or Occupation? Theory and Practice in the French Revolutionaries' Treatment of Civilians outside France," 115.

78. Ibid., 115.

79. Ibid., 130.

80. Gutmann, *War and Rural Life in the Early Modern Low Countries*, 196.

81. Constantin Cazanisteanu, "The Consequences for the Rumanian Principalities of the Ottoman Wars with Austria and Russia," in *East Central European Society and War in the Pre-Revolutionary Eighteenth Century*, edited by Gunther E. Rothenberg, Béla Király, and Peter Sugar (New York: Columbia University Press, 1982), 407.

82. John Theibault, *German Villages in Crisis, Rural Life in Hesse-Cassel and the Thirty Years' War, 1580–1720* (Atlantic Highlands, NJ: Humanities Press, 1995), 157. See also Cunningham and Grell, *The Four Horsemen of the Apocalypse*, 171.

83. Esdaile, *The Peninsular War*, 329.

84. Ibid., 327.

85. Hollis Clayson, *Paris in Despair, Art and Everyday Life under Siege (1870–1871)* (Chicago: University of Chicago Press, 2002), 3, 164.

86. Howard, *The Franco-Prussian War*, 369.

87. Stig Förster, "The Prussian Triangle of Leadership in the Face of a People's War: A Reassessment of the Conflict between Bismarck and Moltke, 1870–1871," in *On the Road to Total War: The American Civil and the German Wars of Unification, 1861–1871*, edited by Stig Förster and Jörge Nagler (Washington, DC: German Historical Institute, 1997), 131.

88. Robert Tombs, "The Wars against Paris," in Förster and Nagler, *On the Road to Total War*, 549.

89. Howard, *The Franco-Prussian War*, 276.

90. Cunningham and Grell, *The Four Horsemen of the Apocalypse*, 193.

91. M. S. Anderson, *War and Society in Europe of the Old Regime, 1618–1789* (New York: St. Martin's Press, 1988), 136, 137.

92. Cazanisteanu, "The Consequences for the Rumanian Principalities of the Ottoman Wars," 405–406.

93. Browning, *The War of the Austrian Succession*, 376.

94. Cazanisteanu, "The Consequences for the Rumanian Principalities of the Ottoman Wars," 405–406.

95. Esdaile, *The Peninsular War*, 161–163.

96. Rowe, *From Reich to State*, 224.

97. Cazanisteanu, "The Consequences for the Rumanian Principalities of the Ottoman Wars," 407.

98. Ibid., 406–407.

99. Theibault, *German Villages in Crisis*, 140–141.

100. Ibid., 141.

101. Ibid., 149.

102. Satterfield, *Princes, Posts and Partisans*, 42–44.

103. Laurence Pope, ed., *Letters (1694–1700) of Francois de Callières to the Marquise d'Huxelles* (Lewiston, NY: Edwin Mellen Press, 2004), 246.

104. Lynn, "How War Fed War," 296–304.

105. T.C.W. Blanning, *The Culture of Power and the Power of Culture* (Oxford: Oxford University Press, 2002), 72.

106. Herbert Langer, *The Thirty Years' War* (Dorset, UK: Blandford Press, 1978), 99.

107. Anderson, *War and Society*, 68.

108. Ibid., 67.

109. Geoff Mortimer, ed., *Eyewitness Accounts of the Thirty Years' War 1618–48* (Chippenham, Wiltshire: Palgrave, 2002), 48. See also David A. Parrott, "Strategy and Tactics in the Thirty Years' War: The Military Revolution," in Rogers, *The Military Revolution Debate*, 227–251.

110. Cunningham and Grell, *The Four Horsemen of the Apocalypse*, 187–190.

111. Ibid., 196.

112. Alan Forrest, *Soldiers of the French Revolution* (Durham, NC: Duke University Press, 1990), 142.

113. Frederick C. Schneid, *Soldiers of Napoleon's Kingdom of Italy: Army, State, and Society 1800–1815* (Boulder, CO: Westview Press, 1995), 82–86.

114. Blanning, "Liberation or Occupation? Theory and Practice in the French Revolutionaries' Treatment of Civilians outside France," 124.

115. Jones, "The Military Revolution and the Professionalisation of the French Army," 155.

116. *War and Society*, 143–144.

117. Cazanisteanu, "The Consequences for the Rumanian Principalities of the Ottoman Wars," 408.

118. Anderson, *War and Society*, 147.

119. Esdaile, *The Peninsular War*, 505.

120. Mortimer, *Eyewitness Accounts of the Thirty Years' War 1618–48.*

121. Cazanisteanu, "The Consequences for the Rumanian Principalities of the Ottoman Wars," 410.

122. Ulrich Wengenroth, "Industry and Warfare in Prussia," in Förster and Nagler, *On the Road to Total War*, 256–262.

123. Mortimer, *Eyewitness Accounts of the Thirty Years' War 1618–48*, 92–93.

124. Guttmann, *War and Rural Life in the Early Modern Low Countries*, 50.

125. Black, "Civilians in Warfare, 1500–1789," 7.

126. Michael Duffy, ed., *The Military Revolution and the State* (Exeter: University Press, 1980), 5.

127. Redlich, *The German Military Enterpriser*, 2: 172–182.

128. Jerry Kowecki, "The General Levy in Eighteenth-Century Poland," in Rothenberg, Király, and Sugar, *East Central European Society and War in the Pre-Revolutionary Eighteenth Century*,193.

129. Isser Woloch, "Napoleonic Conscription: State Power and Civil Society, *Past and Present* 111 (May 1986): 101.

130. Alexander Grab, "Army, State, and Society: Conscription and Desertion in Napoleonic Italy (1802–1814)," *Journal of Modern History* 67, no. 1 (March 1995): 28.

131. Michael Broers, *Europe under Napoleon, 1799–1815* (New York: Arnold, 1996), 104.

132. Michael Rowe, ed., *Collaboration and Resistance in Napoleonic Europe: State Formation in an Era of Upheaval, c. 1800–1815* (London: Palgrave Macmillan, 2003), 3.

133. Grab, "Army, State, and Society: Conscription and Desertion in Napoleonic Italy (1802–1814)," 50.

134. Anderson, *War and Society,* 65.

135. Ibid., 66.

136. Marian Zgórniak, "The Financial Problems of the Polish Military System during the Saxon Period," in Rothenberg, Király, and Sugar, *East Central European Society and War in the Pre-Revolutionary Eighteenth Century,* 184.

137. Duffy, *The Military Revolution and the State,* 4–5.

138. Béla Király, "War and Society in Western and East Central Europe in the Pre-Revolutionary Eighteenth Century," in Rothenberg, Király, and Sugar, *East Central European Society and War in the Pre-Revolutionary Eighteenth Century,* 13.

139. Satterfield, *Princes, Posts and Partisans,*126–127. See also Cunningham and Grell, *The Four Horsemen of the Apocalypse,* 113.

140. Black, "Civilians in Warfare, 1500–1789," 8.

141. Alan Forrest, "Conscription and Crime in Rural France during the Directory and Consulate," in *Beyond the Terror: Essays in French Regional and Social History, 1794–1815* (New York: Cambridge University Press, 1983), 92–107. See also Alan Forrest, *Conscripts and Deserters: The Army and French Society during the French Revolution and Empire* (New York: Oxford University Press, 1989).

142. Lynn, *The Bayonets of the Republic,* 98.

143. Grab, "Army, State, and Society: Conscription and Desertion in Napoleonic Italy (1802–1814)," 28.

144. Stéphane Audoin-Rouseau, "French Public Opinion and the Emergence of Total War," in Förster and Nagler, *On the Road to Total War,* 405–406.

145. Esdaile, *The Peninsular War,* 197.

146. Ibid., 198.

147. Quoted in Blanning, "Liberation or Occupation? Theory and Practice in the French Revolutionaries' Treatment of Civilians outside France," 126.

148. Rowe, *From Reich to State,* 69.

149. Blanning, *The Culture of Power and the Power of Culture,* 141–142.

150. Rowe, *From Reich to State,* 56–57.

151. Dorothy Mackay Quinn, "The Art Confiscations of the Napoleonic Wars," *American Historical Review* 50, no. 3 (April 1945): 438, 441.

152. Ibid., 443, 444.

153. Guiomar, *L'Invention de la guerre totale,* 178.

154. Quinn, "The Art Confiscations of the Napoleonic Wars," 439. See also 441.

155. Ibid., 459, 460.

156. Rowe, *From Reich to State,* 57

TWO

Civilians in the Thirty Years' War

Tryntje Helfferich and Paul Sonnino

THE BEGINNING OF A DISASTER

In the year 1618, a sign of impending disaster appeared in the Holy Roman Empire. According to a contemporary journalist, "a terrible comet with a very long burning tail appeared in the heavens, and was seen with particular terror across most of Europe." This comet was no mere astrological curiosity, for people believed that it was a sign and a warning placed in the heavens by God himself,

> so that the people might see that he would punish them because of their sins, and that he had decided to let loose the rod of his wrath. And so this comet has become a true indication of the future punishment of God. . . . For the elders have said of the comet that none has ever appeared that has not brought with it great misfortune.[1]

The elders were right, for the life of civilians during the period 1618–1648 would be full of misfortune. Scholars argue over the exact numbers of dead, the true percentages of buildings, livestock, and crops lost, and the precise debt load of the cities and states, but it is just as important, or perhaps more important, to understand what the war meant to the people. That the people saw this period as such a radical departure from their always difficult everyday experience of life shows us the absolute horror of the Thirty Years' War.

In 1618, the smoldering problems of the empire, both structural and religious, exploded. The spark came from an unexpected place, and from the hands of a small number of obstreperous Calvinist nobles in the kingdom of Bohemia. These men, claiming that their traditional right to build churches had been violated, saw fit to throw the representatives of their Catholic king, Ferdinand, of the house of Hapsburg, also known as the house of Austria, out an upper-story window of the Hradčany castle in Prague. This "shameful evil act," in the words of one Catholic observer, killed no one, but it soon led to more drastic action, for the rebels planned the even more extreme step of dethroning their king and offering the crown to Frederick V, the Calvinist elector of the Palatinate. Everyone, including his father-in-law, King James I of England, entreated Frederick not to upset the delicate religious and political balance. The elector of Cologne also gave dire warnings of the consequences to the empire and its people should Frederick accept the crown. "If it should be true, that the Bohemians have in mind to set aside Ferdinand and to chose instead a counter-king," he wrote with as much foresight as was shown by the elders who saw the comet, "then one would have make oneself ready for a 20-, 30-, and 40-year war, for the Spaniards and the house of Austria would rather put into play everything that they possess in this world than to give up Bohemia."[2] Other warnings were less clear but just as foreboding. Chroniclers across the empire reported unsettling miracles that year, such as strange lights in the sky, blood and sulfur raining from the heavens, an earthquake at Frankfurt, a bloody sword in the sky, an angel who threatened divine retribution for our sins, a mysterious sign above the church tower at Darmstadt, and rivers of blood that poisoned the fish in the rivers. Some local officials ordered people to attend prayer sessions once or even two times a day.[3] The people of the empire were uneasy, but Frederick, identifying his own glory with that of his religion, ignored every warning and accepted the crown of Bohemia.

The moment Frederick took this dangerous step, every Catholic prince in the empire felt threatened in his possessions. This was especially true for Maximilian, the Catholic duke of Bavaria, who saw the Bohemian revolt as part of a larger plot. "The Bohemian disorders," he wrote, "obviously aim at the extermination of the Catholic religion." But this evil ambition went beyond Bohemia, he believed, for "the heretical electors and princes in the empire also now work to remove the Bohemian crown completely from the house of Austria, in order to turn it over to a heretic and thereby gain the majority in the electoral college, so then they are able to chose a heretical emperor."[4] Facing such a prospect, Maximilian offered his support to Ferdinand, who had in the meanwhile become Ferdinand II, Holy Roman Emperor, for the reconquest of his lands. It proved easy. The battle of White Mountain on November 8, 1620, routed the Bohemian Protestant rebels and chased out Frederick V, earning him, for the rest of his unhappy life, the derisive nickname "The Winter King."[5]

For the people of Bohemia, regardless of their religion, the battle of White Mountain was the beginning of a long agony. A few gullible nobles, attracted by imperial offers of amnesty, returned to find themselves dragged before a judge and quickly executed. It was in many ways worse for the living. The emperor's military commander, Count Albrecht von Wallenstein, proceeded to disregard the people's traditional privileges and extracted every last penny out of them in order to maintain his armies. His most compelling argument was that they had a choice: they could either "contribute" voluntarily or be subject to the pillaging of soldiers, which he could not otherwise control. Tens of thousands of Protestants, including hundreds of nobles, were either expelled or voluntarily emigrated from the kingdom and their property sold or transferred to supporters of the emperor. Wallenstein also engaged in a policy of currency manipulation, setting up a mint that issued millions of debased coins that were then put into circulation at face value—creating instant inflation and collapsing the economy.[6] His promises to control his troops, moreover, were not easy to fulfill, and the people found themselves subjected not only to new taxes but also to the depredations of the soldiers. "One cannot describe more pitifully the extremely distressing and miserable situation here," one man reported, "the plundering and murders have no end. . . . First they began to plunder the houses of the directors and Calvinists, now however it is going on through every single house without distinction."[7] Efforts to hide one's possessions resulted in various forms of maltreatment, and the maltreatment was particularly horrendous if the victim had no more possessions to surrender. And the visits of the soldiers were followed by those of Jesuit missionaries, who reestablished the Catholic hierarchy and threatened further punishment to any who relapsed into heresy. The ruthless elimination of Protestantism from Bohemia frightened and horrified Protestants across the empire. "Because Bohemia was overcome by the emperor and lost all assistance," one Lutheran observer wrote, "it also happened to them that all the preachers in the entirety of Bohemia were evicted . . . under the pretext that the disorder had arisen out of the religion. Thus we Evangelicals always receive injustice from the Catholics."[8]

Ferdinand II and Maximilian might at this point have been satisfied with restoring the religious and political status quo. But, like a great many persons of power inebriated by success, they decided to push their advantage and punish the hapless Frederick. In 1620, the emperor's cousin, the king of Spain, sent his best general, Ambrogio Spinola, up the Rhine, occupying Catholic and Protestant territories alike, including some of the "Winter King's" lands in the Lower Palatinate. Towns in the general's path were plundered, their churches burnt to the ground for easier access to their treasures, the residents fleeing for their lives. Not to be outdone and unwilling to leave all the spoils to the Spanish, Maximilian of Bavaria also sent his general, Johann von Tilly, into Frederick's lands in the Upper Palatinate, where he camped for the winter. The sudden presence of so many armies in the area was a disaster for the people of the region. The soldiers simply took what they needed and wanted from the civilians without regard to their religion. The troops also brought plague into the countryside, and, as hordes of refugees fled the troops, they spread the disease even further. For some, however, the thought of adventure and booty made the life of a soldier an exciting thought. A pastor from the Hessian town of Reichenbach, for example, reported that on January 18, three local lads, Hans Heuß the tailor, Christian Klüppel, and Hans Seidenmacher, had run off to join the war. Their experience was surely not what they had expected. "The first of these," the pastor recorded, "ran away from the soldiers and returned home after a few days, while the other two, along with the sons of the local magistrate, stayed away until 13 April 1620."[9]

As local governments began to mint debased coins to meet the staggering costs of preparing for possible war, inflation spread outward from Bohemia into the rest of the empire. "For all emperors and kings, princes and lords, counts and noblemen, cities and towns, vagabonds and vagrants," one man complained,

minted and were allowed to mint, so there were many and various kinds of money, and one had to have a learned tongue and good eyesight in order to be able to read and see all the engravings. Then a debased and false money arose that had no permanence. For in the beginning it was pretty, as if it was made of pure silver, but thereafter, in the third, forth, fifth, or eighth week, it faded away and went red like copper, all except for the taler and the old money. And because all the coinage was so bad and valueless, no one wanted to be paid any more with such awful money, as was only proper and just. As a result it was worth nothing. Then a great misery arose in all lands.[10]

Prices for food and services quickly became impossibly high, and in some areas the monetary system broke down completely, with people resorting to rough barter instead. In other places, tradesmen abandoned their crafts in a mad rush to profit by exchanging good currency for bad. But bad money, as it always does, chased out the good, and people were left with piles and piles of worthless metal, so that "even the children played in the alleys with the coins, but could buy nothing with them."[11] Currency debasement and rapidly spiraling inflation added a new level of insecurity and anxiety to the lives of people already facing the advance of war and led to mass migrations of peasants leaving their villages in search of work and food.[12]

And the war continued to spread. Imperial armies pushed their advance through Frederick's lands, and in September 1622 Tilly took Frederick's capital, the picturesque town of Heidelberg. While the inhabitants of Prague had been subjected to extortion by a government that intended to keep on exploiting them, Heidelberg was subjected to pillaging by conquerors who did not care if the inhabitants lived or died. "In the old town," one contemporary wrote, "there was a pitiful hue and cry over the massacres, plundering, and extraction of money by tortures such as thumbscrews, kneecapping, flogging, torments, fingernail boring, the scorching of private parts, hangings, burning of soles, and the violation and abduction of women and virgins, and meanwhile the rutting in the suburb was frighteningly out of control, and the rich hospital, known as the Preacher's Cloister, was also attacked, and this plundering continued for three days."[13] After the rough looting of the initial attack, Heidelberg was subjected to a more systematic stripping of its treasures; its famous library was boxed up and sent to the Vatican as a present.[14]

The ravages of war were not limited to Bohemia and to the Palatinate. Christian of Brunswick, a Protestant duke who had decided to take up Frederick's cause, had raised an army in Westphalia, and Frederick's general, Ernst von Mansfield, moved into winter quarters in neighboring Alsace, thereby subjecting large areas of North and West Germany to similar indiscriminate depredation. Ferdinand, the archbishop of Cologne, protested bitterly to the Spanish ambassador about the effect of Christian of Brunswick's invasion and begged the ambassador for assistance. Not only had Christian raised a rough mercenary army against his rightful emperor, the archbishop complained, but also he had invaded the archbishop's lands in Westphalia, Münster, and Paderborn without any provocation. Once there, his soldiers had "captured, stretched, beaten, and 'martyred' some subjects to death," and the people had been so frightened and miserable that men, women, and children had all fled into the woods and the valleys to escape. There the poor people were open to the elements, and many had died from starvation and extreme cold. To make matters worse, while the survivors huddled in the woods, eating what roots and berries they could find, the soldiers looted their homes and farms, taking all their belongings, their livestock, and their food stores and then burning their houses to the ground. Ferdinand reported with outrage that Christian had overpowered not just "entire villages and towns" but also "princely and noble houses and cities," including even the parish churches, and plundered them, ruined them, and finally torched them one after the other. "In sum," he wrote, "because of this the poor innocent people have reached the greatest extremity, and are ruined in body, possessions, and goods to such a degree that it is impossible for them ever to rise again."[15] Mansfield was no better. A pastor from Hesse-Darmstadt reported that the general and his troops had plundered the entire land and had taken high-ranking nobles for ransom.[16]

Although the advance of the armies of Christian and Mansfield must have seemed like the end of the world to the people in their path, their military diversion had little effect on the emperor. Confident in his own victories, he proceeded to exploit them in order to bring about one of the biggest changes in the constitution of the Holy Roman Empire since its inception. In punishment for what he saw as Frederick V's outrageous intervention in Bohemia, in 1623 he summarily deposed him and transferred his electoral title and his lands in the Palatinate to the loyal duke of Bavaria. For an emperor to cashier and replace an elector in such a manner was unprecedented. This act seemed to his opponents to be a clear indication of his intention to establish his supreme authority over the Holy Roman Empire and to transform it from a republic of independent princes and cities into an absolute monarchy.[17] For the common people, however, the intricacies of constitutional politics seemed much less important than their concerns about what this escalating war might mean for their daily

General Gonzáles de Córdoba with Spanish troops besieging Frankenthal, Palatinate, September 27–October 14, 1621. Courtesy of Library of Congress Prints and Photographs Division, Washington, DC.

lives. And they were increasingly worried about the rapid advance of the conflict. Numerous accounts began to appear about further mysterious portents of doom and about divine messages of impending disaster. "During the harvest," one man wrote,

many drops of blood were found on the stalks as we reaped. Indeed, the stalks became completely bloody, which unfortunately signified the bloody war. Also during this summer near Tübingen and Schorndorf in the country of Württemberg, around St. James's Day, fiery balls fell from heaven. On one Sunday this happened three times, in the morning, afternoon, and evening. A published pamphlet was issued about it, which I myself read.[18]

Another account related how in many places, including Strassburg, Heidelberg, Ulm, and Switzerland, there was "in the night a frightening chasm and fiery beacon," and the next day three multihued suns appeared in the sky, completely surrounded by a single rainbow. A similar phenomenon appeared in the skies above Prague only a month later.[19]

INTERVENTION OF FOREIGN POWERS

The plague was now raging everywhere in the empire. There were 16,000 dead in Prague alone, inflation was still disrupting the economic system, and boatloads of refugees were flooding areas yet untouched by war. Yet, to the Catholic princes and to the emperor, it seemed as if the greatest threat to humanity came from the aggression of the Protestants, and to the Protestant princes it was just the opposite. For example, all that the wife of the ousted Frederick V could think about was the possibility of enlisting her brother the new king of England and other Protestant princes in order to defend the righteousness of her husband's cause. As she wrote to a trusted friend, "In England the fleet is almost readie to goe out. . . . My uncle, the king of Denmark doth beginne to declare himself for us, and so doth Sweden."[20] Her expectations about her own brother and the king of Sweden came to naught, but the Protestant princes did find a champion in Christian IV, the Lutheran king of Denmark, who prepared to intervene. To parry his intervention, Catholic armies under Tilly and Wallenstein moved north and occupied the Protestant territories of Magdeburg, Halberstadt, and Hildesheim, despoiling them in the process. They also took the Protestant areas of Osnabrück, Minden, and Verden, installing a Catholic bishop and forcefully restoring Catholic worship.[21] Thus, once the rulers of the empire had abandoned the principle of caution for the principle of escalation, the war rapidly spiraled out of control.

Christian IV had both political and religious reasons for his actions, since he was just as interested in placing his sons in charge of a number of territories around Denmark as in defending the cause of the "Reformation." The king of England, the elector of Brandenburg, and even the Catholic king of France were urging him on, the latter promising him 60,000 *livres* if he would intervene on the side of the Protestants. But the war did not wait to see what Christian would decide. Instead, it continued to spread across the empire, subjecting more and more people to its direct horrors. In the spring of 1625, for example, the Protestant citizens of Ulm, who had been spared direct involvement until then, faced invasion by waves of imperial troops looking for safe quarters and loot. According to one resident:

> On the 24th of March many soldiers fell upon the land of Ulm at Langenau, Öllingen, Setzingen, Nerenstetten and Wettingen, and they inflicted onto the people great plagues and suffering and all kinds of maliciousness. The men were badly beaten and many women were raped. This continued for nine days. . . . [Then] in the harvest time around St. James's Day several hundred cavalrymen fell upon the land. Thus the militia of the land of Ulm had to be called up at Bissingen, Öllingen, Setzingen, Nerenstetten, and Wettingen, for these cavalry were encamped at Langenau, at Rammingen, and at Elchingen. I myself was posted at Setzingen and Öllingen for twelve days. But the cavalry at Rammingen wreaked havoc, for they set fire to the town such that almost fifty buildings were burnt. This continued in the land for fourteen full days, after which they withdrew.[22]

That same year, Christian finally decided to act in defense of the German Protestants. His intervention, however, was short-lived. At the battle of Lutter, on August 27, 1626, he and his Protestant allies were thoroughly defeated by the Catholic armies under Tilly.[23] At least Christian had not stayed long enough in North Germany to cause a great deal of damage, but Wallenstein and Tilly certainly did. By 1627, Wallenstein, with a huge army of 100,000 men, had seized the entire coastline from Jutland to Pomerania, and, as a reward for his services, the emperor again displayed his imperial majesty by cashiering the rebellious duke of Mecklenburg and transferring his duchy and title to Wallenstein.[24]

By now Wallenstein had complete control of the Baltic and had fully developed his system of supporting his army by contributions. But he had even more ambitious plans. It was his intention to expand the economic ties of this area with Spain and to challenge, in the process, the economic dominance of the Swedes and the Dutch, so he made more than a token effort to win over the population. As an example of his moderation, and unlike in the areas of northern Germany that the imperialists considered to have been illegally appropriated by the Protestants, in the long-Protestant Pomerania he did not attempt to impose a change in religion. His social policy, however, more than made up for his religious restraint. He attempted to gain the affection of the upper classes by exempting them from all taxation and, in the process, alienated the peasants and burghers, who were forced to bear the full burden. To the average man and woman, this taxation was an even better reason to resist the occupation than being forced to listen to the sermons of Jesuit missionaries. The fishermen of Stralsund took matters into their own hands and, against the strenuous opposition of the city officials, succeeded in blockading and expelling the imperial garrison from the island of Rügen, a popular act that brought the city under direct attack from the imperialists, who quickly made it pay for its impertinence.[25] But the complaints did not cease, especially as Wallenstein's soldiers began to behave just as badly as those of any other army. A representative of Pomerania, for example, complained that

the poor people in the countryside and in the cities are forced here and there into unnecessary work, and are beaten . . . and when officers or soldiers ride through, the residents of the land who still have a bit of bread are not only forced to give it up without pay, as if everything were common property, but they must also provide their horses . . . which they either never get back or get back completely destroyed. . . . And it is very common that riders and soldiers daily ride or run out of the garrisons to spoil and plunder the villages almost the entire night . . . beat and wound the people until they are eventually almost killed. . . . Along with the spoiling and plundering all kinds of new butcheries and tortures occur in order to determine if someone or another had hidden something. . . . The kind of shameful sin and disgrace that is practiced with the violation of virgins and women is inexplicable, and some virgins, facing such immodest guests, have leaped from the windows and hurt themselves in order to rescue their honor. And there are also numerous examples of old and sick wives and maids raped to death and afterwards eaten by the dogs.[26]

The more segments of society that Wallenstein alienated, the more these individuals yearned for their old masters or a new Protestant savior.

While Wallenstein's troops terrorized the people of the Baltic coast, other armies continued to roam across southern, central, and western Germany. And while the movements of soldiers across territories caused the most damage to the residents, many people also had to face the constant difficulty of long-term occupation. In 1628, in the tiny town of Weidenstetten, for example, residents were forced to house and feed a group of cavalrymen, along with all their servants. "We had to supply them with an unfortunately large amount of provisions," one resident complained, "including several barrels of wine, meat, bacon, and all kinds of magnificent things."[27] But this was only the beginning, for not only did these troops stay for years, but later that summer, several hundred more infantrymen marched through the area and had to be put up in the local villages. "An impossible burden has now been placed on the peasantry throughout the land," a villager wrote, "since we have to buy for the soldiers whatever they want to have, including meat, wine, beer and many other things, whatever they can think of, and the subjects are thus tremendously burdened."[28] In this situation, as in many similar ones across the empire, local government officials met with military leaders to try to minimize the damage. Such agreements benefited both sides. Local governments wanted to limit and standardize the extractions on the people, while military leaders wanted to ensure a compliant population and the continuous payment of contributions. The authorities at Ulm, for example, met with the colonel who commanded the troops quartered in their territory. Their agreement was then printed up and posted throughout the territory so that everyone, both peasants and soldiers, could see its terms, which included provisions

that no peasant had to give anything more to the cavalry than wood, straw, hay, candles, and salt, and in return the lords of Ulm had to give to every single cavalry captain 50 talers. And as a cavalry captain received 50 talers, a lieutenant also received 25 talers, an ensign 20 talers, a corporal 9 talers . . . and every single cavalryman 3 talers. They [the cavalry] had to stick to this agreement firmly and solidly on pain of life and limb.[29]

Of course, such agreements were fine in theory, but they seldom held firmly in practice. With this arrangement in Ulm, for example, a resident complained that the soldiers "only minimally kept to this agreement, and still most horribly tormented and distressed us subjects, and robbed and plundered us on all the streets, so that no one was safe, even riding only a half an hour over the fields."[30]

The success of the emperor being so impressive, he continued to act as if he were the absolute ruler in the empire. In 1628, he installed his younger son, Leopold Wilhelm, as bishop of Bremen, Magdeburg, and Halberstadt, and, in 1629, he pushed Denmark out of the war. His most imperious act, however, was the issuance, that very same year, of the Edict of Restitution. "We, Ferdinand, by the grace of God, Holy Roman Emperor," the edict began,

are determined for the realization both of the religious and profane peace to dispatch our Imperial commissioners into the Empire; to reclaim all the archbishoprics, bishoprics, prelacies, monasteries, hospitals and endowments which the Catholics had possessed at the time of the Treaty of Passau [1552] and of which they have been illegally deprived. . . . Such as hold the archbishoprics and bishoprics, prelacies, monasteries, hospitals, etc., shall forthwith return them.[31]

In other words, according to this edict, anyone who had acquired lands appropriated from the Catholic Church since 1552 was required to return them without receiving any compensation or "be distrained by force." The edict was thus even more incendiary than Wallenstein's social policy because it alienated anyone who had ever acquired such property and so gave a great many such proprietors an added incentive to hold onto their religion and resist what they felt to be a dictatorial act. The edict frightened Protestants across the empire, who read into it even more sweeping changes than it held. As Hans Heberle, a tailor from the Protestant territory of Ulm, described it,

Lutheranism was now abolished everywhere by the emperor, and Catholic property or church property was supposed to be given back to the Catholics. This frightened the Protestant states while greatly pleasing the Catholics. Then there was a great outcry and lack of trust, and everyone was afraid that his goods would be extracted and taken away.[32]

Hans Heberle was wrong that the edict banned Lutheranism, but he was close. Within the edict, Ferdinand stated that "we herewith declare that the Religious Peace [of Augsburg] refers only to the Augsburg Confession as it was submitted to our ancestor Emperor Charles V on 25 June 1530; and that all other doctrines and sects, whatever names they may have, not included in the Peace are forbidden and cannot be tolerated."[33] In other words, Ferdinand had banned Calvinism. This not only horrified Calvinists but also ensured that, in order to preserve their religion, Calvinist princes and states must now keep fighting until God granted them either victory or death.

It seemed, however, as if the emperor was unstoppable and well on the way to establishing his dominance and reestablishing religious unity in the Holy Roman Empire.[34] The new king of England having problems of his own, and the king of Denmark having failed miserably, only one possible Protestant champion still remained. This was Gustavus Adolphus, the Lutheran king of Sweden, a brilliant soldier who had already established his military reputation in Poland. He, too, was alarmed by the rise of imperial power, but he was hesitant to intervene. He did not want to share the fate of Christian IV of Denmark. The Catholic prime minister of France, Cardinal Richelieu, was also extremely concerned. He had already tried to help Christian IV of Denmark in his failed enterprise, and now he set about to tempt Gustavus Adolphus with subsidies if he would only intervene in the empire. After a great deal of soul searching, the king of Sweden concluded that in order to protect the interests of his own monarchy as well as those of his religion, he had no choice but to evict Wallenstein from the Baltic coast. Thus, in June 1630, he set off from Sweden with about 14,000 troops, landing a few days later on the shores of Pomerania. Fortunately for him, Wallenstein's meteoric rise had aroused such jealousy among the Catholic princes that the emperor chose just this moment to dismiss him. Little by little, therefore, Gustavus Adolphus made himself master of eastern Pomerania, meeting little opposition. He also came to terms with France for a treaty that provided him with much-needed financial support for his armies.[35]

The arrival of Gustavus Adolphus was followed by one of the most awful massacres of the Thirty Years' War—the sack of Magdeburg. Magdeburg was a Lutheran bishopric seriously threatened by the Edict of Restitution. Seeing its salvation in the arrival of Gustavus Adolphus, it rebelled against the emperor and threw its lot in with the Swedes. Although its petty forces were quickly defeated by the imperialists in the field, the city promised Gustavus Adolphus that it would withstand a siege until February of the following year, by which time his army could come to the rescue. But the city waited in vain, for while the army of Tilly remained stubbornly camped outside its walls, Gustavus Adolphus was far away, busily taking over the rest of Pomerania and Mecklenburg while attempting to entice various Protestant princes into his alliance. By the morning of May 20, 1631, its defenses at the breaking point, the city council finally decided to come to terms with Tilly. But the council had deliberated on

the surrender for too long, and, as they pondered one last time, imperial troops breached the walls and poured into the city. Having long since
stripped the surrounding countryside of all provisions, and depending on
booty for a large part of their pay, the soldiers plundered the rich city with
abandon, hauling away whatever priceless books, manuscripts, paintings,
tapestries, and treasures they could find. "Whoever they encountered,"
the Swedish ambassador John Adler Salvius reported, "they slew."

They raped wives and virgins, tyrannized young and old . . . and spared no one. . . .
The clergy was most terribly treated. They were first massacred in their library and
then burnt along with their books. Their wives and daughters were tied behind the
horses, dragged into camp, raped, and terribly molested. The church of St. John
was full of womenfolk, whom they locked in from the outside, thereafter throwing
burning torches through the windows. The Croats and Walloons behaved mercilessly, throwing children into the fire and tying the more beautiful and well-off
women citizens to their stirrups, made off with them behind their horses out of
town. They spiked small children onto their lances, waved them around and cast
them into flames. Turks, Tartars, and heathens could not have been more cruel.[36]

By ten in the evening, the entire city was destroyed, burnt by a fire that
spread to every corner. Even in the face of the ongoing brutality of war, the
extent of this destruction shocked observers across Europe and pushed a
number of key Protestant princes, including the electors of Brandenburg
and Saxony and the landgrave of Hesse-Cassel, to throw their lot in with
the Swedes. Contemporary accounts estimated as many as 20,000 residents
of Magdeburg dead, the bodies burnt in the flames or tossed unceremoni-
ously into the Elbe, where "many floated about for a long time, some with
their heads out of the water and others with their hands outstretched as
if to heaven, making a gruesome spectacle for onlookers." Some people
argued that "it was exactly as though these dead people were still pray-
ing, singing and crying out to heaven for vengeance."[37] Salvius's report on
the sack, while expressing horror at the indiscriminate slaughter, refused
to accept any blame for Sweden's failure to come to the aid of the city.
Instead, he blamed the citizenry itself for providing insufficient aid to the
defenders and for complacency. But whoever was responsible for the fall
of the city, however the deadly fire started, and whether or not contemporary rules of war made the sack technically legal, tens of thousands of
innocent people were now dead.[38]

Gustavus Adolphus may have lamented the sack of Magdeburg, but,
like so many other princes of his time, his solution to such atrocities was
to win the war. And in this effort he lived up to his reputation when, along
with the troops of the elector of Saxony, he met Tilly at the battle of Breitenfeld on September 7, 1631, and gained a great victory, scattering the
imperialists before him. And, while his Saxon allies then invaded Bohemia, he moved his own armies more than 200 miles to the west. Within a
year, he occupied the Rhineland, including the Catholic archbishopric of

Mainz, from which he moved south to take Munich, the capital of the duke of Bavaria, the emperor's biggest supporter. In other words, not only did the Swedes manage to retake large areas of North and West Germany from the imperialists; they also advanced into areas that did not greet them as liberators. By his treaty with France, Gustavus Adolphus had promised that he would not disrupt the practice of Catholicism in areas he occupied, and, while he and his officers generally kept this promise, the Swedish troops were less interested in mollifying the French court than in securing the supplies and food they desperately needed. They were also quite willing to extract money from the common people by threatening their religious leaders. In the town of Salem, near the Rhine, for example, the Swedish soldiers

caught eight or nine of the monks, together with a number of horses and traps or coaches, into which they all had to get, and they took them with them to Ravensburg as prisoners. There they were to be held until such time as a ransom or protection money of 6000 taler was paid, which had to be promptly on the 28th, first thing in the morning. . . .This 6000 taler was paid on the 28th of April, and the monks were set free again, although the time until the money arrived must have been long enough for them, as they were frequently threatened that if the ransom did not follow they would have to hang.[39]

While Gustavus Adolphus had promised to restrain violence against Catholics, he had not promised not to assist Protestants who now wanted to practice their religion in Catholic areas, and he also had no problem with extracting large forced loans from the Jews or forcing the Catholic populace of the Rhineland and Bavaria to support his army through organized contributions.[40]

The extractions of contributions, the looting, and the quartering of soldiers angered the common people and their leaders, and in some areas the peasants organized themselves to resist their invaders. An English observer reported, for example, that in southern Germany

some boors in Swabia being 10,000 strong have assembled themselves together, they have taken again Leutkirch and Wangen, they have with them some pieces of ordnance . . . This week the afore mentioned boors did overcome and surprise 50 Swedish soldiers . . . [and] these boors when they had mastered them, did cut off their ears and noses, chopped off their hands and feet, and put out their eyes, and so left them. . . . As soon as the king of Sweden was advertised of the cruell insolencies of these boors he was much displeased, and so much the more because he saw that his soldiers would not put it up but presently cried revenge and fired their villages, insomuch that in one day there were seen 200 several fires blazing at once.[41]

Thus, while Gustavus Adolphus tried to limit the damage caused by his troops, in this case they proceeded out of a spirit of vengeance and in return for 50 slain troops took 200 villages. This principle of an eye for an eye also guided some Protestant civilians who had been newly liberated from Catholic overlords. A perfect example of this is what happened in January 1631 when the Saxons invaded Bohemia and occupied the city of Prague:

Fifteen cornets of cavalry and thirteen companies of infantry were brought into Prague and quartered. Thereafter the Lutherans, who up to now had been dispossessed and forced to go around in misery, returned to the cities and the countryside and into their houses and possessions, which had been taken from them by the Catholics. The peasants also began to join the Saxons, plundering their overlords and ecclesiastical possessions, and whenever they met their lords they beat them almost to death. They did the same to the imperial soldiers whenever they fell into their hands.[42]

While these two examples of Swabia and Prague show how some peasants came together into bands on their own initiative, either to resist invaders or to wreak vengeance on prior oppressors, other peasant armies were more organized. In Ulm, for example, which was only a small Protestant city-state with no standing army to defend it, the city council required every town within its territory to contribute a number of able-bodied men for a defensive militia. As we saw earlier, however, this peasant army had not proven to be particularly effective and had been disbanded years before. Yet the reinvigoration of the war caused by the entry of the Swedes forced the city council to reconsider in 1631. One peasant recalled the events of that year:

The 10th day of June we, as the militia, once again had to take up arms and were called to Ulm to the armory courtyard. And they wanted to make us into real soldiers, for there we had to swear loyalty to the troop, and they read aloud to us in the strongest possible terms all the articles of war. Then we had to stand with our hands raised and to promise to comply with them, as is traditional in war. After this we were transferred [elsewhere in the city] where several tents were pitched and we were given beer and bread as rations.[43]

Although the city council seemed to hope that treating the peasants as if they were "real soldiers" might make them more effective, they were not. This was not so much a product of their lack of skill, however, but a result of their minuscule numbers in the face of actual armies. Having endured the continuous plundering by Catholic troops since 1625, the city council gladly signed a formal treaty of alliance with the Swedes in February 1632. As part of this agreement, the burghers agreed to support a garrison of Swedish troops under the command of Colonel Patrick Ruthwen, a Scottish earl in the Swedish service. "And thereafter," a resident reported, "the 28th day of February, the government asked the burghers whether they would want to be Swedish, and this was accepted from the heart with joy. The 14th day of March the young fellows in the land of Ulm were put under the Swedish troops, so that resistance could be offered to the enemy."[44]

Within a short span of time, therefore, the situation in the Holy Roman Empire had changed completely. In 1629, Ferdinand II seemed to be on the brink of establishing his hegemony and restoring Catholicism. Three years later, Gustavus Adolphus was poised to seize control of the empire and build up within it a Protestant state with a state. Cardinal Richelieu, in France, began to worry about what he had wrought, and he was not the only one. In his panic, Ferdinand recalled Wallenstein, the only man who might be able to stop the Swedish onslaught. Wallenstein managed to rally the Catholic and imperial armies, and he confronted Gustavus Adolphus on November 16, 1632, at the battle of Lützen. In the midst of this historic battle, Gustavus Adolphus met his death, even though his army emerged victorious. His supporters were devastated, his enemies exultant.[45]

THE LINGERING AGONY

The death of Gustavus Adolphus did not result in the disappearance of the Swedes from the war. Indeed, deprived of his moderating control, and under such commanders as the freebooter Duke Bernard of Saxe-Weimar, the Swedish armies became on the one hand more German and on the other hand more violent. For example, after a siege of the imperial city of Regensburg in November 1633, Bernard's mercenary troops not only abolished Catholicism and looted the churches but also moved on to plunder the countryside mercilessly, destroying all the houses and fields. The response of the people to such incursions was the same as it had ever been. Most fled into the forests and wild areas; some few attempted to resist. The residents of the monastery at Salem are a good example of this second group. Facing repeated raids on food and cattle by Swedish troops, the monastery raised a mixed force of 400 professional soldiers and around 150 "badly mounted Haylgenberg farmers with halberds, boar spears, . . . badger-catching forks, clubs and cudgels . . . with the intention of going out to meet them, greet them, attack them and defeat them."[46] Luckily for the inhabitants, the Swedes moved on to easier targets. Their conduct in Bavaria and along the Rhine produced some of the most grisly tales of torture that came out of the war. One contemporary reported that in order to extract the meager possessions from the peasantry, the Swedish troops used tortures such as the *capitum prensatio,* in which they bound the head of their victim tighter and tighter until his eyeballs popped out. Another torture was the *haustum suecicum,* or "Swedish drink." Here the troops tied the hands and feet of the victim and tossed him to the floor, forced open his mouth, knocking out his teeth in the process, then poured liquid manure or urine down his throat until he was full to bursting. A third was the *digitorum compressio,* in which the soldiers fastened the fingers of their victim in a vice and tightened it until blood spurted from the fingernails. These tortures were not reserved for Catholics, however, but were also used against any Protestant who might be hiding money, food, or livestock. One chronicler also took pains to note that the phrase "the Swedish drink" did not mean that the Swedes alone practiced it. Indeed, he argued, the name could be construed in the opposite way, because the imperialists often used this torture on Swedish prisoners.[47]

While the death of Gustavus Adolphus did not end the Swedish intervention in the empire, it did produce a resurgence of his enemies. By 1634, the imperialists and their Spanish cousins had managed to reorganize their armies, and when they faced the depleted and poorly led Swedes at the battle of Nördlingen in November, they completely defeated them. The ruined Swedish army fled the battlefield, and residents of neighboring regions followed suit. "Because [the Swedes] had lost everything," a peasant from the countryside near Ulm reported,

their entire army was ruined and put to flight, so that the fleeing cavalry were already with us at midday. Then as we saw this we did not delay for long. Whoever could run, ran, so that we might still reach [the city of] Ulm that same day. This was absolutely necessary, since the enemy was at our throats. . . . Then we had to leave behind everything that we had, and when we could only escape with our wives and children and our lives, we were happy to let the rest go, so great was the necessity. In the evening we came to the city, many thousand people from all over, and we camped over night in front of the [closed gates of the] city, and in the morning of the 28th of August we were let into the city of Ulm.[48]

Those who made it to safety inside walled cities were the lucky ones. As the imperialists advanced against the defeated Swedes, their victorious troops pillaged the countryside, killing and torturing anyone they could find. A minister of the town of Calw, in Würtemberg, described the great fright of the common people as they fled.

I joined a band of women and children soon amounting to more than 200 people. Like ants we scurried over hills and rocks. . . . After going about 20 miles as if swept on by the wind we arrived in the depth of night at Gernsbach, to the great consternation of the citizens there, who at first thought we were enemies. . . . Since the enemy was also active in these parts and pillaging the whole neighbourhood, and since we were nearly encircled, we decided to make an attempt to ask the victor for mercy. But to our further consternation we had to flee once again into the hills where no one could readily follow us. From there we wandered around, divided into smaller bands. . . . We were [finally] called back in a letter from our friends, since everything, as far as the times allowed, was back in order, which accorded with the enemy's own best interest. When I saw my beloved town of Calw in ashes and rubble . . . I felt a cold shudder and I brooded repeatedly on that which I neither can nor wish to repeat now.[49]

Such scenes played out in town after town, and any that dared resist the imperial forces faced harsh retaliation. When the residents of the small town of Geißlingen, for example, tried to defend themselves, they were viciously attacked, and hundreds of them were killed. As a further caution, the soldiers "also cut off the head of their minister and robbed the little town blind."[50] The town of Bietigheim suffered under the attentions of three separate armies—the Spanish, the Bavarian, and the imperialists, and at one time residents could clearly see 16 different neighboring towns up in flame. The residents of Bietigheim were doubly cursed, however, for not only did they face the approaching soldiers, but their own city officials fled, leaving the residents "without help or advice." Like the residents of Calw, therefore, the citizens of Bietigheim decided to flee into the woods and fields, but the soldiers used dogs to hunt them out.[51]

Civilians had just as much to fear from their "defenders" as they did from the enemy troops. As the Swedes fled Nördlingen, for example, the frightened troops did nothing to help their allies but instead took their supplies wherever they could get them. Thus, one peasant complained that whatever the Swedish troops "could grab from us as we fled, that is what they did as they fled, so that we had both [armies] at our throats."[52] The imperialists were just as indiscriminate, and one chronicler from Überlingen reported bitterly that "the imperialists have brought more desolation and ruin to this land in the last ten days alone . . . than the enemy did in almost a full year."[53] This was not a new phenomenon, of course. Even back in 1621, the people of the Palatinate had complained that the Palatine soldiers were worse than the Spanish invaders. According to one report, "the [Palatine] soldiers . . . opened cabinets, cupboards, and chests and confiscated everything, stole the fruit from the cold storage and the stakes from the vineyard, ripped out the doors and made huts from them, shot cows and pigs and devastated everything. Thus the Palatine 'defenders' were called 'devastators.'"[54] Yet, while some things were the same as they had been in 1621, the differences were much more striking. In 1621, the war had been confined to Bohemia and the far eastern reaches of the empire on the one hand and the dual Palatinates on the other. But over the years, the war had inexorably spread, first northwest, then north and northeast, then south, then everywhere in between. By 1634, therefore, the stain of war had spread throughout the entire empire, leaving almost no one unsullied.

On top of his military victories, the emperor now managed a diplomatic one. In order to reclaim the support of the Protestant princes, he moderated his stance on the matter of religion and agreed to repeal the controversial Edict of Restitution if they would join him in resisting the foreign enemies. This diplomatic advance worked, and nearly all of the German princes signed on to a peace made at Prague in 1635. The peace was greeted with joy by Catholics and Protestants alike. When the good news reached the city of Ulm, for example, a peasant who had taken refuge there reported that

On Sunday after the sermon all the bells were tolled together and salvos or shots of joy were fired from great cannons around the entire city and from every bastion. . . . Then I, with my wife and children, moved from the city back to our home, as did the entire countryside, after the miserable blockade that we had endured for so long . . . camped in the city on top of each other, enduring such great hunger and grief that I will forbear to write of it, since it would take me far too long to describe.[55]

Similar scenes played out across the empire, as the common people thanked God for their deliverance. The people of the Holy Roman Empire were now in a position to breathe and weigh their losses.

By this point, the empire presented a patchwork of devastation. First, there were areas that in one violent moment had been utterly destroyed, such as Magdeburg, and areas that had suffered repeated or continual despoliation, such as Bohemia, Württemberg, and the Rhineland. Things were so bad in the countryside around Ulm, for example, that agriculture had almost ceased, and, in the words of one resident, "the Heidhof and Zimmerlau forests grew together into an area which, in my time, had all been open land. Then it had been a common field, on which I myself had harvested crops. Now it has become a forest, so that whoever wants to go to Bernstadt now has to go through a forest which did not exist previously."[56] Second, there were areas that had been sacked or despoiled on only a few occasions and had been able to survive such events much as they had survived previous natural disasters. In this category one could list the Protestant city of Leipzig, which, despite being conquered and fleeced multiple times, was too valuable as a trading center for anyone to want to damage it irrevocably. The Catholic city of Regensburg, seat of the *Reichstag* and of the elections to the imperial throne, was another such area. Only 10 months after being ravaged by Bernard of Saxe-Weimar, it was retaken by the imperialists, and the citizens rapidly managed to recover and rebuild. Third, and last, there were areas of the empire that either had escaped the war entirely unscathed or had even prospered. Examples of this category were the imperial capital of Vienna, the Catholic city of Cologne, and the great free imperial city-state of Hamburg. Hamburg, protected by its status as neutral ground for the diplomatic maneuvering of the warring parties, thrived during the war. It also became an increasingly important financial and commercial center, challenging Amsterdam as the main focus of Iberian commerce and attracting Protestant, Catholic, and Jewish immigrants from across Europe. Such growth and prosperity was the exception, however, for 17 years of war had left much of the empire ruined, its cities and towns depopulated by war, plague, and famine and its financial and agricultural resources exhausted.[57]

The Peace of Prague promised to end the ravages of war in the empire, but Cardinal Richelieu, the French prime minister, had different ideas. "It is certain," he had written on hearing of the Battle of Nördlingen, "that if the [Protestant] party is ruined, the entire power of the house of Austria will fall on France."[58] Once again, in the mind of a European statesman, the interests of his state prevailed over the suffering of humanity, and this time, remarkably, the interests of his state prevailed even over the potential triumph of his religion. He set about to raise a large army, hired Bernard of Saxe-Weimar, and prepared to take the battle to the enemies. And so, just as the Habsburgs seemed to be on the verge of restoring some sort of peace and stability, this Catholic cardinal almost singlehandedly stepped in to rekindle the flames. But Richelieu was not quite alone. A small number of Calvinist princes, including the landgrave of Hesse-Cassel and the Prince Palatine, had either refused or been excluded from the Peace of Prague. The alliance of France with both Sweden and these few, but powerful, German states meant that, despite the emperor's victories, the war would go on.[59]

One clear difference by this point in the war, however, was that, by now, the empire had been so ravaged and its economy so strained that armies had much more trouble living off the land. This made the size of armies smaller but did little to alleviate the misery of the people. And as if unpredictable episodes of war were not enough, the residents of the empire also had to face inflation and frequent famine. "And because of this famine," one peasant wrote,

many hideous and loathsome things were eaten by the poor people, as namely all kinds of things that did not make sense: dogs and cats, mice and dead livestock, horse meat, so that the knacker and butcher got their meat from dead livestock, such as horse, dog, and other animals, and people scrambled with each other for it and considered it to be delicious. All kinds of herbs from the open country were also considered good: thistle, nettle, water hemlock, buttercup. . . . In sum, all kinds of herbs became good, for hunger is a good cook, as one says in the proverb.[60]

Famine hit the poor the hardest, of course, but you can't eat money, and numerous chronicles reported with wonder that even the children of the rich went hungry.[61] The effects of famine were also more subtle than mere death or suffering. A pastor from Hesse remarked, for example, that the famine had made almost every marriage unfruitful, "so that even among the youngest married couples no children were brought forth." Such difficult circumstances also "cooled the love between married couples and others," he wrote, "since no one was any use to anyone else: a husband moved away from his spouse into another land in order to look for bread; children moved away from their parents, and some of them never saw each other again."[62]

Weakened by hunger and constant fear, all efforts at hygiene foiled by repeated flights into the woods and crowded refugee conditions in the cities, the common people also began to fall prey in increasing numbers to disease, especially the plague. The connection among famine, flight, and plague seemed clear to even the lowliest peasants, but there was little they could do.[63] Over the course of the year 1635, more than 15,000 people died of the plague in the city of Ulm alone. Seven thousand died in the city of Frankfurt on the Main, including 222 Jews, mostly children, from the ghetto.[64] In smaller towns, the numbers of dead were also smaller, but the percentages just as—or even more—devastating. In the town of Biberau, for example, only twenty-five people out of three hundred survived the epidemic.[65] In the small towns of Bietigheim and Bönnigheim, the town deathbook recorded 149 deaths in the year 1632, but 1,614 in 1635, with most of these caused by the plague that appeared in the town between July and November. The number lost in this one year alone amounted to around 35 percent of the population, with the first victim being a nine-year-old girl, Anna Hornmold. By September 1635, the pastor of Bietigheim was almost beyond despair. "Oh Lord," he wrote, "say to the Angel of Ruin: it is enough, now remove your hand, for the sake of Jesus Christ, Amen."[66] Yet even though the peasants were sick, dying, and starving, soldiers from both sides continued to demand food and money. The pastor of the town of Groß-Bieberau wrote that people dying of plague were not safe even in their own homes but that instead "the sick were thrown out of their beds so that they could be searched, and the sick were also beaten, since the robbers hoped to get some money or bread out of them." Since there were so many dead, and the number of dead grew so quickly, many people remained unburied for a long time. The pastor recorded that one day he had been alerted by miserable cries to a young girl lying sick in bed with her long-dead mother, covered in worms. His kindness in arranging the mother's burial led other desperate townspeople to deposit their dead at his doorstep during the night.[67] Foreign observers were shocked by the widespread destruction. Visiting the empire on a diplomatic mission, an English diplomat recorded that all the towns from Cologne to Frankfurt were "battered, pillaged, and burnt," with "wretched children" sitting huddled on their doorsteps "almost dying of hunger."[68]

Although his empire was dying out from under him, the emperor maintained the upper hand militarily and also got the electors to name his son Ferdinand "king of the Romans," a title that assured him the succession to the empire as Ferdinand III in the year 1637 upon the death of his father, Ferdinand II. As with his father, the new emperor's biggest priority was countering the threat of the Swedes and the French. And he was not alone. To the rising chorus of wails and complaints, many princes responded with their usual pious repartee about how they wanted peace but their evil enemies did not.[69] Indeed, all the evidence from Brandenburg demonstrates that the elector and the nobility exhibited very little sympathy for their peasants who had attempted to escape the ravages of war.[70]

The depredations and the quartering of troops were common problems for the people of both the countryside and the city, but city residents also suffered from a unique horror—siege. The siege of Breisach in the autumn of 1638 by Bernard of Saxe-Weimar, for example, cut the city off from its food supplies for almost four months. Prices soared, and nearly all the house pets were eaten. Those with the least suffered the most, and some reports claimed that people even resorted to cannibalism. According to one contemporary,

On 24 November a soldier under arrest in the prison died, and before the warder in charge could order his burial the other prisoners had taken the body, cut it up and eaten it. Two corpses were dug up and cut open. The innards were taken out and eaten. In one day three children were consumed. The soldiers promised a pastry-cook's boy a piece of bread if he followed them to camp. But when he got there, they cut him up and ate him. On 10 December eight well known burghers' children alone disappeared in the fishers' district, presumed eaten, they could never be traced, not to mention all the children of beggars and strangers whom no one knew anyway. . . . On 12 December another prisoner died and before the warder in charge could have him buried, the other prisoners fell onto the corpse and tore at it with their teeth, eating the raw flesh. . . . On the last day before the defenders marched out, a bowl of sauerkraut went for a golden ring. . . . No wonder that we're dying, when such atrocities are God's punishment to Germany.[71]

Thus, the people of the Holy Roman Empire, both in the cities and in the countryside, continued to suffer and die. And it seemed to them that no one, not even Almighty God himself, wanted to stop the carnage.

The great promises of the Peace of Prague had now long since proved themselves to have been only a cruel joke, and the people's joy at the arrival of peace all the more emotionally devastating for being so quickly and brutally crushed. Germans bemoaned the fate of their country "that was once so rich, so full of plenty, so abounding with multitudes of people, so glorious for arts, so renowned for pleasantness, for strength, for our many, great and beautiful cities." "[O]h how my soul mourns to see her excellence thus departed," one Lutheran sermon exclaimed. "You are all witnesses. . . .The sword has not marched without other judgments to accompany it, as heavy or heavier than itself; as fire, famine, pestilence; and has not yet blunted, but is moving on as furiously as if it had scarcely begun its work."[72]

Such general pessimism was one thing, but locals were also at pains to demonstrate the actual numbers of their losses to their seemingly unfeeling rulers. "At the beginning of the invasion by Tilly in 1623," one Hessian village reported in 1639,

this village had 172 hearths, but after the terrible Croatian arson only 72, including the tiniest, remained and in the Götzian passage another 12 burned down and other houses and barns were set on fire. Even though another 13 tiny houses now have been built, it does not help at all, and it is truly pitiable that we poor people have not had our contribution reduced by a single *Heller* despite the great damage, and we once again beg for God's sake and in all submissiveness, that that might occur.[73]

Yet, as we have seen before, the imperialists were not alone in their brutality. The 1640 seizure of areas of the Bohemian countryside by the Swedes was followed by "burning, plundering, destroying, and overturning of the towns and villages." The Swedish troops "not only found and confiscated all the crops and everything else that was necessary to support human life ... but also all ruined and chopped down all the fruit trees."[74] The destruction wreaked by soldiers on both sides was so complete in some areas that the wild animals even began to reclaim the land as their own. In the winter of 1640, one peasant described how, "as punishment, God sent us evil animals into the land to devour our sheep and cattle. Before the war it was a wonder if one saw a wolf," he wrote,

> but now and in these years it is not unusual for us to have seen many together, for they run everywhere, young and old. They run among the livestock, even when two or three men are with the livestock, and take from the herd nanny goats and sheep. And they do not allow themselves to be taken, even if one goes after them with full force. Yes, they even come into the villages and in front of the houses and take cats and dogs away, so that one can no longer have any dogs in the villages.[75]

Under the pressure of such widespread misery and complaints, in 1641, the French, the Swedes, and the imperialists finally agreed to hold a peace conference. But this was mere words, and the war went on. People even began to think that the war would never end. In June 1642, a pastor from the small town of Reichensachsen described the utter hopelessness of the people and the endlessness of the war. "Is there even one house, one alley, one corner, one street, one field, one road, one trail, one footpath, one hill, one hedge, one mountain, one valley," he wrote, "that has not been sprinkled with our blood and marked by the blood of the killed?"

> And those of us who still live and remain here ... what else are we but a repast for fire and the sword, which await us. .... You have become like a common whore, whoever thinks of you wants to quarter by you! ... In addition, they open their mouths up wide against you—that is your reward—whistle at you, blacken your teeth and say "he ha" we have plundered and hunted you and we like it, we have treated you like discarded water and spurned you. .... I say to you all who pass by, Look for yourself and see if there is any pain that has passed us by, for the Lord has filled me with woe on the day of his anger, he has sent a fire from hell to my bones and let it boil, he has tied a net around my feet and knocked me down, he has made me desolate, so that I must mourn daily. I the pastor and all who pass by you may say: O Reichensachsen ... your suffering is great as a sea, who can heal you?[76]

Only peace would end such suffering, but decades had passed and peace was still elusive. Its prospect seemed almost fantastical, a time when "our sons grow up in their youth like plants and our daughters like the bay trees ... our sheep bear a thousand and a hundred thousand in our villages."[77]

It was not until 1643 that the representatives of the various princes actually began to assemble. Catholics met in the Westphalian town of Münster, Protestants in the Westphalian town of Osnabrück. By this time the popular discontent with the war was such that, in the words of one contemporary, "not only the people made great complaints, but also the cities, villages, towns, houses, open country, fields, trees, and vineyards. Yes, the livestock themselves, if they could speak of it, would have witnessed, told, and complained about it."[78] Yet, in spite of such misery, or perhaps because of it, in some places a new spirit of toleration was emerging. A French officer serving with the French army in Lorraine in 1643, for example, described just such an "extraordinary" situation, which he saw while passing through the city of Vaudrevange, which was situated on the border of Lorraine. The city "is inhabited by equal numbers of Huguenots [Calvinists] and Catholics," he wrote, and

the Catholic church also serves as the church for the Huguenots. The [Catholic] curate and the minister live in perfect harmony with each other. On Sunday, the Catholics hear mass from eight to ten in the morning, and at ten the Catholics leave to make place for the Huguenots, greeting each other most courteously, and in the same pulpit as the curate has preached to the Catholics, the minister preaches to the Huguenots. And if one Sunday the Catholics have come in at eight o'clock, the next Sunday they come in at ten. There is such perfect equality that after having eaten with the curate, the minister came to invite me to dinner as well.[79]

This willingness of Catholics and Protestants to live together in "perfect equality" may have been a rare phenomenon, but it is a significant one. It shows both that 26 years of war had not removed all vestiges of humanity from the average man and woman and that the very idea of religious difference had become less offensive and disturbing over the years. This same Frenchman had reason to appreciate this fact, for by 1644 he had become a prisoner of war in Augsburg, a city occupied by the imperialists but also inhabited by a good number of Lutherans. As he describes his ordeal:

We were kept for three months in cells, with only as much light as could come in through some air holes, sending out appeals for alms into the city, and since they are rather charitable in that country, there were some good women who brought us bread, beer, and cider in their aprons, which they passed down through the air holes. We also asked for charity from the monks, who were all-powerful in this city, but we only got rebuffs from them, and the Lutherans behaved more charitably towards us than these monks, who prided themselves on being good politicians.[80]

This episode is also quite fascinating for the way in which the participants' actions do not follow directly from their religious affiliation. The French prisoners, though Catholics, were comforted by their allies in the war, the Lutherans. The monks, though Catholics, had no sympathy for their enemies, the French, and instead preferred to flaunt their loyalty to the imperialists.

At Münster and Osnabrück, meanwhile, the parties continued to waste time, always looking for the next battle to change the odds in their favor and so increase their diplomatic leverage, to the point where even the chaplain of one of the French plenipotentiaries got impatient. Delivering a sermon on the passion on March 30, 1646, he had Jesus Christ speaking from the cross to the Catholic monarchs of Europe in the following words:

I have made you my lieutenants in this world in order to dispense justice on other men. I have put you in a position that is barely below that of my angels, I have crowned you with honor and with glory. . . . I have given you immense riches, numerous peoples, no end of subjects. How have you disposed of them, how have you governed them, how have you treated my creatures who are made in my likeness as well as yours? I have given you great armies on land and sea in order to make you formidable to the Turks and Infidels, to keep heretics in their duty, to protect and defend my churches; however, they ruin my temples, the violate my altars, they turn Christian provinces into deserts, while the enemy of my name is not satisfied with usurping the country which I have today consecrated with my blood and which was formerly conquered so heroically by your fathers, but is extending his frontiers everyday and building his mosques in the unfortunate Crete.[81]

And while these monarchs continued to destroy Christendom in their push for what they saw as the greater good, and while the diplomats continued to discuss the particulars of territorial transfers and financial reparations, the peasants and townspeople continued to be forced to support the war with money, food, and the sweat of their brows. "In this year of [16]47," the mayor of the town of Allensbach wrote,

we had to give [the garrison at Hohent]wiel a monthly contribution of ten florins, together with three tuns of wine, . . . four wagonloads of grain, . . . and in the spring two thousand vine stakes, . . . while instead of hay and straw we regularly paid the captain of cavalry Hans Jerg Widerholt in cash, 86 florins and 6 batzen. The same year . . . we supplied [the garrison at] Constance with 2½ tuns of wine, many wagons of wood for watch fires, labourers for working parties and digging fortification works every day, and 100 hundredweight of hay. Likewise to Niclaus, Baron von Gramont, commandant of Zell, two florins service money every month, and 20 kegs of wine at the beginning of the year, as well as labourers and fortification workers at that time, and we had afterwards to pay out 16 batzen a week for the labour service.[82]

Yet, with the people of the Holy Roman Empire feeding the war machine, there was little incentive for the people in political power to rush into a peace, and it was concluded only when the Catholic and Protestant princes of the empire finally decided to unite in order to pressure the French, the Swedes, and the emperor into reaching some sort of compromise. Finally, on October 24, 1648, the Peace of Westphalia was signed by the powers in the city of Münster.

If one considers how close the house of Hapsburg had come to establishing its domination over the Holy Roman Empire, the treaties that the powers signed in Münster marked the dismal failure of this dynasty's ambitious

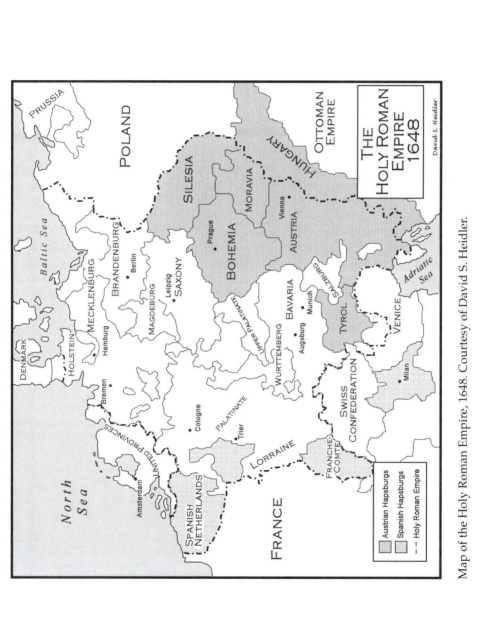

Map of the Holy Roman Empire, 1648. Courtesy of David S. Heidler.

designs. If one considers how close the house had come to total extinction at the hands of the Swedes, the Peace of Westphalia marked a reprieve. By this peace, the emperor retained his hold on the kingdom of Bohemia. Probably the biggest gainer among the Catholic princes, however, was the duke of Bavaria, who managed to keep not only his new electoral title but also the territory of the Upper Palatinate. Some Protestant princes, such as the elector of Brandenburg, also gained territories, but the unfortunate son of the "Winter King" had to consider himself lucky to be restored in the western half of his father's lands, the Lower Palatinate, and to accept for himself the newly created position of eighth elector of the Holy Roman Empire. In future imperial elections, therefore, the Catholics retained the majority. But the foreign powers now also became a force in the empire. The French obtained the province of Alsace and the Swedes the eastern part of Pomerania, the archbishopric of Bremen, the bishopric of Verden, and other territories, which gave them possession of a good deal of the Baltic coastline.

For the average man and woman, however, it was less the change of a distant sovereign than the religious settlement that would mark a shift in their lives. In some ways, the Peace of Westphalia merely confirmed the Peace of Augsburg of 1555. In both instances, a number of cities continued to enjoy mixed magistracies, and those individuals who cared enough to do so could still exercise the right of emigration. But in other ways the peace updated the arrangement at Augsburg and attempted to freeze it. The framers of the Peace of Westphalia were one with the people of the empire in wanting no more religious conflict. Any prince still had the right to change his religion, but he lost the right to change the religion of his people. The Protestant cities and princes were permitted to keep whatever church lands they might have grabbed up to the year 1624, but from now on they could grab no more, so that to all intents and purposes the "Reformation" was over. Bohemia, the Upper Palatinate, and other territories that the Catholics themselves had possessed up to that date were now secure in the hands of their overlords. One brief article in the peace explicitly gave to the Calvinists in the Holy Roman Empire the same rights as those enjoyed by Lutherans, even though Jews and other religious minorities were expressly excluded. Nevertheless, another remarkable article went so far as to state that any Catholics or Protestants who wished to change their religion must "be patiently tolerated and have freedom of conscience in their homes without investigation or disturbance." Out of the agony of mutual destruction and a desire to put an end to the insanity emerged the glimmer of the modern idea of toleration.[83]

The news of the peace took a while to trickle into the countryside, but, when it did, the rejoicing throughout the Empire was enormous. In Karlstadt, when the news of the peace was published, the citizens held a procession through the city, and there was celebratory singing and the ringing of the church bells and shots fired into the air.[84] In Ulm, one man reported that "we celebrated the festival [of thanksgiving], as formally and with such a will as ever we had Christmas day, and God be praised and thanked." The war had been hard, he wrote, and "such a miserable business that even a stone would have been moved to pity, not to mention a human heart. For we were hunted like wild animals in the forests. . . . Because of this we cannot sufficiently praise and laud God for the noble peace which we have lived to see."[85] And just as a miraculous comet had marked the beginning of the war, so, too, did one mark its end. According to Andreas Kothe, councilor of the Westphalian town of Wiedenbrücker, in November 1648 a "great comet was seen in the heavens, appearing in the east at eight in the evening." This comet, he wrote, "was seen across all of Europe, and had a long tail . . . and was seen for thirty evenings." The meaning of this was clear, for "the German shriek in the [Holy] Roman Empire has lasted thirty years," ended only "by the grace of God."[86]

Now that the war was over, it was finally time to begin the long process of rebuilding. But this would not be an easy task. Not only did it take years to disband all the soldiers and even longer for various states, cities, towns, and individuals to pay off their war debts; as survivors and refugees slowly began to return to their homes, many of them—especially in the countryside—found things in ruins. A resident of the village of Weidenstetten, for example, reported that, while he and his neighbors "returned home with every joy and moved back home and to our houses," those houses needed to be "put back together, for they were, in part, badly smashed and the windows, ovens, and doors were destroyed."[87] Across the empire, entire families had been wiped out, entire villages destroyed, and the agricultural basis on which everything rested seriously strained. The town of Bietigheim, for example, in addition to the destruction of its wells, its mill, its city walls, and 41 percent of all of its other structures, had also lost 79 percent of its inhabitants and 58 percent of its acres under cultivation.[88] In all, the population of the empire had dropped from around 20 million before the war to approximately 16 million thereafter, the biggest population drop since the great plague of the fourteenth century. It would take another half century, at least, for the civilians of the Holy Roman Empire to recover from the ravages of the Thirty Years' War.[89]

NOTES

1. Johann Philipp Abelinus and Matthaeus Merian, *Theatrum Europaeum*, vol. 1 (Frankfurt am Main: Wolffgang Hoffman, 1662), 100–101. For another account of the comet sighting, see *Die Reichenbacher Chronik (1599–1620) des Pfarrers Martin Walther*, cited in Rudolf Kunz and Willy Lizalek, eds., *Südhessische Chroniken aus der Zeit des Dreissigjährigen Krieges* (Heppenheim: Verlag Laurissa, 1983), 111.

2. *Zeitung aus Böhmen, Mähren, Österreich und anderen Ländern mehr*, 1619, nr. 42, cited in Hans Jessen, *Der Dreissigjährige Krieg in Augenzeugenberichten* (Düsseldorf: K. Rauch, 1963), 70.

3. Guenther Bentele, *Protokolle einer Katastrophe: zwei Bietigheimer Chroniken aus dem Dreissigjährigen Krieg* (Bietigheim-Bissingen: Stadtarchiv Bietigheim-Bissingen, 1984), 179–181; *Die Reichenbacher Chronik*, cited in Kunz and Lizalek, 113, 115.

4. Kurt Pfister, *Kurfürst Maximilian von Bayern und sein Jahrhundert* (München: F. Ehrenwirth, 1948), 180 cited in Jessen, 71.

5. C.V. Wedgwood, *The Thirty Years' War* (Garden City, NY: Anchor Books, 1961), 69–129.

6. Geoffrey Parker, ed., *The Thirty Years' War*, 2nd ed. (London & New York: Routledge, 1997), 88–90.

7. Titellose Berliner Zeitung, 1621, Nr. 50, cited in Jessen, 93–94.

8. Gerd Zillhardt, *Der Dreissigjährige Krieg in zeitgenössischer Darstellung: Hans Heberles "Zeytregister" (1618–1672), Aufzeichnungen aus dem Ulmer Territorium: ein Beitrag zu Geschichtsschreibung und Geschichtsverständnis der Unterschichten* (Ulm & Stuttgart: Stadtarchiv; Kommissionsverlag Kohlhammer, 1975), 101. For more on the situation in Bohemia, see Parker, *The Thirty Years' War*, 83–92. For the similar effects of the war on lower Austria in this period, see Erich Landsteiner and Andreas Weigl, "'Sonsten finden wir die Sachen sehr übel aufm Landt beschaffen'. Krieg und lokale Gesellschaft in Niederösterreich (1618–1621)," in *Zwischen Alltag und Katastrophe. Der Dreissigjährige Krieg aus der Nähe*, ed. Benigna von Krusenstjern and Hans Medick, *Veröffentlichungen des Max-Planck-Instituts für Geschichte* (Göttingen: Vandenhoeck & Ruprecht, 1999).

9. *Die Reichenbacher Chronik*, cited in Kunz and Lizalek, 120.

10. Zillhardt, 98–99.

11. Bentele, 181–182.

12. See, for example, Govind P. Sreenivasan, *The Peasants of Ottobeuren, 1487–1726. A Rural Society in Early Modern Europe* (Cambridge: Cambridge University Press, 2004), 289.

13. Conrad Memmius and Sigismund Latomus, *Relationis historicae semestralis autumnalis continuatio. Jacobi Franci historische Beschreibung der denckwürdigen Geschichten. alles auss überschickten Lateinischen, Italienischen, Frantzosischen, Hoch- und Nieder-Teutschen* (Frankfurt am Main: Johann Görlin, 1668), cited in Jessen, 143–145.

14. Wedgwood, 156.

15. For Christian of Brunswick's depredations see StA Praha, RA Valdštejnové, A II, 34, Ferdinand, Elector of Bavaria and Archbishop of Cologne to Count Franz Christoph Khevenhüller, 6 July 1622, cited in Miroslav Toegel, ed., *Der Kampf des Hauses Habsburg gegen die Niederlande und ihre Verbündeten: Quellen zur Geschichte des Pfälzisch-Niederländisch-Ungarischen Krieges, 1621–1625*, vol. 3, *Documenta bohemica Bellum Tricennale illustrantia* (Prague: Nakladatelství Československé akademie věd, 1976), 128–130.

16. *Die Bieberauer Chronik (1579–1654) des Pfarrers Johann Daniel Minck*, cited in Kunz and Lizalek, 239–240. For Mansfeld's behavior see also Memmius and Latomus, 18, cited in Jessen, 160–161.

17. Wedgwood, 145–159; Samuel Pufendorf, *An Introduction to the History of the Principal Kingdoms and States of Europe* (London: Thomas Newborough and Martha Gilliflower, 1700), 303. See also Samuel Pufendorf, *The Present State of Germany* (London, 1696), 152–153.

18. Zillhardt, 110.

19. Abelinus and Merian, vol. 1, 619.

20. E. Benger, *Memoirs of Elizabeth Stuart, queen of Bohemia, daughter of King James the First. Including sketches of the state of society in Holland and Germany, in the 17th century* (London: Longman Hurst Rees Orme Brown and Green, 1825), 230–233.

21. Stüve, *Geschichte des Hochstifts Osnabrück,* vol. 2 (Osnabrück: H. T. Wenner, 1980), 34–58.

22. Zillhardt, 113–14.

23. Paul Douglas Lockhart, *Denmark in the Thirty Years' War, 1618–1648: King Christian IV and the Decline of the Oldenburg State* (Selinsgrove, PA: Susquehanna University Press, 1996), ch. 6.

24. For more on Christian and Wallenstein see Parker, *The Thirty Years' War,* 71–81.

25. Herbert Langer, "Heeresfinanzierung, Produktion und Märkte für die Kriegführung," in *1648—Krieg und Frieden in Europa,* ed. Klaus Bussmann and Heinz Schilling (Münster & Osnabrück: Veranschaltungsgesellschaft 350 Jahre Westfälischer Friede mbH, 1998); Herbert Langer, *Stralsund 1600–1630: Eine Hansestadt in d. Krise u. im europ. Konflikt* (Weimar: Böhlau, 1970), 229–242.

26. Jessen, 218–220.

27. Zillhardt, 120–121.

28. Ibid.

29. Ibid.

30. Ibid., 122. For another example of soldiers only half-heartedly keeping to such agreements after the Thirty Years' War, see Geoff Mortimer, *Eyewitness Accounts of the Thirty Years War, 1618–48* (Houndmills, UK: Palgrave, 2002), 48.

31. Gerhard Benecke, *Germany in the Thirty Years' War,* ed. A.G. Dickens, *Documents of Modern History* (London: Edward Arnold, 1978), 14.

32. Zillhardt, 127.

33. Benecke 14.

34. Peter Wilson, *From Reich to Revolution: German History, 1558–1806,* ed. Jeremy Black, *European History in Perspective* (Houndmills, UK: Palgrave MacMillan, 2004), 127; Parker, *The Thirty Years' War,* 83–88.

35. Michael Roberts, *Gustavus Adolphus: A History of Sweden, 1611–1632,* vol. 2. (London: Longmans, 1953), 305–328, 345–444.

36. Salvius, Letter to the Riksråd, Hamburg, May 1631, cited in Benecke, 34–6. For additional descriptions of the sack of Magdeburg see Johann Philipp Abelinus and Matthaeus Merian, *Theatrum Europaeum,* vol. 2 (Frankfurt am Main: 1646), 368–70.

37. Otto von Guericke, *Die Belagerung Eroberung und Zerstörung der Stadt Magdeburg am 10./20. Mai 1631,* ed. Friedrich Wilhelm Hoffmann and Horst Kohl, vol. 6, *Voigtländers Quellenbücher* (Leipzig: R. Voigtländer, 1912), cited in Mortimer, 70.

38. For the failure of the Swedes to save Magdeburg, see Roberts, 496–502. For more on the meaning of the siege and sack of the city to contemporaries, see Hans Medick, "Historisches Ereignis und zeitgenössische Erfahrung: Die Eroberung und Zerstörung Magdeburgs 1631," in *Zwischen Alltag und Katastrophe. Der Dreissigjährige Krieg aus der Nähe,* ed. Benigna von Krusenstjern and Hans Medick, *Veröffentlichungen des Max-Planck-Instituts für Geschichte* (Göttingen: Vandenhoeck & Ruprecht, 1999). For the classic argument that the fire was actually caused by Falkenberg to keep the city from falling into the hands of the imperialists, see Karl Wittich, *Magdeburg, Gustav Adolf und Tilly,* vol.1 (Berlin, 1874). For the argument that the sack was perfectly legal, see Geoffrey Parker, "Early Modern Europe," in *The Laws of War: Constraints on Warfare in the Western World,* Michael Eliot Howard et al., eds. (New Haven; London: Yale University Press, 1994).

39. F. von Weech, ed., *Sebastian Bürster's Beschreibung des schwedischen Krieges 1630–1647* (Leipzig: Hirzel, 1875), 20–22, cited in Mortimer, 51.

40. For a contemporary account of the impact of the Swedes on the region see Werner Zapotetzky, *Was noch geschieht, muss man abwarten: Karlstadt im Dreissigjährigen Krieg: die sogenannte "Satz'sche Chronik" im Stadtarchiv* (Karlstadt: Historischer Verein Karlstadt, 1999). See also The Treaty of Barwalde, Article VI, January 13, 1631, cited in Jean Dumont, ed., *Corps universel diplomatique du droit des gens*, vol. 6.1 (Amsterdam, The Hague: 1728), 1–2. For more on the treatment of the Jews by the Swedes, see Jonathan Irvine Israel, *European Jewry in the Age of Mercantilism, 1550–1750*, 3rd ed. (London; Portland, Or.: Littman Library of Jewish Civilization/ Vallentine Mitchell, 1998), 77–83.

41. Benecke, 69.

42. Abelinus and Merian, vol. 2, 485–486.

43. Zillhardt, 133–134.

44 Ibid., 139–140.

45. Wedgwood, 316–320; Roberts, 666–672.

46. Weech, 33, cited in Mortimer, 52–53.

47. Rupert Sigl, *Wallensteins Rache an Bayern. Der Schwedenschreck. Veit Hösers Kriegstagebuch* (Grafenau: Morsak Verlag Grafenau, 1984), 127–8, 151. The depredations of the Swedes are also mentioned in Mortimer, 45–58, 165. For another contemporary account of Swedish atrocities in this period, see *Die Bieberauer Chronik*, cited in Kunz and Lizalek, 252–254.

48. Zillhardt, 150.

49. Johann Valentin Andreä, *Ein Schwäbischer Pfarrer im Dreissigjährigen Krieg*, ed. P. Antony and H. Christmann (Heidenheim: 1970), 80–83, cited in Benecke, 85–87.

50. Zillhardt, 151.

51. Bentele, 192.

52. Zillhardt, 150.

53. A. Semler, ed., *Die Tagebücher des Dr. Johann Heinrich von Pflummern 1633–1643*, in *Beihefte zur Zeitschrift für die Geschichte des Oberrheins* 98 (1950): 25, cited in Mortimer, 53–54.

54. Abelinus and Merian, vol. 1, 537–538.

55. Zillhardt, 159.

56. Ibid., 167.

57. For a discussion of a hard-hit area see Wolfgang Von Hippel, "Eine südwestdeutsche Region zwischen Krieg und Frieden—die wirtschaftlichen Kriegsfolgen im Herzogtum Württemberg," in *1648—Krieg und Frieden in Europa*, ed. Klaus Bussmann and Heinz Schilling (Münster & Osnabrück: Veranschaltungsgesellschaft 350 Jahre Westfälischer Friede mbH, 1998), 329–336. See also John C. Theibault, *German Villages in Crisis: Rural Life in Hesse-Kassel and the Thirty Years' War, 1580–1720*, ed. Thomas A. Brady, and Roger Chickering, *Studies in German Histories* (Atlantic Highlands, NJ: Humanities Press, 1995). For more on Hamburg, see Rainer Postel, "Hamburg zur Zeit des Westfälischen Friedens," in *1648—Krieg und Frieden in Europa*, 337–343.

58. For Richelieu's memoir, see Achives des Affaires Étrangères, Correspondance Politique *Suède 3*, fols. 265–266, *Advis donné au Roy Sur le Sujet de la bataille de Nordlingen perdue par les Suedois six heures apres en avoir receu la nouvelle par le Sr de Mire.*

59. For more extended discussions of Richelieu's justification of his policy of involvement, see Paul Sonnino, "From D'Avaux to dévot: Politics and Religion in the Thirty Years' War," *History 87*, 286 (April 2002): 192–203.

60. Zillhardt, 161.

61. See, for example, F. Heymach, ed., *Aufzeichnungen des Pfarrers Plebanus von Miehlen as den Jahren 1636/37*, vol. 38, *Annalen des Vereins für nassauische Altertum-skunde und Geschichtsforschung* (1908), 276, cited in Mortimer, 79.

62. *Historica des Pfarrers Johann Daniel* Minck, cited in Kunz and Lizalek, 261. For more on the difficulty of everyday life in such times, see Ruth E. Mohrmann, "Everyday Life in War and Peace," *1648—Krieg und Frieden in Europa*, 319–327.

63. Zillhardt, 161; Bentele, 188.

64. Zillhardt, 162; Israel, 77.

65. *Die Bieberauer Chronik*, cited in Kunz and Lizalek, 256.

66. Bentele, 64–65.

67. *Die Bieberauer Chronik*, cited in Kunz and Lizalek, 254–255.

68. Francis C. Springell and William Crowne, *Connoisseur and diplomat: the Earl of Arundel's embassy to Germany in 1636 as recounted in William Crowne's Diary, the Earl's letters and other contemporary sources with a catalogue of the topographical drawings made on the journey by Wenceslaus Hollar* (London: Maggs, 1963), 59–76.

69. See, for example, the arguments of the landgravine of Hesse-Cassel, Amalia Elisabeth, who made it clear that while she was distressed at the horrible sufferings of her people, she saw her God-given duty to preserve her Church and the liberties of the German states as more important, whatever the cost in blood and treasure. Hessische Staatsarchiv Marburg 4d Nr. 50, fol. 50–51, Amalia Elisabeth (letter in her hand) to Vultejus, 7/17 March 1639. For more on Amalia Elisabeth, see Tryntje Helfferich, "The Scepter Rests Well in the Hands of Woman': Faith, Politics, and the Thirty Years War," PhD Dissertation (University of California, 2003).

70. William Hagen, "Seventeenth-Century Crisis in Brandenburg: The Thirty Years' War, The Destabilization of Serfdom, and the Rise of Absolutism," *American Historical Review* 94, no. 2 (1989): 302–325.

71. Benecke, 56–7. See also Zillhardt, 175–7.

72. Benecke, 54–5. See also Hessische Staatsarchiv Marburg 4d Nr. 38, Residents of the town of Scherffe to the Hessian Secret Council, November 10/20, 1638.

73. Theibault, *German Villages*, 156.

74. Memmius and Latomus, 78, cited in Jessen, 383.

75. Zillhardt, 182.

76. Theibault, 159.

77. Ibid., 160.

78. Zillhardt, 191.

79. Louis de Pontis, *Mémoires*, ed. Andrée Villard (Paris: H. Champion, 2000), 558–559.

80. Pontis, 580.

81. François Ogier, *Journal du Congrès de Munster*, edited by Auguste Boppe (Paris: E. Plon Nourrit et cie, 1893), 225–226.

82. F.J. Mone, ed., "Allensbacher Chronik von Gallus Zembroth," in *Quellens-ammlung der badischen Landesgeschichte*, ed. F.G. Mone (Karlsruhe: Macklot, 1863), 577, cited in Mortimer, 49.

83. *Die Westfälischen Friedensverträge vom 24. Oktober 1648. Texte und Überset-zungen* (Acta Pacis Westphalicae. Supplementa electronica, 1). (http://www.pax-westphalica.de/ [2006]). See in particular *Instrumentum Pacis Osnabrugensis,* Article V, §34.

84. Zapotetzky, 90.

85. Zillhardt, 224–24.

86. Andreas Kothe and Franz Flaskamp, *Die Chronik des Ratsherrn Andreas Kothe: eine Quelle zur westfälischen Geschichte im Zeitalter des dreissigjährigen Krieges* (Gütersloh Ger.: L. Flöttmann, 1962), 25–26.

87. Zillhardt, 225. A discussion of the ambivalence of the people of Augsburg in response to the peace is in Claire Gantet, "Die ambivalente Wahrnehmung des Friedens. Erwartung, Furcht und Spannungen in Augsburg um 1648," in *Zwischen Alltag und Katastrophe: Der Dreissigjährige Krieg aus der Nähe,* ed. Benigna von Krusenstjern and Hans Medick, Veröffentlichungen des Max-Planck-Instituts für Geschichte (Göttingen: Vandenhoeck & Ruprecht, 1999). For an example of the costs to the peasantry of war debts and reparations, see Sreenivasan, 292–304.

88. Bentele, 104, 105, 112.

89. Parker, *The Thirty Years' War,* 210–212. For more on the process of recovery, see Theibault, *German Villages,* 193–220. For his discussion of demographic losses in the war, see John Theibault, "The Demography of the Thirty Years' War Revisited: Günther Franz and his Critics," *German History* 15, 1 (1997), pp. 1–21. Sreenivasan, for example, points out that the monastery of Ottobeuren only returned to its pre-war population in the eighteenth century. Sreenivasan, 291.

FURTHER READING

Abelinus, Johann Philipp, and Matthaeus Merian. *Theatrum Europæum, oder Warhaffte Beschreibung aller denckwurdigen Geschichten.* 6 vols. Frankfurt am Main: Wolffgang Hoffman, 1643–1652. Volumes of an important contemporary periodical covering in detail the major events of the Thirty Years' War. Illustrated with beautiful engravings by Matthaeus Merian.

Benecke, Gerhard. "Germany in the Thirty Years War." In *Documents of Modern History,* edited by A. G. Dickens. London: Edward Arnold, 1978. Collection of translated primary sources for Germany during the Thirty Years' War.

Benger, E. *Memoirs of Elizabeth Stuart, Queen of Bohemia, Daughter of King James the First. Including Sketches of the State of Society in Holland and Germany, in the 17th Century.* 2 vols. London: Printed for Longman Hurst Rees Orme Brown and Green, 1825. Biography written in the nineteenth century, including many personal letters of Elizabeth of Bohemia, wife of Frederick V.

Bentele, Guenther. *Protokolle einer Katastrophe: zwei Bietigheimer Chroniken aus dem Dreissigjährigen Krieg.* Bietigheim-Bissingen: Stadtarchiv Bietigheim-Bissingen, 1984. Thematically organized study of the Thirty Years' War in Württemberg. The author's analysis is followed by the full texts of two local chronicles.

Dumont, Jean, ed. *Corps universel diplomatique du droit des gens.* Vol. VI, 1. Amsterdam: P. Brund, J. Wetstein, and G. Smith, 1728. Classic eighteenth-century compendium of European diplomatic treaties.

Gantet, Claire. "Die ambivalente Wahrnehmung des Friedens. Erwartung, Furcht und Spannungen in Augsburg um 1648." In *Zwischen Alltag und Katastrophe. Der Dreissigjährige Krieg aus der Nähe,* edited by Benigna von Krusenstjern and Hans Medick, 357–376. Göttingen: Vandenhoeck & Ruprecht, 1999. Discussion of the ambivalent reception of the Peace of Westphalia in Augsburg.

Hagen, William W. "Seventeenth-Century Crisis in Brandenburg: The Thirty Years' War, the Destabilization of Serfdom, and the Rise of Absolutism." *American Historical Review* 94, no. 2 (1989): 302–335. Discussion of the relationship between peasants and rulers in Brandenburg-Prussia during the Thirty Years' War. Attempts to trace the social origins of absolutism of the region in the seventeenth century.

Helfferich, Tryntje. "'The Scepter Rests Well in the Hands of a Woman': Faith, Politics, and the Thirty Years' War." Ph.D. Dissertation, University of California at Santa Barbara, 2003. Study of the early reign of the landgravine of Hesse-Cassel, Amalia Elisabeth. Investigates the interaction of faith and politics in driving the war.

Hippel, Wolfgang von. "Eine südwestdeutsche Region zwischen Krieg und Frieden—die wirtschaftlichen Kriegsfolgen im Herzogtum Württemberg." In *1648—Krieg und Frieden in Europa*, edited by Klaus Bussmann and Heinz Schilling, 329–336. Münster & Osnabrück: Veranschaltungsgesellschaft 350 Jahre Westfälischer Friede mbH, 1998. A careful consideration of the economic effects of the war using data from the duchy of Württemberg.

Israel, Jonathan Irvine. *European Jewry in the Age of Mercantilism, 1550–1750*. 3rd ed. London; Portland, OR.: Littman Library of Jewish Civilization/Vallentine Mitchell, 1998. Study of the history and culture of the Jews in early modern Europe. In particular, chapter 5 covers the period of the Thirty Years' War, analyzing its effect on such things as population growth and dispersal, economic activity, and legal status. Makes some very intriguing and surprising arguments.

Jessen, Hans. *Der Dreissigjährige Krieg in Augenzeugenberichten*. Düsseldorf: K. Rauch, 1963. Hundreds of primary source snippets on the Thirty Years' War and its immediate aftermath.

Kothe, Andreas, and Franz Flaskamp. *Die Chronik des Ratsherrn Andreas Kothe: eine Quelle zur westfälischen Geschichte im Zeitalter des dreissigjährigen Krieges*. Gütersloh Ger.: L. Flöttmann, 1962. Brief chronicle of the city councilman Andreas Kothe, from the town of Wiedenbrück, beginning in 1623 and continuing through until 1651, when the chronicle is taken up by his sons.

Kunz, Rudolf, and Willy Lizalek, eds. *Südhessische Chroniken aus der Zeit des Dreissigjährigen Krieges*. Heppenheim: Verlag Laurissa, 1983. Collection of four edited chronicles from the area of southern Hesse. Demonstrates both the everyday concerns and the war-related problems of the common people during the war.

Landsteiner, Erich, and Andreas Weigl. "'Sonsten finden wir die Sachen sehr übel aufm Landt beschaffen.' Krieg und lokale Gesellschaft in Niederösterreich (1618–1621)." In *Zwischen Alltag und Katastrophe. Der Dreissigjährige Krieg aus der Nähe*, edited by Benigna von Krusenstjern and Hans Medick, 229–272. Göttingen: Vandenhoeck & Ruprecht, 1999. Discussion of the economic and social effects of the war in lower Austria during the period 1618–1621.

Langer, Herbert. "Heeresfinanzierung, Produktion und Märkte für die Kriegführung." In *1648—Krieg und Frieden in Europa*, edited by Klaus Bussmann and Heinz Schilling, 293–299. Münster & Osnabrück: Veranschaltungsgesellschaft 350 Jahre Westfälischer Friede mbH, 1998. Study of the practicalities of making war in this period. Includes discussions of military financing, production, and markets.

———. *Stralsund 1600–1630. Eine Hansestadt in d. Krise u. im europ. Konflikt.* Weimar: Böhlau, 1970. An excellent economic-social analysis of the impact of the Thirty Years' War on a Baltic seaport.

Lockhart, Paul Douglas. *Denmark in the Thirty Years' War, 1618–1648: King Christian IV and the Decline of the Oldenburg State.* Selinsgrove, PA: Susquehanna University Press, 1996. Useful monograph on the political and military history of the kingdom of Denmark during the period of the Thirty Years' War.

Medick, Hans. "Historisches Ereignis und zeitgenössische Erfahrung: Die Eroberung und Zerstörung Magdeburgs 1631." In *Zwischen Alltag und Katastrophe. Der Dreissigjährige Krieg aus der Nähe,* edited by Benigna von Krusenstjern and Hans Medick. Göttingen: Vandenhoeck & Ruprecht, 1999. Article analyzing the contemporary meaning of the siege and sack of the city of Magdeburg by the imperialists in 1631.

Mohrmann, Ruth E. "Everyday Life in War and Peace." In *1648—Krieg und Frieden in Europa,* edited by Klaus Bussmann and Heinz Schilling, 319–327. Münster & Osnabrück: Veranschaltungsgesellschaft 350 Jahre Westfälischer Friede mbH, 1998. Study of the everyday aspects of life among the people of the empire during the war. Focuses on material culture, the everyday necessities of life, and the effects of the war.

Mortimer, Geoff. *Eyewitness Accounts of the Thirty Years War, 1618–48.* Houndmills, Basingstoke, Hampshire; New York: Palgrave, 2002. Social and literary history of the war from the point of view of contemporaries. Includes sections on both military and civilian life and attempts to come to a general understanding of how contemporaries perceived the war as a whole.

Ogier, François. *Journal du Congrès de Munster.* Edited by Auguste Boppe. Paris: E. Plon Nourrit et cie, 1893. Informative journal by the chaplain of the Count d'Avaux, one of the three French plenipotentiaries at the Congress of Westphalia.

Parker, Geoffrey. "Early Modern Europe." In *The Laws of War: Constraints on Warfare in the Western World,* edited by Michael Howard et al., New Haven; London: Yale University Press, 1994. Succinct treatment of the laws of war in early modern Europe.

———, ed. *The Thirty Years' War.* 2nd ed. London; New York: Routledge, 1997. Classic general survey of the war, edited by Parker with a team of scholarly contributors.

Pontis, Louis de. *Mémoires (1676).* Edited by André Villard. Paris: H. Champion, 2000. Extremely revealing memoirs by a lower-ranking officer in the French army during the Thirty Years' War. Unusual revelations about the characters of Cardinal Richelieu and Louis XIII.

Postel, Rainer. "Hamburg zur Zeit des Westfälischen Friedens." In *1648—Krieg und Frieden in Europa,* edited by Klaus Bussmann and Heinz Schilling, 337–343. Münster & Osnabrück: Veranschaltungsgesellschaft 350 Jahre Westfälischer Friede mbH, 1998. Snapshot of Hamburg in the period of the Thirty Years' War and Peace of Westphalia.

Pufendorf, Samuel. *An Introduction to the History of the Principal Kingdoms and States of Europe.* London: Thomas Newborough & Martha Gilliflower, 1700.

Pufendorf, Samuel, and Edmund Bohun. *The Present State of Germany.* London: Printed for Richard Chiswell, 1696. Microform. Two classic works by one of the leading scholars of seventeenth-century Europe. Includes analysis of the history and culture of the states of Europe and of the Holy Roman Empire.

Roberts, Michael. *Gustavus Adolphus; A History of Sweden, 1611–1632.* 2 vols. Vol. II. 1626–1632. London: Longmans, 1953. Classic and still unsurpassed study of Gustavus Adolphus and the history of Sweden in this period. Volume II covers the Swedish intervention in the war.

Sigl, Rupert. *Wallensteins Rache an Bayern. Der Schwedenschreck. Veit Hösers Kriegstagebuch.* Grafenau: Morsak Verlag Grafenau, 1984. Transcription of the chronicle of Veit Höser, the abbot of the cloister of Oberalteich in Bavaria (d. 1634).

Sonnino, Paul. "From D'Avaux to *dévot:* Politics and Religion in the Thirty Years' War." *History* 87, no. 286 (April 2002): 192–203. A contribution by an obscure American historian to the classic question of political versus religious motives during the Thirty Years' War.

Springell, Francis C., and William Crowne. *Connoisseur and Diplomat: The Earl of Arundel's Embassy to Germany in 1636 as Recounted in William Crowne's Diary, the Earl's Letters and Other Contemporary Sources with a Catalogue of the Topographical Drawings Made on the Journey by Wenceslaus Hollar.* London: Maggs, 1963. Diary of an English diplomat who visited the empire in 1636.

Sreenivasan, Govind P. *The Peasants of Ottobeuren, 1487–1726: A Rural Society in Early Modern Europe.* Cambridge: Cambridge University Press, 2004. Impressive work of scholarship on the peasants living in the Bavarian monastery of Ottobeuren.

Stüve, C. *Geschichte des Hochstifts Osnabrück.* 3 vols. Osnabrück: H. T. Wenner, 1980. Thorough description of events in the archbishopric of Osnabrück from 1250 to 1647.

Theibault, John. "The Demography of the Thirty Years' War Revisited: Günther Franz and His Critics." *German History* 15, no. 1 (1997): 1–21. Discussion of the controversy over the extent of the population losses in the war.

Theibault, John C. *German Villages in Crisis. Rural Life in Hesse-Kassel and the Thirty Years' War, 1580–1720.* In *Studies in German Histories,* edited by Thomas A. Brady and Roger Chickering. Atlantic Highlands, NJ: Humanities Press, 1995. Study of the life of the peasantry in Hesse-Cassel before, during, and after the war.

Toegel, Miroslav, ed. *Der Kampf des Hauses Habsburg gegen die Niederlande und ihre Verbündeten: Quellen zur Geschichte des Pfälzisch-Niederländisch-Ungarischen Krieges, 1621–1625.* Vol. III, *Documenta bohemica Bellum Tricennale illustrantia.* Prague: Nakladatelství Československé akademie věd, 1976. Third in a series of books dedicated to cataloging the relevant contents of the archives of Bohemia and Moravia. Most sources appear merely as bibliographic records with brief summaries of their contents; others include full transcriptions.

Wedgwood, C. V. *The Thirty Years War.* Garden City, NY: Anchor Books, 1961. The classic and still unsurpassed description of the Thirty Years' War by one of England's greatest historians.

Die Westfälischen Friedensverträge vom 24. Oktober 1648. Texte und Übersetzungen (Acta Pacis Westphalicae. Supplementa electronica, 1), http://www.pax-westphalica.de/. Indispensable texts of the treaty between the French and the empire and the Swedes and the empire, which concluded the Thirty Years' War. Presented both in the original Latin and in a variety of European languages.

Wilson, Peter. "From Reich to Revolution: German History, 1558–1806." In *European History in Persepctive*, edited by Jeremy Black. Houndmills; New York: Palgrave Macmillan, 2004. Study of the political, economic, cultural, and social development of the empire from 1558 until its fall in 1806.

Wittich, Karl. *Magdeburg, Gustav Adolf und Tilly*. Vol. 1. Berlin: Carl Duncker, 1874. Classic discussion of the sack of Magdeburg. Argues that the fire was actually caused by Falkenberg to keep the city from falling into the hands of the imperialists.

Zapotetzky, Werner. *Was noch geschieht, muss man abwarten: Karlstadt im Dreissigjährigen Krieg: die sogenannte "Satz'sche Chronik" im Stadtarchiv*. Karlstadt: Historischer Verein Karlstadt, 1999. A chronicle that details the events of the war in Karlstadt from the attack of the Swedes in October 1631 to the conclusion of the peace in 1648.

Zillhardt, Gerd, *Der Dreissigjährige Krieg in zeitgenössischer Darstellung: Hans Heberles "Zeytregister" (1618–1672), Aufzeichnungen aus dem Ulmer Territorium: ein Beitrag zu Geschichtsschreibung und Geschichtsverständnis der Unterschichten*. Ulm & Stuttgart: Stadtarchiv; Kommissionsverlag Kohlhammer, 1975. Excellent, detailed, and even gripping chronicle of a peasant from the area around Ulm. Edited with extensive notes and useful introductory material.

THREE

Matrices: Soldiers and Civilians in Early Modern Europe, 1648–1789

Dennis Showalter

The period between the Thirty Years' War and the French Revolution witnessed the development in Europe of two social categories that have remained central to Western society's self-definition ever since: soldiers and civilians. Through the history of the West and the history of the world, societies have shared war's risks and outcomes in common. The man who fell in battle, the woman enslaved as her home burned, the child dying in the ruins of a sacked city—their fates were a simple matter of time and place. The medieval world attempted, with limited success, to organize a theologically based order of those who fought and those who worked or prayed under the warriors' protection. In the sixteenth century, a civil variant of that paradigm emerged. In its ideal form, it included only two categories in the context of war: those paid to fight, the soldiers, and those who paid them, the civilians

Had it only been that simple! Images of limited wars fought in a vacuum by marginal men while normal people went peacefully about their business no longer survive even in textbooks. War has been restored to the center stage of early modern Europe. To date, that process has focused on the "high history" of states and strategies, cultures and philosophies. It had a human dimension, as well. The armies that fought the wars and the societies that endured them were not separate compartments. Civilians and soldiers came from the same population; early modern Europe had no warrior classes. As a consequence, part of this essay addresses the formation and organization of armies, and part is presented from the soldiers' perspective. At the same time, civilians and soldiers remained fundamentally different—a gap that would begin closing only when civilians began developing from subjects to citizens and from noncombatant victims to affirmative participants in an emerging culture of total war.

FROM CIVILIANS TO SOLDIERS

Central to the relationships of soldiers and civilians in early modern Europe was the increasing ability of states to mobilize resources from all levels of society in exchange for furnishing protection and stability. In the rural aristocracies, the backbone of European military systems for centuries, martial values were increasingly discounted. A father might see to his son's instruction in the arts of the duel but was less likely to provide instruction in the crafts of war. Civic elites might join municipal guards or serve in sieges and similar emergencies. But the fascinating, complex, demanding processes of making money or developing the specialized knowledge associated with the secular "learned professions" of law and medicine led to a distancing from warmaking as a life choice.

Governments were perfectly willing to assume the responsibility. What Jan Glete calls the "fiscal-military state" was a complex structure of de facto and de jure contractual relationships able to integrate and sustain a broad spectrum of otherwise discordant domestic interests to the end of raising and managing money. The money, in turn, was used to raise and support armies. All but a vanishingly small amount of European public budgets between 1648 and 1789 was devoted to sustaining armed forces. The resulting burdens imposed on the ordinary people and the developing commercial and industrial classes are remarkable for the equanimity with which they were accepted.[1]

The distinguishing characteristic of early modern armies was their size. Military superiority can be achieved in only two ways: quality and number. Early modern Europe was characterized by the consistent movement not only of personnel but also of ideas among armies. What one learned or developed, another could discover almost immediately.[2] The obvious response, then, was to increase the number of soldiers. And, while the increase in available funding was modest by later standards, it seemed like endless wealth to governments whose treasuries had historically been consistently near empty. Finally, no one was sure exactly how much the new armies would cost, and in what ways. In most cases, optimism triumphed over caution. France was the exemplar. A peace establishment of around 10,000 soldiers at the end of the sixteenth century increased fifteenfold over the next hundred years.[3] Even lesser military powers fielded forces of strengths unprecedented since the days of Imperial Rome: 100,000 for the Dutch Republic, 100,000 for Sweden, 80,000 for Prussia, and 90,000 for England, all in the early 1700s,

Early modern armies hemorrhaged men—at least on paper. John Lynn has highlighted the significant differences between official strengths and men in ranks, in an environment where administration was rudimentary and peculation unabashed. One of the most common, and most profitable, scams involved captains putting false names on the roster and pocketing the wages of these phantom soldiers. Should a muster be held, there was seldom a problem finding stand-ins for a day, ready enough to perform the service for a drink and a few cents.[4] The trick was so common that it helped define a word in the English language. A "faggot" in eighteenth-century slang was one of those soldiers who existed on paper only—a make-believe man.

Even in peacetime, inadequate paperwork compounded the traditional causes of declining strength: disease and desertion. Recruiting thus became the central issue in practical terms that confronted early modern armies. How best to put enough men in the ranks, and keep them there, to sustain the state's place in the continent's pecking order?

In the Middle Ages, states had increasingly preferred to build armies from building blocks by enlisting men from social backgrounds and geographic regions believed to foster particular military qualities or skills.[5] Those still existed even in the eighteenth century: Scottish Highlanders; German hunters and foresters, the *Jaeger*; and Austrian *Grenzer*, to mention the most familiar. But, as Western societies grew increasingly homogenized, the number of such specialists fell far below those needed by the ever-emptying regiments.

The answer was as obvious as it was uncongenial. Armies that had been built around warriors needed to reconfigure with civilians. In the good old days, recruiting a *Landsknecht* (German mercenary) company or a Scottish regiment for service under Gustavus Adolphus resembled a rural hiring fair. Conditions might in general have favored the employer, but the job-seekers had some preexisting qualifications and some negotiating opportunity.[6] After the Thirty Years' War, showmanship and artifice came to the fore—on the grounds that general recruiting in civilian communities depended on deception.

R. Lee Ermey, a Marine drill instructor turned actor *(Full Metal Jacket)*, memorably described himself as "a stand-up comic," whose major challenge was to get the attention of his charges. Early modern recruiters assumed similar personae. The Irish dramatist George Farquhar established contemporary archetypes in *The Recruiting Officer*. Published in 1706, repeatedly revived for stage and television in recent years, it features "Captain Plume" asking a crowd of yokels what they think of "a purse of gold out of a Frenchman's pocket after you have dashed out his brains with the butt of your fire-lock, eh?" The play is dominated, however, by "Sergeant Kite," who exhorts his audience: "if any 'prentices have severe masters, any children undutiful parents: if any servants have too little wages or any husband too much wife, let them repair to the noble Sergeant Kite. . . . "[7]

The sergeant describes his career path:

I was born a gypsy; there I learned canting and lying. I was bought by a nobleman; there I learned impudence and pimping. I turned bailiff's follower; there I learned bullying and swearing. I at last got into the army, and there I learned whoring and drinking. So that if your worship pleases to cast up the whole sum, you will find the sum total will amount to a recruiting sergeant.[8]

A kite is a bird of prey that prefers carrion. Recruiters usually held open house in taverns, seeking to create a convivial, masculine atmosphere that encouraged signing an enlistment contract, accepting "the King's shilling," and sometimes merely drinking the local ruler's health at the recruiter's expense. Misrepresentation was so common as to be universal and ranged from promises of rapid promotion or commissioning as officers to describing membership in some kind of elite unit when reality was ground-pounding in the infantry. One British cavalry regiment warned prospective recruits that, because the regiment's horses were young, the men were not allowed to hunt more than once a week![9]

By no means all of the recruits thus obtained were from what modern jargon dubs the "underclass": the can't-copers and no-hopers. A declining child mortality rate meant an increasing number of sons surviving to an age requiring that something be done for them and with them. Urban guild regulations made it increasingly difficult for journeymen to set up their own establishments—acquiring master status by marrying a master's widow was a staple of bawdy humor and an uncomfortable everyday prospect for too many twentysomethings. Teachers grew tired of beating the same fragments of knowledge into unwilling heads. Clerics lost vocations. Jugglers, actors, and puppeteers found themselves in uniform as a consequence of injury, rheumatism, or loss of the touch that made an audience throw money. Like Jane Eyre, such men might well reason that if they could not have liberty, they could at least seek new servitude.

In France and elsewhere on the continent, seigneurial recruitment was a common variation of the individual approach. Officers would take up to six months' leave, return home, and come back with a trail of recruits from family estates. Wives, mothers, and siblings participated in the process, which included structural pressure involving matters like fees and lease and, at times, more exotic inducements as well—such as a kiss from the lady of the manor. A captain's sister won praise from no less an exalted expert than a Marshal of France: "there is not a trick that she does not know" when it came to transforming civilians into soldiers.[10]

The next step in filling depleted ranks involved turning to "masterless men"—vagabonds and pimps, the chronically unemployed, even brigands—though these last seem to have more often been men living from hand to mouth, pilferers of laundry and chickens, than hardened "gentlemen of the road." From sweeping the streets and countryside, it was a short step to emptying the jails. "Emptying" is an exaggeration. The idea of extending the concept of honor to common soldiers may have been embryonic, but it was strong enough to create a reluctance to treat military service as an alternate form of punishment. Nor were officers exactly over-joyed at having their ranks completed by antisocial criminals. Thieves, alcoholics, and brawlers were a constant source of friction, making life far more miserable than it had to be for their better-behaved comrades, and for the officers, as well. Recruiters preferred inmates whose offenses were the kind that in later centuries inspired judges to offer defendants a choice between incarceration and enlistment. In the France of Louis XIV, smugglers and debtors were particular favored. Debtors were likely to be victims of bad luck or bad management, and suitably appreciative if their creditors could be constrained to resign their claims in favor of the state. Smuggling was widely considered a victimless crime; smugglers had an image as bold adventurers, outside the law but not alienated from society. Men sentenced to the galleys were enrolled only in extreme emergencies—and then kept under heavy guard.[11]

The custodial/rehabilitative model of prison is a nineteenth-century innovation. Early modern societies could not afford to keep large numbers of healthy men out of the workforce for long periods, and convicts suitable for the army were correspondingly scarce. The next step in supplement-ing volunteers involved, logically, compulsion. This existed on two tracks, both most comprehensively developed in France. Aristocratic feudal service, the *ban* and the *arrière ban,* might long have been vestigial but still remained on the books. Kings of France called out levies as late as 1689, with predictable results. The 40-day limitation on service beyond the frontiers bore no relation to the actual nature of early modern war. The men who responded personally, as opposed to paying compensation, were poorly armed and unresponsive to discipline as early modern armies understood it.[12]

Commoners as well were expected to serve the king in his wars. Partial call-ups to meet particular emergencies were a familiar last resort. In France, local levies watched roads and fords. They provided labor for sieges, 20,000 and more men for a complex investment. Their carts and animals hauled supplies—sometimes even with some compensation involved.

The second track of direct civilian service in arms involved militias. Throughout Europe, a variety of organizations, rural and urban, local and provincial, provided armed men for police and security purposes. In the cities, service, based on residence location or guild membership, was often compulsory but also enough of a mark of status that members took pride in doing well when fighting for their home towns. Rural militias could in emergencies provide large numbers of bodies at limited cost. They played enough of a role in France's Wars of Religion that during the next century the revived monarchy was at pains to bring them under state control. Louis XIV summoned local militias for state service in the Dutch Wars—a process similar to that of federalizing state National

Guard units in twentieth-century America. Provinces and cities were also required to recruit and support from their own resources units for general service—though money rather than men was likely to be the true medium of compliance.

Beginning in 1688, the local organizations began giving way to a royal version initially designed to provide low-cost auxiliary troops and then to funnel replacements into line regiments. Depending on raising armies by conscription, the new system was correspondingly unpopular, and not only because it allowed buy-outs. Determining service by a lottery system, the *tirage au sort*, was widely considered unjust in civil society because of the same randomness that has made draft lotteries acceptable in the twentieth century. A man's fate should be determined by his merits and his needs—not by some piece of paper pulled from an urn. In short, France's royal militias in their successive forms were generally and legitimately considered by professional soldiers and social theorists alike as doing more harm than good to both military effectiveness and state-subject relations.[13]

Across the Rhine, in the lands of the Empire, militias remained attractive to the small and middle-size territories. Their persistence reflected two fundamental facts. One was theological. Protestant rulers and their people shared a belief that aggressive war—and at this period "defensive war" was something of an oxymoron—violated Christian principles. Men summoned from the plough and the counter were hardly likely to be interested in defying that particular command of scripture. The second was economic. No German ruler was in a position after the Peace of Westphalia to maintain operationally effective standing armies with public resources. Bavaria, which kept as many as 20,000 men under arms during the Thirty Years' War, after 1648 reduced its army to a few companies of garrison and security troops.

Militias seemed a reasonable compromise. They could be called up long enough to receive at least some training. They made useful garrisons for the small fortresses thickly scattered across the Empire. They could be used as recruitment or replacement pools for the paid professionals engaged for emergencies. Brandenburg and Saxony, to cite two of the best-known examples, depended on militia-based systems through the Thirty Years' War. They did so, however, in the face of experience and despite a comprehensive pattern of disappointing performance best illustrated by the token fight—less than 30 minutes on the field, followed by panic and rout—put up by the Saxon militia at Breitenfeld.[14]

An alternative recruiting system developed in eastern Europe. First impressions might suggest more differences than similarities among the soldiers produced by Sweden's allotment system, the uniformed serfs of Petrine Russia, and the cantonists of eighteenth-century Prussia. What they shared was their refinement of the concept of the civilian soldier. Sweden, Russia, and Prussia fielded neither militias of civilians in arms nor professional armies of paid fighters on the French and British models.

Instead, they turned to their own people, the peasants in particular, for the raw material of a new subcategory of army: the uniformed subject.

Beginning in the reign of Gustavus Adolphus, Sweden raised its infantry by the "allotment system." Groups of farms furnished a soldier, provided him with an enlistment bonus, food, clothing, a yearly wage, and either a small plot of land or living space on one of the farms. In peacetime, the soldier worked his own land and labored on the other farms in the group. In war, his neighbors assisted his family. If the soldier died or was disabled, the group provided a replacement. Recruits might be younger sons of the community or outsiders, even foreigners, persuaded to participate. In either case, they were able to achieve, at least in principle, a stable place in the village community while contributing to its ongoing welfare.

The system had a number of favorable military side effects. Recruits were assigned to locally based regiments, giving them a sense of place denied the more cosmopolitan soldiers of other armies. Localization also facilitated a stable command system, and training methods that on an assembly-line basis turned farm boys into soldiers at least the equal of the best mercenary regiments.

Sweden's conscription system also guaranteed a steady supply of volunteers for the native Swedish cavalry regiments: service on horseback was widely preferred to being conscripted as a foot soldier. In broader terms, the allotment system was so socially acceptable that it became demographically dysfunctional. As Sweden developed into a warfare state, with campaigns lasting longer and longer and occurring ever farther from home, the steady drain of about 2 percent of the male population each year led to a gradual decline in the male population. One parish with 488 males between 15 and 60 in 1621 counted only 288 in 1639. Of almost 300 conscripts during that period, only 15 returned home. Such statistics meant land unworked, families unrenewed, and social bonds disrupted. The army's costly connection with the people meant that it had to be used with caution. Even during the Thirty Years' War, native Swedish regiments were disproportionately on home service or in garrisons. Offensive campaigns needed to be planned carefully and justified at high policy levels before being undertaken. Even then, and despite significant increases in Sweden's overall population through conquest, under a warrior king and fighting fool like Charles XII (1697–1718), Sweden essentially conquered itself to death in the first quarter of the seventeenth century.[15]

Whatever its long-term structural problems, Sweden's army demonstrated consistent and embarrassing superiority to a Russia whose army was an unstable compound of irregular cavalry, Cossack, and aristocrat, an uninspired mass of randomly recruited and uninspired infantry ostensibly organized on Western lines, and the once elite corps of musketeers, or *streltsy*, that by this time had ossified into a hereditary caste of urban craftsmen and tradesmen, much as had their rough counterparts, the janissaries of the Ottoman Empire.

Tsar Peter I, Peter the Great, replaced these vestiges and fragments with a system designed on the Swedish model, with every 20 "hearths" furnishing a recruit and replacing him when necessary. Initially, landowners and village councils chose among serfs made eligible for service as a class by the Law of 1705. Later, the task of determining eligibility was assumed by state authorities. Recruiting and volunteering on the Western model were prohibited; landowners and officials alike feared the possible loss of control over a serf population even then called "the dark people"—a reference to their backwardness, not their color. Service was for life; discipline was harsh, conditions Spartan. Even then, life in the regiment was frequently easier than life in the village—and not necessarily that much shorter. As the officer corps's initially rock-bottom standards improved, the Russian serf soldiers developed a stoic endurance that in many ways ran counter to the military ethos of the period. Quick movement was not their forte. No one could accuse them of having imagination or initiative. But few were eager to meet Russians face to face in a pitched battle—at least after the first time Frederick the Great himself was taught a lesson at Zorndorf by green-coated men who had to be killed twice and then knocked down before they realized they were dead.[16]

From the commencement of his reign, in 1713, to his death, in 1740, Prussia's King Frederick William I worked to increase the size and efficiency of the army he considered essential to Prussia's continued existence. Since the Thirty Years' War, Prussia had depended for manpower on volunteers, most of them coming from Prussian territory. Local sources, however, faced unfamiliar strains as the king's demands for recruits increased. Landlords perfectly willing to see the last of a troublemaker protested at losing steady hands to crimps. By the 1720s, domestic recruiting parties increasingly resembled press gangs. It was a common German practice for recruiters to operate across state lines, but Prussian methods so resembled manhunts that Hanover came close to declaring war in 1729. Other states made recruiting for the Prussian service a capital offense, on a par with parricide and witchcraft.

The most obvious solution to the army's appetite for men was to tap Prussia's own resources on a long-run, systematic basis. Frederick William I began by conditioning his subjects to recognize their particular obligation to support the military, whether it was the aristocracy providing sons as officers, merchants and burghers paying heavy taxes, or those who had nothing else providing blood and sinew in the ranks. As early as 1713, an edict proclaimed that civilians leaving their administrative districts (*Kreise*) without permission were considered deserters. Over the next 20 years, further declarations regularized domestic recruiting procedures. They culminated in the decrees of 1732–1733 that established the basic features of the Prussian canton recruiting and conscription system. Every regiment was assigned a specific recruiting district. All males were entered in the recruiting rolls at age 16. If the regiment did not fill its ranks by voluntary enlistment, eligible cantonists were called up to complete the numbers.

The key word was "eligible." While every male was registered, only those who met the height requirement of 5'7" (170 cm) or taller, were nonnoble and not the sons of officers, did not directly own a farm, or came from families worth less than 10,000 *Thalers* were eligible for induction. That reduced the number of eligibles in a regimental pool to about 18 percent of the male population. As an example, in one company-size recruiting area of 771 hearths, there were approximately 135 households that met the minimum requirements for conscription at any time during the cantonal era. This population filled a yearly cantonal requirement of about three soldiers—scarcely a high blood tax by any standards.[17] While call-ups were increased during war, by the time of the canton system's abolition, in 1813, fewer than half of all those registered in the entire Kingdom of Prussia had actually found themselves in uniform—a percentage that allowed ample margins for those seriously committed to avoiding service.

Prussia's developed recruiting policies closely prefigured the selective service system practiced in the United States in the 1950s and 1960s. Prussia's economy could not spare its most vigorous element for even a few of their most productive years. Nor could the state properly train every eligible man. A process of random selection seemed as irrational to Prussia's monarchs as to America's Congress. Moreover, once the conscripted cantonist learned his new craft, he was eligible to be returned to civilian life and the civilian economy for an average of 10 months a year, spending only two with the colors to refresh memory and reflexes. All these factors combined to produce tractable, if not enthusiastic, soldiers—much like their American counterparts two centuries later.[18]

The final form of recruitment developed between the Thirty Years' War and the French Revolution was the subsidy system. With war becoming a constant and wars lasting longer, the major combatants sought increasingly to increase their strength by turning to lesser states. The first step in that process was usually an alliance that involved an exchange of men for money. Sovereignty was not best served by permitting foreign recruitment of mercenaries in the traditional way, through contractors. Instead, the lesser states themselves assumed the responsibility of raising regiments whose costs were assumed by the larger, presumably richer party to the alliance.

As early modern states sought advantage in diplomatic flexibility, alliance agreements developed into a pattern of auxiliary service. Instead of disbanding their forces at the end of a war or a campaign, the German states sought contracts for future employment in locations as far away as North America, South Africa, or India if the terms were right. Few major campaigns were conducted in western Europe between 1675 and 1748 in which auxiliaries and subsidy contingents did not compose up to half the orders of battle on one side. Even established states like Denmark concluded subsidy treaties with more ambitious, more affluent neighbors. Pressures developed to make the subsidy arrangements permanent, sustaining them in times of peace as well as war. While finance ministers and, in England, parliamentary delegates tended to scotch such plans on grounds of cost, war ministries appreciated and acknowledged these "special relationships." These could range from the option for first refusal generally favored by Britain to the longstanding relationship France developed with the Swiss cantons that provided some of its best infantry. Hesse-Cassel maintained a subsidy relationship with the Estates of the Netherlands after 1688 and, through King William, developed a similar one with England.

Since the relative marketability of auxiliary forces depended largely on their effectiveness, successful suppliers rapidly learned the wisdom of professionalizing their systems. At the same time, recruiting and maintaining the numbers called for in the subsidy treaties put unparalleled strains on state administrations. Addressing these issues could involve reconfiguring not only governments but societies. Again, Hesse-Cassel is a good example. Initially, its rulers sought to use subsidies to maintain an army large enough to sustain an independent foreign policy. The limits of that vision were demonstrated during the Seven Years' War, when the state was repeatedly occupied and placed under contribution by the French. The resulting near-breakdown of society highlighted the worth of subsidies and the "special relationships"that went with them, despite the accompanying limits on freedom of diplomatic action, and the risks of being double-shuffled by the stronger power.

Charles Ingrao's "Hessian mercenary state" began with the *Landgrave* centralizing the collection and disbursement of military payments at the turn of the eighteenth century. It developed as the state encroached steadily on peasant society in search of both manpower and the funding necessary to bridge the gap between the amount of the subsidies and the actual costs of fulfilling the treaties. Military taxation and military recruitment, to be effective, required increasingly developed recordkeeping—and increasingly comprehensive enforcement of the network of laws regulating military service and its ramifications. By the last quarter of the eighteenth century, the entire population of Hesse-Cassel was organized to support the army, which was the major source of public income. The concepts of "civilian" and "soldier" had become artificial constructs. All men between 16 and 30 were listed on rolls kept by local bailiffs and were liable for service in their local regiment when that should become necessary.

In practice, those owning more than 250 *Thalers* in property fulfilled their obligation with money instead of blood. Craftsmen, workers in vital industries, and men essential to the prosperity of their farms or families were also exempted—indeed, if someone in those categories enlisted, his case might be investigated to make sure he was a "true volunteer." On the other hand, the state went so far as to encourage a steady supply of marginalized "have-nots" by adjusting patterns of inheritance and employment. Parents were held responsible for sons who emigrated, even being imprisoned until the miscreants reported for duty.

In terms of numbers, Hesse-Cassel maintained a field army of around 12,000 muskets for hire, supported by the same number in garrison units. These men were usually employed, Prussian style, in the economy— usually in family enterprises—but stood available as replacements and reinforcements. One out of 4 households was represented in the army; in Prussia the figure was 1 of 14.

One result of this fusion of military and civilian was steady, profitable work for architects and construction workers, as Cassel became a show-place of public works and public buildings. Another was the positioning of the government as a primary source of profit—not exactly through corruption, but through mutually acceptable arrangements among gentlemen. Not all the subsidy money, moreover, went for public works or private aggrandizement. Hesse produced its own uniforms and weapons as far as possible, and the numbers of craftsmen and skilled workers correspondingly steadily increased. Government experts improved peasant agriculture, especially by encouraging potato cultivation and sheep raising. Wool manufacturing expanded the textile industry to a point where weavers were described as being able to eat meat and drink wine on a daily basis. By modern standards, one may speak of involuntary servitude. It was also an interesting, not unsuccessful, exercise in making war support peace.[19]

SOLDIERS AMONG THEMSELVES: DISCIPLINE, DRILL, AND HONOR

The development of standing professional armies is usually presented in the general context of an early modern "military revolution," in which varying combinations of tactical and technological developments were best implemented by trained, disciplined soldiers permanently organized in small, flexible units. Specifically, the standing army is usually associated with a Dutch Republic condemned to permanent war with an exponentially richer and stronger Habsburg Spain. From there the system spread throughout Europe. Sidetracked temporarily as the Thirty Years' War slid into anarchy, it later reemerged to set the military tone for more than a century.[20]

In setting that tone, the professional army also established new lines of demarcation between the soldier and the civilian. First was discipline. In *The Face of Battle*, John Keegan repeatedly raises the question why men fight when the common sense of self-preservation urges flight. The conditions of battle between 1648 and 1789, however, often made running the most dangerous option. If casualties for an army that stood its ground could be murderously high, breaking in the face of an enemy might well bring annihilation, particularly at the end of a long and bitter day, when mercy was unlikely to be a common behavior. Discipline, in short, was a survival mechanism.

Underlying the issue of discipline was a general characteristic of eighteenth-century society. It was hierarchic, but not especially deferential. Bowing to the landlord and the pastor was taken for granted and understood. Taking orders from someone of one's own social standing and close to one's own age because of a few lines of braid on his sleeve was a much more dubious proposition. The kinds of grass-roots, small-group cooperation engendered by the factory system, compulsory schooling, and team sports was foreign to ordinary people in the Age of Reason. The authority of the junior officers and noncommissioned officers who directly supervised an army's daily routines could not be taken for granted. It had to be sustained and reinforced at every turn, in ways even the most stubborn rear-ranker could understand.[21]

Drill, and the soldiers' affirmation of it, was a major factor in instilling discipline. Twenty-first-century readers, accustomed to dismissing drill as mindless hut-two-three-four may find it unlikely that soldiers whose predecessors scorned to soil their hands with digging would turn out willingly, even enthusiastically, for a turn on the parade ground. From the beginning of his service, every early modern infantrymen had one truth hammered into him from every quarter: the unskilled or unwilling soldier in an eighteenth-century formation directly endangered his comrades, as well as himself. Any recruit who did not understand drill's practical importance was likely to become the subject of direct and uncomfortable enlightenment by the old soldiers of his company.

A second factor in drill's popularity was its role as a social bond. Anthropologists suggest that collective movement of large muscle groups arouses affirmative echoes of primitive hunting groups. Drill was also likely to be the first ongoing play, in the sense of an activity undertaken without immediate purpose, that many seventeenth-century men had in their lives. Especially when executed to music, as was increasingly the case, drill performed many of the same functions that dance, in the complex, highly structured forms of the period, did in the ballrooms and courts of early modern Europe.[22]

Drill was, finally, a source of status. The private soldier who mastered the arcanae of military movements and military bearing tended to take pride in the accomplishment. His chances for tangible signs of approval, such as promotion to corporal, depended heavily on his ability to meet the standards of his community—standards, it may be observed, no more artificial than their civilian counterparts—which, at this period, focused heavily on the drill ground.

A sense of honor also set soldiers apart from the civilian world. They copied their military superiors in everything from fighting duels to keeping mistresses. The swords many infantrymen carried until well into the eighteenth century were more than increasingly vestigial 10-pound weights. A Prussian regiment deprived of them as a punishment before the Battle of Leignitz went into action, charging the Austrian line without orders and shouting "Honor or death!" Frederick the Great not only returned the swords but purchased new hat braiding for the whole regiment at his own expense, itself a thing to be marveled at given his well-known parsimony.[23]

"For if we go it's one to ten/But we return all gentlemen" promises the most familiar English recruiting song. James Graham, Marquis of Montrose, expressed the sentiment elegantly in his well-known couplet "He either fears his fate too much / Or his deserts are small / That puts it not unto the touch / To win or lose it all." Often described as a pre-battle toast, it was in fact part of a love poem—an ironic reflection of the familiar connections between Ares and Aphrodite. But the two couplets expressed the same truth: life is more than the sum of its routines. The very act of volunteering was described as lifting the recruit out of the common ruck, not only because it involved taking up arms, but even more because it was an exercise of the choice considered a major, frequently envied, prerogative of the upper classes.[24]

Discipline, drill, honor—these set Europe's early modern soldiers apart from civilians, not only on their own terms but because they were chosen values—even if the "choice" meant no more than not deserting. The soldier could, and did, see himself as heir to a right even the medieval church agreed accrued to those entitled to bear arms: the right of conquest.[25] To civilians, the collective, anonymous aspect of a regiment on parade or on the march, the prompt obedience, the automatic deference to authority— these unfamiliar behaviors were often more frightening, and proved more dangerous, than the short-term smash-and-grab medieval *chevauchée* and the random pillaging of the Thirty Years' War.

SOLDIERS AMONG CIVILIANS

Soldier-civilian interaction in its simplest form involved what John Lynn calls the "tax of violence": seizing needed resources by force or the threat of force.[26] This tax was usually collected in "friendly" territory and was often situational. Armies preferred to supply their marches in as orderly and systematic a fashion as possible. The optimal alternative, particularly for long moves, developed and tested in the sixteenth century on the Spanish Road from Italy to the Low Countries, was a chain of permanent supply centers, restocked as needed from local sources that were—at least theoretically—paid in cash. The next-best choice was the *étape*, a designated location on the route where the troops halted and merchants delivered supplies for bulk sale. Lodging was structured by regulation and compensated by certificates that could be used to fulfill tax liabilities.

This was all well enough—when it worked. Even with Spain's resources underwriting the Spanish Road, breakdowns on its route were frequent.

In states less well organized and financed, any system tended toward the random. Hungry, unpaid soldiers might plunder the countryside at random and loot friendly towns as though they were enemy strongholds taken by storm. Exemption from quartering was everywhere prized. Communities tried to buy themselves free even at the highest prices. Better-off individuals were often willing to pay premiums to neighbors who agreed to assume their unwanted guests. Taverns and brothel keepers hoping for windfall profits often found soldiers readier to pick fights with the inn's civilian customers than to pay their own scores—and negotiation over sums owed, while manageable with one or two men, was usually impossible when a dozen were involved and none wished to lose face before the rest by seeming to back down.

Soldiers quartered with families could at a minimum be expected to demand food, drink, and services above and beyond those legally and customarily specified. Soldiers in a playful mood baited respectable householders by smashing crockery and putting their boots on chairs and beds. Soldiers were a source of physical infection, bringing with them alien germs and exotic diseases, not all of them venereal. Soldiers brought moral infections, as well: the strong language and swaggering attitudes that impressed young boys, the open contempt for systematic work that was every respectable parent's nightmare. Soldiers broke hearts, and worse. For every "Maid of Fif-e-o" who refused her martial suitor and sent him into a terminal decline, there were too many like the "Captain bold in Halifax / Who dwelt in country quarters [and] / Seduced a maid who hanged herself / One Monday in her garters."

The tax of violence, as Lynn calls it, reached its heyday in the first half of the seventeenth century. Thereafter, while it never disappeared, it steadily declined in extent and degree as quartering grew more systematic and better defined. Officers who in earlier years identified sufficiently with the rank and file and who derived much of their command authority from the assent of the commanded, were reluctant to test a fragile authority by interfering. Experience showed, however, that discipline sacrificed on the march or in garrison was not easily restored for battle. At the same time, governments seeking to reassert authority badly shaken by the behavior of their armies took the side of their subjects. Officers were punished for tolerating disorder in quarters. Soldiers were required to compensate victims of pilfering or breakage, at least in theory.

The laws governing quartering and billeting nevertheless offered ample room for everyday friction. In France, they dated back to the days of Joan of Arc. Firewood, salt, and vinegar, a bed and a candle, linens, cookware, wine as a matter of course were required. Increasingly, items of consumption were compensated in cash. That made the system no more popular. Most of the friction, however, involved domestic disputes, rather than pregnant daughters. In the German town of Goettingen, for example, a soldier enjoyed puttering around the kitchen, to the growing irritation of his involuntary hostess. One day, when he attempted to warm a dish in the oven, he was informed that he was interfering with the preparation of dinner for the family. He called the housewife a "sassy, brutal broad." She kicked him in the shins. He pushed her into the wall. The husband and son appeared and told the soldier to shut his big mouth. Words like ox, villain, and jackass were freely exchanged among all participants. Unlike in other similar situations, no blows were struck. No one reached for a club or a knife. Yet the pattern of townsmen seeing themselves unjustly exploited and soldiers feeling cheated by strangers was the same whether manifested as tragedy or, as in this case, as farce.[27]

An alternate solution developed in the small German states, whose authorities, in the relatively quiet circumstances of German "home towns," were well practiced in dealing with minor domestic squabbles. It amounted to a system in which civilians who could afford it paid the soldiers assigned to them a cash sum equal to the legal cost of billeting. The soldiers then sought other quarters in the poorer sections of town as renters making their own terms. A bed and a chest were often enough to satisfy them—it left more money for important things like beer. Their landlords, usually themselves from the poorer elements, were pleased to have the extra income. Their domestic circumstances, moreover, were likely to be more flexible than those of the prosperous classes and, as such, more accommodating to outsiders.

So far, so good. But the pressures that system put on low-rent housing did nothing to increase the soldiers' popularity among apprentices and day laborers. Small wonder that Austria, for example, shifted responsibility for quartering troops to the state in 1749 and even before then preferred to house its men in barracks or "quasi barracks" such as abandoned monasteries. Even in Prussia, where most of the soldiers lived at home most of the time, most garrison towns featured "private barracks," essentially rooming houses for soldiers.

And yet soldiers quartered among civilians often found useful social niches. Like their predecessors the *Landsknechte* and the *tercios* (basic infantry formation of Spanish and imperial armies in the 16th and 17th centuries; forerunners of regiments), they were reasonably decent men most of the time. In Germany's increasingly "well-ordered police states," where every form of commerce was regulated, soldiers worked "off the books," making doors and cupboards for their hosts and "helping out" craftsmen from tailors to carpenters. Soldiers were useful in other ways, as well. Responsible for guard duty at town gates, they could facilitate smuggling on a large scale; grain, cloth, and brandy were commonly smuggled items. With production, consumer sales, and business dealings largely conducted in family homes, quartered soldiers provided security and muscle, both the literal and the euphemistic kind. Two or three burly grenadiers carrying cudgels sent an unmistakable message to neighborhood busybodies and officious constables. And, since these were widely regarded as victimless crimes, good citizens seldom found moral problems in buying at reduced costs "off the back of a wagon" and wearing gloves to carry away the "hot" merchandise.

Acculturation was facilitated in small states and city states, which tended as a rule to attract an herbivorous species of soldier, more concerned with bed, board, and a quiet life than with seeking reputation at the cannon's mouth or getting into payday fights. In Germany, local authorities regularly sought veterans of the Prussian service to smarten up their easygoing contingents. These men, however, tended to consider service in the small states and city-states a form of active retirement, with the result that things went on pretty much as before.

Marriage between soldiers and civilians was everywhere legally restricted or forbidden, less because of what soldiers did than because they were "outsiders." Nevertheless, in Goettingen between 1721 and 1755, almost two-thirds of the soldiers who married legally wed civilian spouses. Other forms of bonding remained open, as well. The most common was standing godparents, at a time when that office had major secular as well as spiritual implications. Again, in Goettingen, three-fourths of the godparents of soldiers' legitimate children were civilians. Soldiers occasionally were able to accumulate the money to buy a house and thereby acquire the civic rights that accompanied the ownership of property.

CIVILIANS IN WAR

Civilians between 1648 and 1789 benefited only indirectly from the universal exhaustion of the Thirty Years' War and the accompanying sense that Europe had come close to self-destruction.[28] The laws of war as they developed after 1648 tended to focus on the conduct of armies and to define noncombatant rights in that context.[29] This was not much— but it was better than nothing at all. When an army took the field, its camps were governed by military law and military custom. Far more than in a town, soldiers were masters in their own realm. But camps were also primary—sometimes the only—sources of cash and negotiable small items—for example, lace, in the words of Friedrich Schiller, "ne'er purchased at Leipzig fair." Soldiers also had a reputation as free spenders, willing to take their chances at games of chance. Camps were corresponding magnets for locals with something to sell or with a pair of dice and a good rap to draw players. Liquor and prostitutes, in passing, were high-end items usually "managed" by the camp provost; the risks accompanying their unauthorized vending were too high to be practical. Schiller, in *Wallensteins Camp,* gives one common scenario: a peasant seeking to get a bit of his own back with crooked dice escapes hanging not from any sense of mercy or fellow-feeling but from a consensus that any soldier who has sunk so low as to gamble with a peasant has no claim for redress.

Camps after the Thirty Years' War grew far more disciplined, with little room for unobserved soldier-civilian interaction. They were replaced by two other mutually alienating behaviors: foraging and requisitioning. Almost as soon as the tents were pitched, detachments of infantry under an officer or sergeant were dispatched to bring in straw for the soldiers' bedding. When the weather was cold, firewood became a necessary item. Sometimes entire villages would be demolished against a backdrop of cries and protests. Larger detachments of cavalry ranged farther afield seeking fodder for horses unable to sustain their strength by simple grazing. Part of the force would establish outposts around the chosen area. Then some troopers would cut grass while others collected hay and grain from peasant barns. Foraging parties almost always included an officer or two, and their conduct was carefully regulated—at least by the standards of the Thirty Years' War. The peasants, for example, usually delivered a certain amount of forage instead of the troopers' collecting it. Threats aimed at those who were noncompliant, however, were dire—and occasionally implemented. Nor did superiors worry much about the near-magical disappearance of fowl and other small edibles into saddlebags or cloaks.

Contributions and requisitions also became art forms during the eighteenth century. Contributions are best compared with modern protection rackets. They involved an invading force whose members allowed a town or locality to avert pillage or destruction by making payments in goods or cash and promissory notes—which were usually redeemable in every bank in Europe. Requisitioning involved demands made on a community for the delivery of certain amounts of food, supplies, and other material goods by a certain deadline. Unlike contributions, requisition might be accompanied by a claim for reimbursement—usually partial. That claim's negotiability depended on the ability of a village mayor to journey to the capital city of the issuing army—unless a merchant or gent accompanying the invaders was generous enough to redeem the voucher—again, at a reasonable discount of 50 percent or more.

The "virtue" of foraging, requisitioning, and, to a lesser extent, seeking contributions was that, in principle, at least, something remained behind. Armies expecting to be back in a year or two or three had no interest in finding a desert populated by starving, desperate men seeking vengeance by any possible means. Marauding was a slightly different story. It involved allowing the camp followers—soldiers' women, servants, hangers-on, and usually a few stragglers to provide guns and nerve—to pillage the countryside in the neighborhood of a moving army. Marauding could reflect a breakdown of discipline. It could be tolerated as a means of keeping a region in submission. Or it could be accepted as a recognized means of making up for pay and rations undelivered. In the former cases, detachments of cavalry carrying some extra rope eventually restored order. In the latter, sounding an alarm often was enough to bring men within hearing range back to the ranks, if only to escape a flogging or worse for being absent. The French in particular developed a name for helping themselves right up to the near side of the hangman; their reputation for self-sufficiency was not entirely a post-Revolutionary occurrence.[30]

The conditions of early modern battle also weighed heavily on civilians. Medieval battles were smaller in scale and conducted by preference on open terrain. The growing size of armies led them to operate in areas where it was easier to obtain food and forage. That meant developed regions, where villages were close together and people densely congested. The growing power of missile weapons led to an awareness of the value of fieldworks. From fieldworks to fortified villages was a simple, obvious step, particularly as the increasing proportion of firearms put a premium on shelter of any kind. The thick walls characteristic of European architecture, impervious to all but the heaviest guns, made even isolated farmhouses potential strong points. As armies' numbers grew and their persistence increased, one assault seldom settled the issue—a half-dozen and more became the norm by the eighteenth century. The resulting devastation was complete. The extended battlefields meant opportunities for last-minute evasion were limited. In turn, civilians died for the offense of being in the way.

After 1648, strategy continued to contribute heavily to soldier-civilian antagonism. The French scouring of the Palatinate in 1689, because of the relatively greater efficiency of the forces involved, came closer to crippling permanently the region's infrastructure than any similar event of the Thirty Years' War. Its memories endure in the age of the European Union. Its motives were in part strategic: the desire of Louis XIV, in the context of his newly adopted defensive strategy, to create a *glacis* (buffer zone) protecting France from invasion. They were in part economic: to punish the region for failing to deliver contributions designed to strain the economy to its limit. And they not least reflected the fact that the Sun King had forgotten, if he ever knew, the difference between war and meanness.[31]

Similar scorched-earth operations, though on a smaller scale, continued through the next century. It took Frederick the Great to execute another in the grand style, against Saxony during the Seven Years' War. Again, in a combination of strategy and punishment, Prussian troops systematically scoured the countryside year after year for men, money, and movable goods, extending to stripping gilt from doors.

The gulf between armed men in uniform and everybody else was, however, most vividly manifested in sieges. Sieges by their nature bore heavily on civilians in the contexts of famine and disease. The food supplies of the surrounding area, on which the community usually drew, were either consumed or destroyed—sometimes even by defenders seeking to deny them to besiegers. Hungry men and women were easy victims of every kind of disease, and vectors of their transmission. Bombarding an entire area, as opposed to targeting the defenses specifically, was forbidden by the laws of war, and Frederick the Great incurred corresponding criticism when he shelled the city of Dresden almost to rubble in 1760. But errors were inevitable given the state of gunnery, and few towns survived a

Ruins of Heidelberg Castle, destroyed by the French in 1689, loom behind the statue of the Virgin Mary in the Grain Market. Courtesy of Erich G. Pohl, Heidelberg.

siege without suffering extensive "collateral damage," as it is called today. Civilians, moreover, were almost always conscripted as labor, clearing rubble and dousing fires under high-risk conditions. Any remaining sense of loyalty to a cause or solidarity with a garrison was usually eroded as the proportion of rats and household pets in civilian diets increased.

The elaborate structure of negotiations developed in the early modern period for surrendering a fortified place once a "practicable breach" had been established stipulated specifically that, in case of an assault, neither garrison nor inhabitants had any claim to mercy. The logic of "surrender or face the consequences" is usually described as being based on the argument that once the final outcome of a siege became certain, the defenders were morally and materially responsible for forcing the besiegers to carry the fortress by assault. The "law of sack" had deeper roots as well, reaching into antiquity. It took near-berserk courage to storm defended walls. The fictional rifleman in the television version of *Sharpe's Company* who mutters "Time to go mad!" before the 1812 assault on Badajoz speaks near-literal truth.[32] The victors and the survivors of such fighting were not to be brought to order by the mere beat of a drum.

One of the ironies of a storm was that the garrison was frequently able to withdraw into a citadel or other redoubt, then hold out until cooler heads prevailed and gallows were reared in what used to be the marketplace—seldom longer than a day or so. Civilians lacked that option. But attempts by local civic and religious authorities to encourage surrender usually foundered on the nature of the officers chosen as fortress commandants: elderly, anal-retentive types, whose sense of duty was as narrow and shortsighted as their vision, seldom inclined to do anyone any favors. And should the commandant be willing, for example, to allow women and children to leave, the opposing commander was almost certain to drive them back within the walls.[33]

The concept of civilians as noncombatants was further increasingly obscured as Europe experienced its first extended experience of "unconventional warfare." Previously confined to frontier areas like the Baltic, the Balkans, and Reconquista Spain, it emerged in the continent's heartland during the second half of the seventeenth century, introduced not by civilians as might be expected but by armies compensating for strategic overextension by tactical irregularity. The French used partisans consistently from the Dutch Wars, for screening, scouting, and small-scale raiding. Some were true irregulars; more were detachments from regular units. In the eighteenth century, they took permanent form as combined-arms infantry-cavalry formations. Austria countered by bringing its border guard troops, the *Grenzer*, into Europe's mainstream wars. These formations earned a combined reputation for ferocity in battle and plundering in camp that led other armies to begin raising specialist light troops as a countermeasure. These "partisan regulars" were in principle kept under command, but it was generally agreed that, without the promise of some loot, volunteers were not always forthcoming. The French threatened "excesses" with life sentences to the galleys. In practice, however, the contents of pockets and saddlebags were seldom scrutinized carefully—after all, it was only civilian property.

Partisans serving under direct military command increasingly encountered civilian resistance based on a combination of charismatic local leadership and collective identity, a sense that there was nothing to lose by making a fight, and, not least, the growing proliferation of military-type small arms in a market depressed by the Treaty of Westphalia. To mention only a few, near-random examples, Swedish troops in Courland in 1658 encountered systematic resistance. The Polish Wars were characterized by irregular combat on a large scale. In 1690s, Ireland, Jacobite supporters, the rapparees, caused major logistical problems for King William's army.[34] Guerrillas were so effective in the Iberian Peninsula during the War of the Spanish Succession that, a century later, French officers sought precedents in their earlier experience for combating greater insurgency.

In Europe, immediate massive reprisals were the norm for dealing with armed nonsoldiers and also served as a means of distinguishing them from recognized members of the soldiers' guild, which is to say civilians. Events in the New World, particularly in British North America, initially replicated that pattern. European settlers found themselves in an efflorescently hostile physical environment, inhabited by a people whose everyday ways of living seemed alien and whose principles of conduct seemed barbarian. They had, however, the beginnings of a model and a method for meeting the challenge. The model was Ireland: another alien environment and another unworthy race, able to achieve liberty only at the price of submission. The method was unlimited war. That meant pitched battles when possible and "little war" when they were not. No significant distinctions were made between combatants and noncombatants; "shock and awe"—or simply terror—were used to break not merely the capacity but the will of warrior peoples to cease fighting permanently and to force them to accept the consequences as preferable to annihilation.[35]

So, at least, states current academic wisdom. Its detailed accuracy is less important than what it logically implies: that British North America should have developed as a martial, even a militarized society along the lines of Austria's Military Border, the Anglo-Scottish frontier, or the no-man's-land of the Cossack steppe. What happened instead was just the opposite. Militias based on general manhood service rapidly gave way to specialized formations composed of and led by men who knew what they were doing in the operationally complex conditions of forest warfare. The farmer, the blacksmith, the shopkeeper was well content to abide at home and compound for his service with money. Cash in hand on enlistment and promises of land on discharge were an appealing combination to the ambitions and the adventurous. "Nothing ventured, nothing have" was the mantra of many a recruit to the Indian Wars from Georgia to Canada.[36]

The British colonies' preference for regulars remained unaltered by such catastrophes as the battle at the Monongahela and the costly failure to storm Fort Ticonderoga. The colonies were quite content to have their own "provincial" regiments relegated to second-line and labor missions. After all, they were not men of war but civilians in all but formal definition, while British professionals adapted admirably to the unfamiliar conditions of North America.[37]

The development of these rangers, as they were generally called, along the lines of sixteenth-century *Landsknechte* or eighteenth-century *Grenzer* was aborted by another internal dynamic of the colonies: a fundamental preference for "real soldiers," regulars, to do the fighting. Characteristic of the North American wars were the increasing demands of the locals for support from the regular armies of their respective home countries. French Canada, though hardly a pacific society, for a variety of reasons—not least the relatively small size of its population vis-à-vis the First Canadians— had never fought indigenous people on the scale or with the enthusiasm of their southern neighbors. The Canadian militia, and the colonial service companies raised by the Naval Ministry, were sufficiently acculturated to be formidable bush fighters. Yet the near-token regular regiments, white coats and all, that the home government managed to send became the backbone of Canada's long rear-guard struggle.[38]

That pattern persisted through the American War of Independence. For all the recent focus on that conflict's revolutionary aspect, an emerging America's first-line Continental Army was a force recruited in good part from the marginalized, the disadvantaged, and the ambitious, whose effectiveness was in more or less direct ratio to its acculturation to the professional methods developed in Europe. Its second-line state militias depended heavily on the services of patriots with property, yet proved more effective in organizing men and supplies than as field forces.[39] It must be noted, however, that, unlike the situation in Europe, men freely shifted between militia and Continental service. One military result of this fluidity was that by the end of the war, particularly in the South, militia regiments gave good accounts of themselves under commanders who understood how to use them.[40] In social and cultural contexts, the early modern dichotomy between soldier and civilian never became as pronounced in the American colonies as in Europe—a fact confirmed by, among many other points of evidence, the Second Amendment to the Constitution and a large number of bumper stickers celebrating the virtues of an armed public.

CIVILIANS FROM SUBJECTS TO CITIZENS

The defining figure of early modern dynastic war was Louis XIV, and war's defining concept was *gloire*. The War of Devolution and the Dutch War, the Nine Years' War of 1689–1697, the War of the Spanish Succession—each had practical aspects, yet essentially all were wars of *gloire*. *Gloire* was personal, involving a code of honor fulfilled with panache. It was also a public concept, justifying rights asserted and authority exercised. *Gloire* required constant renewal and constant manifestation. As they grew more efficiently managed, these wars correspondingly assumed a form John Lynn calls "war as process."[41] The devastation of the Palatinate between 1683 and 1689 exceeded any comparable event of the Thirty Years' War without generating any direct results. Battles and sieges seldom yielded more than local, temporary results. With, however, no fundamental motive to strive for an end-game, there were no compelling reasons to challenge the methods.

That perspective changed in the eighteenth century as "war as process" developed into limited war. Europe's rulers and generals did not see the reconstruction of war as a passionless instrument of state policy, restricted in time, scope, and scale, as an end in itself. It was, rather, a precondition to the focus that would restore purpose and decision to what seemed an increasingly sterile, increasingly expensive activity—a dynastic plaything anomalous in an Age of Reason.[42]

The relationship of focus and decision was first illustrated in a civilian context during the Jacobite Rebellion of 1745.[43] The British government and British public opinion moved through two approaches to dealing with the invasion or insurgency: "savagery" and "rebellion." The first was rooted in a centuries-old-fear that had all too often been justified in the history of brutal wars and border reiving (the stealing of goods,

Monument de la Place des Victoires.

Louis XIV, Monument de la Place des Victoires. Tableau
historique et pittoresque de Paris. Courtesy of the
Special Collections and Archives, U.S. Military Academy
Library, West Point. Photo by James Holland, Jr.

especially cattle) that did much to shape the Anglo-Scots relationship.
With the Act of Union not half a century old, the Highlanders in particular,
who formed the core of Charles Stuart's army, were seen as alien and
sinister "Sons of Murder," in the words of one contemporary poem.
While all of Scotland suffered under British occupation in the aftermath of
Culloden, the Highlands were singled out for special treatment in a series
of "military executions," punitive raids that began with the seizure of

weapons, then escalated into comprehensive destruction and confiscation of property. Some English politicians and pamphleteers spoke of creating a comprehensive famine that would eradicate the Highlands' population. Bridges were demolished, boats were sunk, an already marginal economy imploded. As part of the "reconquest," Cumberland's army implemented systematic violence against women.[44] Even the most latitudinarian codes of warfare exempted unarmed women from attack.

Yet this apparent rejection of any concept of "civilian" was in fact part of its fundamental redefinition. The manhandled women stood accused—not, as might be expected, of aiding or concealing rebels but of helping fugitives to escape justice. Instead of traitors to the crown, the women of the Highlands were accessories to crime. After the Reformation, religious heresy had moved in the direction of an individual choice that could be abjured. It now became possible, in England at least, for political rebellion to be processed as an individual decision, subject to specific punishment. Before the 1745 Rising, and even after its scale became apparent, George II and his ministers made plans to defeat it by using criminal proceedings. The Duke of Cumberland's army marched north with orders not to harrow the land indiscriminately but to carry out investigations, arrest suspects, and hold them for trial. After Culloden, thousands of Charles Stuart's soldiers were jailed, hundreds tried, and dozens executed, to say nothing of the hundreds exiled to America.

This is a far cry from the general image of suppression so brutal that it gave the nine of diamonds the nickname "curse of Scotland" on the mythic grounds that Cumberland wrote on it his order that there be no quarter given at Culloden. The policy was in fact easier stated than applied. So many prisoners were taken that even identifying them proved difficult. Surnames in the English sense had not made much headway in the Highlands. Making cases against the prisoners strained the judicial system to its limits and beyond. Nor did the soldiers greet this departure from custom with enthusiasm. Among government institutions, armies remain perhaps the least fitted to undertake criminal trials. Few eighteenth-century British officers had anything but rudimentary knowledge of the relevant laws and procedures. Many, probably most, believed that rebels in arms should not be given quarter. Certainly Cumberland remained unwavering in his insistence on a government monopoly of armed force. At Culloden in particular, Scots were killed indiscriminately, in hot blood and cold— especially Highlanders. The government, however, remained adamant in granting military status as prisoners of war only to the detachment of French troops that had accompanied Charles. The rest were criminal suspects, at least officially.

The trials were held in English courts. The best defense was to stand mute and rely on the prosecution's case to collapse from lack of evidence. Claims to be treated as prisoners of war were consistently disallowed as irrelevant. Coercion, the claim that a defendant had been compelled by a landlord or a clan chief, also received short shrift. Significant for this essay, however, is the practical advance represented by the Jacobite trials in developing the concept of "civilian." Rebellion was a capital crime—but a civil crime. Thus, the status of civilian was developing an expanded legal definition—but only in the context of a military victory decisive in good part because of its limited, focused objective of breaking armed resistance.

That was only one side of the story. On the continent, the most comprehensive and sophisticated application of the theory of limited war was implemented by Prussia's King Frederick II. Frederick believed that war should be short and brutal enough to deter future challenges from the defeated party or anyone else. Between 1740 and 1763, he applied that principle with singleminded determination. Prussia confronted Europe in arms and survived. It might even be said to have emerged victorious—but at a price that left the state shaken to its physical and moral foundations. In the course of the Seven Years' War alone, Prussia lost 13,000 houses destroyed and 60,000 horses dead. In the province of Pomerania, one-fifth of the population died of hardship and disease. Sixty thousand more died or disappeared in Neumark-Brandenburg, the heart of the kingdom. When all the losses were reckoned, even given the army's 180,000 dead, a Prussian soldier was arguably safer than a Prussian civilian.[45]

Statistics can be presented indefinitely to make a common point. By the end of the Seven Years' War, any concept of the civilian as a protected noncombatant, supporting war indefinitely through the meager surpluses of a preindustrial economy, had been reduced to the vaguest of theoretical principles. Wherever armies marched, they took their gloves off—and did so as a matter of policy. The Russians set new standards for devastating occupied territory during their repeated invasions of eastern Prussia. In the Rhineland, French generals stripped countryside and towns more comprehensively than had ever been done a century earlier. The civilian was no less war's victim in 1756 than in 1648. Civilians had learned to adapt, building with wood instead of stone to facilitate rebuilding, farming in the expectation of losing crops and animals more or less regularly, reducing investment to the bare minimum necessary to sustain local economies. These compensations pointed a clear way to decivilizing by the slow route, as opposed to the catastrophic immediacies of the Thirty Years' War.

It was in those contexts that fundamental redefinitions of war and civilians' place in war began emerging. Partly as a legacy of Rome and partly from its own spiritual and social dynamic, the West had historically accepted both war and killing as normative. Violence was considered an appropriate way of defending personal interests and personal honor. Intellectuals from Thomas More to John Locke interpreted war as a logical result of the existence of a number of sovereign states that recognized no higher authority to settle disputes among them. Hugo Grotius, whose writing repeatedly asserted the fundamental distinction between lawful and unlawful combatants, those who could be killed and those who must be protected, also accepted war as an instrument of state policy and justified its waging on grounds so general as to be virtually universal. Pacifism was a fringe position, widely suspected as touching the edges of heresy.[46] Nor, it should be said, had nonviolence and negotiation been part of the stock in trade of the peoples and governments Europe had encountered in the previous millennium or so. Prussians and Lithuanians, Mongol and Muslims had their own justifications for ferocity that matched anything Western Europe could show and throw.

Nevertheless, as the eighteenth century progressed, to an increasing number of nonparticipants, the ostensibly limited and ordered conflicts hailed as progressive invited interpretation as homicidal theatrics, a set of rituals meaningful to their initiates the soldiers but harmful to everyone else. An emerging secular intelligentsia increasingly conscious of its independent status, increasingly dedicated to proving the pen mightier than either the sword or the scepter, interpreted war as not merely irrational but unnatural. Man in his natural state might be positively benevolent

Hugo Grotius, author of *The Rights of War and Peace*, often called the founder of international law. Courtesy of Kansas State University Libraries.

toward his fellows, or he might be too timid or too self-regarding to be aggressively belligerent. In either case, natural man was definitely unwar-like unless stimulated by the artificial sanctions and encouragements offered by society.

War also violated the natural economic order. Theories that the wealth of a state depended on expanding its influence by force had been given the lie most recently by the impoverished people and the empty treasury bequeathed by Louis XIV to his successor—along with the rueful con-fession that he had loved war too much. Continental physiocrats and British laissez-faire theorists alike argued that economic development naturally followed peaceful paths, determined by positive synergies of needs and desires. War only distorted natural processes of production and exchange.

There was, however, another face of war in the Enlightenment's world-view. At least since the Age of Augustine, European moral and intellec-tual traditions had incorporated an idea of progress based on the triumph of righteousness. That end could be reached only through suffering and destruction, purging society of its baseness. It was not to be sought lightly. But, in the pursuit of such ultimate moral objectives as true peace and true justice, war might be understood as a cruel necessity and a moral good. Montesquieu, for example, argued that the armed forces of a state should evolve from being the tools of monarchs to being the instruments of communities' desire for justice. Jean-Jacques Rousseau also seems to have regarded war, at least potentially, as an arbiter of right.[47]

Some idea of the consequences of this development emerged in Corsica, where Pasquale Paoli led revolts first against Genoa, then against France that developed along the lines of a republican war, mobilizing Corsicans as citizens to fight for justice, liberty, and equality without counting the cost.[48] Defeated but never subdued and never reconciled, the island met a fate that prefigured too many ideologically based death grapples in later centuries as its energies turned toward resistance and its defining institu-tion became the *Union Corse*.

In the context of republican wars, the concept of the civilian changed essentially. The medieval definition of "those who worked," the fiscal-military state's concept of passive "subjects," was giving way to the notion of a "Third Estate," which included a rapidly increasing community of lawyers, journalists, and part-time or free-lance intellectuals who cultivated a proactive, positive image best expressed in the pamphlet of the Abbé Sieyès. "1st. What is the third estate? Everything. 2nd. What has it been heretofore in the political order? Nothing. 3rd. What does it demand? To become something therein."[49]

By 1789, the Third Estate was on the verge of moving from participation in society to participation in the state to sharing in governance—to becoming a citizen. And, in a final irony, the touchstone of citizenship for the next century and beyond would be military service. The army's specialists

This frontispiece of *The Rights of War and Peace*, Amsterdam 1670, displays three figures: Justice, War, and Peace. Courtesy of Kansas State University Libraries.

might set the norms and define the terms. Citizens in arms did the fighting at no cost to their civic identity. To generalize a point made specifically about the Virginia militia, they were "soldiers when they chose to be so."[50] "When we assumed the soldier," in George Washington's words, "we did not put aside the citizen." The aphorism foreshadowed and defined the uniformed civilians who made up the mass armies that would fight Europe's wars in the coming century and a half. That, however, is a story for later chapters in this volume.

NOTES

1. Jan Glete, *War and the State in Early Modern Europe: Spain, the Dutch Republic, and Sweden as Fiscal-Military States, 1500–1660* (London: Routledge, 2002).

2. For this process of informal technology transfer see B. S. Hall, *Weapons and Warfare in Renaissance Europe: Gunpowder, Technology, and Tactics* (Baltimore: Johns Hopkins University Press, 1997).

3. John A. Lynn, "Recalculating French Army Growth during the Grand Siècle, 1610–1715," *French Historical Studies* 18 (1994): 881–906.

4. A good description of the scam and its contexts in Geoffrey Parker, *The Army of Flanders and the Spanish Road, 1567–1658* (Cambridge: Cambridge University Press, 1972), p. 161.

5. Dennis E. Showalter, "Caste, Skill, and Training: The Evolution of Cohesion in European Armies from the Middle Ages to the 16th Century," *Journal of Military History* 57 (1993): 407–430.

6. See the overview by Reinhard Baumann, *Das Soeldnerwesen im 16. Jahrhundert im bayerischen und sueddeutschen Beispiel: Eine Gesellschaftsgeschichte Untersuchung* (Munich: Woelfle, 1978).

7. George Farquhar, *The Recruiting Officer*, reprint ed (Manchester: Manchester University Press, 1986), 62, 98.

8. Ibid., 105 (slightly edited).

9. Richard Holmes, *Redcoat. The British Soldier in the Age of Horse and Musket* (New York: HarperCollins, 2001), p. 140. The poster in question dates from 1809, but in spirit it belongs to this chapter.

10. John Lynn, *Giant of the Grand Siècle. The French Army 1610–1715* (Cambridge: Cambridge University Press, 1997), 348–356, 358–363. The quotation is from p. 355.

11. Ibid., 357–358.

12. Ibid., 369–371.

13. Jacques Gebelin, *Histoire des milices provinciales (1688–1792): le tirage au sort sous l'ancien régime* (Paris: Hachette, 1882), remains the most detailed study.

14. Helmuth Schnitter, *Volk und Landesdefension.Volksaufgebote, Defensionswerke, Landmilizen in den deutschen Territorien von 15. Bis zum 18. Jahrhunderts* (East Berlin: Militaerverlag, 1977).

15. A. Aberg, "The Swedish Army from Luetzen to Narva," in *Sweden's Age of Greatness, 1632–1718*, edited by M. Roberts (London: Longmans, 1973), 265–287; J. Lindegren, The Swedish 'Military State,' 1560–1720," *Scandinavian Journal of History* 10 (1985): 305–336.

16. John Keep, *Soldiers of the Tsar: Army and Society in Russia,1462–1874* (Oxford: Clarendon Press, 1985).

17. Jürgen Kloosterhuis, ed., *Bauern, Bürger und Soldaten: Quellen zur Sozialisation des Militärsystems im preußischen Westfalen 1713–1803*, 2 vols. (Münster: 1992), 61, 67–68; and "Zwischen Aufruhr und Akzeptanz: Zur Ausformung und Einbettung des Kantonsystem in die Wirtschafts-und Sozialstrukturen des preussischen Westfalen," in *Krieg und Frieden: Militaer und Gesellschaft in der Fruehen Neuzeit*, edited by Bernard R. Kroener and Ralph Pröve (Paderborn: Schöningh, 1996), 167–190.

18. The long-standard rural-oriented analysis of Otto Busch, *Military System and Social Life in Old-Regime Prussia*, trans. J. Gagliardo (Atlantic Highlands, NJ: Humanities, 1997), is now complemented and challenged by the more urban-oriented account

by Martin Winter, *Untertanengeist durch Militaerpflicht? Das preussische Kantonsystem in brandenburgischen Staedten im 18. Jahrhundert* (Bielefeld: Verlag fuer Regionalgeschichte, 2005). See as well Willerd Fann, "Peacetime Attrition in the Prussian Army, 1713–56: Some Statistical and Interpretive Problems," in ibid., 23 (1990), 76–84. Robert Rush, "'Der Gute Kamerad': The Life of a Prussian Soldier in the Army of Frederick William I," a paper presented at the 2006 meeting of the German Studies Association, is an insightful overview.

19. My analysis is based on Charles Ingrao, *The Hessian Mercenary State* (Cambridge: Cambridge University Press, 1987); Rodney Atwood, *The Hessians* (Cambridge: Cambridge University Press, 1980); and Peter K. Taylor, *Indentured to Liberty. Peasant Life and the Hessian Military State, 1688–1815* (Ithaca, NY: Cornell University Press, 1994). Generally valuable in this context is Peter Wilson, "Social Militarization in Eighteenth-Century Germany," *German History* 18 (2000): 1–39.

20. Barry Nickle, "The Military Reforms of Prince Maurice of Orange," PhD dissertation, University of Delaware, 1975, is an overview worth the difficulty of obtaining it. *Exercise of Arms. Warfare in the Netherlands, 1568–1648*, edited by M. Van der Hoeven (Leiden: Brill, 1997), is an anthology of useful case studies on subjects ranging from battle history to public finance.

21. This issue is addressed in various contexts of the French Revolution in *Re-Creating Authority in Revolutionary France*, edited by Bryant T. Ragan and Elizabeth Williams (Rutgers, NJ: Rutgers University Press, 1992). Cf. as well Robert Darnton, *The Great Cat Massacre and Other Episodes in French Cultural History* (New York: Basic Books, 1984), especially the title essay.

22. William H. McNeill, *Keeping Together in Time: Dance and Drill in Human History* (Cambridge, MA: Harvard University Press, 1995); Kate van Orden, *Music, Discipline, and Arms in Early Modern France* (Chicago: University of Chicago Press, 2005).

23. Christopher Duffy, *The Army of Frederick the Great* (New York: Hippocrene, 1974), 193–194.

24. Caroline Cox, *A Proper Sense of Honor: Service and Sacrifice in George Washington's Army* (Chapel Hill: University of North Carolina Press, 2004), analyzes key aspects of the subject in an American context.

25. Fritz Redlich, *De praeda militari: Looting and Booty, 1500–1815* (Wiesbaden: Steiner, 1956).

26. Lynn, *Giant of the Grand Siècle*, 184–217. The forthcoming work by Maren Lorenz, *Das Rad der Gewalt: Militaer und Zivilbevoelkerung in Norddeutschland nach dem Dreissigjaehrigen Krieg (1650–1700)* (Vienna: Boehlau, 2007), describes a situation in which postwar change was little more than cosmetic. Myron Gutmann, *War and Rural Life in the Early Modern Low Countries* (Princeton: Princeton University Press, 1980), suggests that rural environments facilitated higher levels of mutual accommodation than did towns.

27. The following presentation is based on Ralf Pröve, "Der Soldat in der 'guten Buergerstube': Das fruehneuzeitliche Einquartierrungssystem und die soziooekonomischen Folgen," in Koerner and Pröve, eds., *Krieg und Frieden*, 191–217; and Ralf Pröve, *Stehendes Heer und staedtische Gesellschaft im 18. Jahrhundert: Goettingen in seine Militärbevolkerung 1713–1756* (Munich: Oldenbourg, 1995). The anecdote is from Pröve, "'Guten Buergerstube,'" 207–208.

28. On that general subject, see most recently the extended essay by Theodore K. Rabb, *The Last Days of the Renaissance and the March to Modernity* (New York: Basic Books, 2006).

29. P. Haggenmacher, *Grotius et la doctrine de la guerre juste* (Paris: Presses Universitaires, 1983).

30. There is a useful overview in Christopher Duffy, *The Military Experience in the Age of Reason* (London: Routledge, 1987), 165 ff.; and an excellent case study in George Satterfield, *Princes, Posts, and Partisans. The Army of Louis XIV and Partisan Warfare in the Netherlands (1673–1678)* (Leiden: Brill, 2003), 42–88. Cf. also Ronald Ferguson, "Blood and Fire: Contribution Policy of the French Army in Germany (1688–1715)," PhD dissertation, University of Minnesota, 1970.

31. John A. Lynn, "A Brutal Necessity? The Devastation of the Palatinate, 1688–1689," in *Civilians in the Path of War,* edited by M. Grimsley and C. Rogers (Lincoln: University of Nebraska Press, 2003), 79–110.

32. Bernard Cornwell, *Sharpe's Company* (London: HarperCollins Publishers Ltd., 1983); *Sharpe's Company,* directed by Tom Clegg (1995).

33. The nature of siege warfare at this period is best presented in Christopher Duffy, *The Fortress in the Age of Vauban and Frederick the Great, 1660–1789* (London: Routledge, 1985).

34. Cf. Lynn, *Giant of the Grand Siècle,* 538–546; Johannes Kunisch, *Der kleine Krieg: Studien des Heerwesen des Absolutismus* (Wiesbaden: Steiner, 1973); and Martin Rink, *Vom Partheygaenger zum Partisanen. Die Konzeption des kleinen Krieges in Preussen 1740–1813* (Frankfurt: Lang, 1999), the latter with a European dimension that belies its title.

35. John Grenier, *The First Way of War: American Warmaking on the Frontier, 1607–1814* (Cambridge: Cambridge University Press, 2005), and Armstrong Starkey, *European and Native American Warfare, 1675–1815* (London: UCL, 1998), are the best overviews.

36. The standard case study is Fred Anderson, *A People's Army: Massachusetts Soldiers and Society in the Seven Years' War* (Chapel Hill: University of North Carolina Press, 1984). Cf. Harold Selesky's complementary *War and Society in Colonial Connecticut* (New Haven: Yale University Press, 1990).

37. Cf. King Parker, "Anglo-American Wilderness Campaigning 1754–1764: Logistical and Tactical Developments," PhD dissertation, Columbia University, 1970); and Stephen Brumwell, *Redcoats: The British Soldier and War in the Americas, 1755–1763* (Cambridge: Cambridge University Press, 2002).

38. Cf. W. J. Eccles, "The Social, Economic, and Political Significance of the Military Establishment in New France," *Canadian Historical Review* 52 (1971): 1–22; and Martin L. Nicolai, "A Different Kind of Courage: The French Military and the Canadian Irregular Soldier during the Seven Years' War," *Canadian Historical Review* 70 (1970): 53–75.

39. Charles Royster, *A Revolutionary People at War: The Continental Army and American Character, 1778–1783* (Chapel Hill: University of North Carolina Press, 1979); and Charles Neimeier, *America Goes to War: A Social History of the Continental Army* (New York: New York University Press, 1996).

40. A point well developed in John Buchanan, *The Road to Guilford Court House: The American Revolution in the Carolinas* (New York, 1999).

41. Cf. John A. Lynn, *The Wars of Louis XIV* (London: Longmans, 1999), 27–40, 367–376.

42. See particularly Armstrong Starkey, *War in the Age of Enlightenment, 1700–1789* (Westport, CT: Praeger, 2003).

43. The following account is based on Geoffrey Plank, *Rebellion and Savagery: The Jacobite Rising of 1745 and the British Empire* (Philadelphia: University of Pennsylvania Press, 2006). Jeremy Black, *Culloden and the '45* (New York: St. Martin's Press, 1990), is the best of the works taking a more conventional approach to the rebellion and its aftermath.

44. Maggie Craig, *Damn' Rebel Bitches: The Women of the '45* (Edinburgh, UK: Mainstream Pub, 1997).

45. Dennis E. Showalter, *The Wars of Frederick the Great* (London: Longmans, 1996).

46. Joan Tocke, *The Just War in Aquinus and Grotius* (London: S.P.C.K, 1965); and Karma Nabulsi, *Traditions of War: Occupation, Resistance, and the Law* (Oxford: Oxford University Press, 1999).

47. The "Republican Tradition of War," with its focal points of hope and heroic action, is developed in Nabulsi, *Traditions of War,* 177 ff.

48. Thadd Hall, *France and the Eighteenth-Century Corsica Question* (New York: New York University Press, 1971), remains useful. Cf. Peter Adam Thrasher, *Pasquale Paoli: An Enlightened Hero* (London: Constable, 1970).

49. Abbé Sieyès, *What is the Third Estate?* in *A Documentary Survey of the French Revolution,* edited by John Hall Stewart (New York: The Macmillan Company, 1951), 42.

50. James Titus, "Soldiers When They Chose to Be So: Virginians at War, 1754–1763," PhD dissertation, Rutgers University, 1983.

FURTHER READING

Anderson, Fred. *A People's Army: Massachusetts Soldiers and Society in the Seven Years' War* (Chapel Hill: University of North Carolina Press, 1984). Definitive on the nature of civil-military relations.

Cox, Caroline. *A Proper Sense of Honor: Service and Sacrifice in George Washington's Army* (Chapel Hill: University of North Carolina Press, 2004). Evaluates the nature of honor in the Revolutionary army.

Glete, Jan. *War and the State in Early Modern Europe. Spain, the Dutch Republic, and Sweden as Fiscal-Military States, 1500–1660* (London: Routledge, 2002). Excellent analysis of the emergence of the fiscal-military state.

Grenier, John. *The First Way of War. American Warmaking on the Frontier, 1607–1814* (Cambridge: Cambridge University Press, 2005). Makes a strong case for the early origins of total war in North America.

Holmes, Richard. *Redcoat. The British Soldier in the Age of Horse and Musket* (New York: HarperCollins, 2001). Anecdotal and perceptive narrative of the army's internal dynamic and social role.

Keep, John. *Soldiers of the Tsar: Army and Society in Russia, 1462–1874* (Oxford: Clarendon Press, 1985). Material on the Petrine reforms is detailed and useful.

Lindegren, J. "The Swedish 'Military State,' 1560–1720." *Scandinavian Journal of History* 10 (1985): 305–336. Seminal article establishing the long-run negative effect of conscription on Sweden's population.

Lynn, John. *Giant of the Grand Siècle. The French Army 1610–1715* (Cambridge: Cambridge University Press, 1997). Definitive on its subject; especially good on civil-military relations.

Parker, Geoffrey. *The Army of Flanders and the Spanish Road, 1567–1658* (Cambridge: Cambridge University Press, 1972). Still the standard work on the early modern Spanish army, focusing on its role in the Eighty Years' War with Holland.

Showalter, Dennis E. *The Wars of Frederick the Great* (London: Longmans, 1996). Develops the social-contract aspects of the Prussian military state.

Wilson, Peter. "Social Militarization in Eighteenth-Century Germany." *German History* 18 (2000): 1–39. Stresses the growing synergies of armies and societies in the German states during the eighteenth century.

FOUR

Civilians and Warfare during the French Revolutionary Wars

Michael Rowe

War was immutably bound up with the French Revolution. Indeed, recent historiography has reaffirmed the linkage not only in the traditional sense that the Revolution led directly to the outbreak of general war in 1792–93, involving all the Great Powers with the temporary exception of Russia. Rather, it has highlighted the foreign-policy dimension to the outbreak of the French Revolution in the first place: the loss of prestige and legitimacy suffered by the Bourbon monarchy during the Seven Years' War at the hands of Britain and Prussia and the subsequent failure of France to intervene to save the Dutch "Patriots" from Prussian intervention in 1787. Given the symbiotic relationship between the Revolution and war from the very beginning, it is a challenge indeed to abstract the one from the other and to avoid drifting into an account of the Revolution itself. The attempt will nevertheless be made. Despite the cogent argument that the cycle of war and revolution started well before 1792 or 1789,[1] this chapter focuses on the so-called Revolutionary Wars. These are generally split into two groups: the First Revolutionary War (also known as the War of the First Coalition), which started with the French declaration of war on Austria on April 20, 1792, and ended with the conclusion of the Treaty of Campo Formio between France and Austria on October 17, 1797, and the Second Revolutionary War (or War of the Second Coalition), which flared up at the very end of 1798 and ended with the Peace of Lunéville, signed by France and Austria on February 9, 1801.[2]

These wars were fought on a grand scale. All of Europe's Great Powers—the so-called Pentarchy of Austria, Britain, France, Prussia, and Russia—

became embroiled at one time or another, as well as second-division players like Spain, the United Provinces, Piedmont-Sardinia, the Ottoman Empire, Naples, and Bavaria. However, neither in this respect nor in terms of their duration were these wars especially revolutionary. Armed conflict involving all the Great Powers had occurred in the past, including, most recently, the Seven Years' War (1756–63). Nor were the Revolutionary Wars especially novel in terms of the theaters of operation. On the contrary, the areas that saw the heaviest fighting in the 1790s, namely the Low Countries, western Germany, and northern Italy, had traditionally served as receptacles of Europe's armies throughout the early modern period. As for their extension overseas, the Seven Years' War had in many respects been more impressive in this regard, with fighting in the 1750s and early 1760s extending to the Indian subcontinent, the Philippines, the Caribbean, and North America. The destruction of most of the French colonial empire in that conflict, and of the larger part of the British Empire in North America in the following war, meant that the Revolutionary Wars were centered on Europe to a greater extent than their immediate predecessors. The only geographical novelty was the brief foray into the Middle East, with Bonaparte's ill-fated expedition to Egypt.

More plausibly, the Revolutionary Wars are termed such because they were the first major conflict to follow the outbreak of the French Revolution in 1789. Above all, they were fought on the one side by a polity that claimed to be founded upon a whole new set of principles bound up with the concept of the sovereign nation. Of course, whether or not this was a French rhetorical smokescreen designed to obscure ruthless self-interest of a type typical of the other Great Powers is another matter.

The present chapter is split into eight sections. The first remains at the level of ideas and declarations. It briefly examines the state of ideas concerning warfare, in particular the treatment of civilians in warfare, on the eve of the French Revolution. It proceeds to look at how the French revolutionaries, through their statements, viewed warfare in general and the place of civilians in warfare in particular. The second and third sections, in contrast, are concerned with practicalities and action. They focus on the operational challenges that confronted the French army as it embarked upon war in the 1790s, examining in particular logistical problems. Questions relating to organization, political motivation, and discipline, which all had a bearing on how civilians might be treated, are also considered here. The fourth section, in its analysis of the French revolutionary army's administrative policies in the occupied territories, combines both theory and practice. This part includes a more general discussion of life under French military occupation in the 1790s, in the Austrian Netherlands, the United Provinces, Italy, Spain, and the Rhineland. It was not only foreign civilians who were confronted by the armies of the French Republic: the inhabitants of parts of France itself learned what it meant to be under occupation. Their experience, and especially that of those living in the

Vendée, is the subject of the fifth section. France's Old-Regime enemies too made some advances into neighboring territories or else faced domestic rebellions in the 1790s. In order to understand what, if anything, was "revolutionary" about the behavior of the revolutionary French army, it is necessary to examine the actions of these avowedly conservative forces. This is done in the sixth section. The final two sections consider the extent to which the Revolutionary Wars might be regarded as the globe's first total war, prefiguring the conflicts of the twentieth century.

ENLIGHTENMENT IDEAS ON CIVILIANS AND WARFARE

When it came to war, as in so many other fields, the French revolutionaries saw themselves as the practitioners of that mode of thought known as the Enlightenment. The Enlightenment was generally hostile to war. This was hardly surprising given its strong humanitarian ingredient, which manifested itself in the condemnation of a whole range of practices still common in the eighteenth century, such as cruel and unusual punishment, torture, slavery, and the maltreatment of vulnerable groups such as orphans, the mentally ill, and religious minorities. Aversion to pointless violence and cruelty extended even to the treatment of animals. War, an activity that produced untold violence and cruelty, inevitably attracted condemnation. This extended to armies, as practitioners of violence—a violence targeted not only at enemy armies, or indeed enemy civilians, but also at the ordinary rank and file who served within them and at civilians in states whose governments despotically resorted to military force to suppress opposition.

Many cultured Europeans viewed a military career as something distasteful on the eve of the French Revolution. Most of Italy's elite, for example, had nothing but contempt for soldiering, which was best left to "fools and foreigners." The same was true for much of German-speaking Europe. There were, of course, exceptions, such as the Prussians and the Piedmontese, who honored and practiced the military arts and stood condemned for it by their neighbors.[3] Disdain for the military was hardly surprising given that early modern armed forces often served as dumps for criminals and outcasts. Given all this, it is surprising that leading thinkers like Rousseau, Montesquieu, and Diderot devoted considerable time to military matters, and not only in order to condemn. Count Hippolyte du Guibert's *Essai générale de tactique,* a technical manual on infantry drill, became something of a bestseller and earned for its author great fame in the literary salons of France.[4] Of course, publications devoted to warfare were nothing new. The previous two centuries had already witnessed an explosion of publications—pamphlets, books, treatises—devoted to this subject. Yet the treatment of civilians tended to be a neglected component. An exception was Emmerich von Vattel (1714–1767), who made an important contribution in detaching the "law of war" from the concept of "just war." This he elaborated in his most important work, *Le Droit des gens* (1758). Vattel recognized that for the law of war to work, both belligerents needed to be counted as equal for that purpose. He did not, however, go so far as to argue *against* the notion that the entire enemy populace should be regarded as enemies: "When the ruler of the State, the sovereign, declares war upon another sovereign, it is understood that the whole Nation is declaring war upon the other Nation. . . . The two Nations are therefore enemies, and all the subjects of one Nation are enemies of the subjects of the other." However, Vattel quickly moved on to distinguish between two different types of enemy, combatants and noncombatants, the latter encompassing those not able to offer resistance. These should not be deliberately mistreated, though Vattel was realist enough to concede that they might suffer through the "accidental" consequences of war, something that left plenty of scope for suffering. He was prepared, for example, to excuse forced requisitioning and even a scorched-earth policy. It should be stressed that Vattel's criteria for noncombatant immunity were based not on age or sex but on nonparticipation in war-making. In an age of total war, therefore, all might be considered a legitimate target following Vattel's logic.[5]

Vattel was but one element of the Later Enlightenment, which, in its optimism, believed that war might become more "civilized" and possibly be abolished altogether. Indeed, there was evidence that it was becoming more civilized, at least in most of Europe. "At the present day war is carried on by regular armies," wrote Vattel,

the people, the peasantry, the towns-folk, take no part in it, and as a rule have nothing to fear from the sword of the enemy. . . . They live in safety as if they were on friendly terms with the enemy; their property rights are even held sacred; the peasants go freely into the enemy camp to sell their provisions, and they are protected as far as possible from the calamities of war.[6]

This was no doubt overly optimistic. During the Seven Years' War, Claude Louis Comte de Saint-Germain (later war minister under Louis XVI) described the war zone in Hesse as being littered with massacred civilians, including women and children, who had resisted pillage.[7] Yet, Vattel was essentially correct about the contrast between war in his time and war in previous eras. Nor did the establishment of a new order in France in 1789 appear to reverse this civilizing process—in fact, quite the contrary, if the plethora of early revolutionary statements on foreign policy and war was to be believed. The new French constitution (1791) pledged that the "French nation renounces to undertake any war with a view to make conquests, and will never employ its forces against the liberty of any people."[8] Wars of conquest were for kings, not free peoples. Rousseau had already shown the way here with his dismissal of war as essentially something ordinary people were forced into by governments.[9]

One of the few who struck a note of dissent at this juncture was Edmund Burke, who predicted in advance of the revolutionary wars that a new age of conflict distinguished by great brutality was at hand:

The mode of civilized war will not be practised; nor are the French who act on the present system entitled to expect it. They, whose known policy is to assassinate every citizen whom they suspect to be discontented by their tyranny, and to corrupt the soldiery of every open enemy, must look for no modified hostility. All war, which is not battle will be military execution. This will beget acts of retaliation from you; and every retaliation will beget a new revenge. The hell-hounds of war, on all sides, will be uncoupled and unmuzzled. The new school of murder and barbarism, set up in Paris, having destroyed (so far as in it lies) all other manners and principles which have hitherto civilized Europe, will destroy also the mode of civilized war, which more than anything else, has distinguished the Christian world.[10]

There were warning signs supporting Burke's predictions: the revolutionaries' ideological zeal; their total commitment to achieving their ends; their execration of the enemy; the seemingly random acts of violence and lynch-mob justice that accompanied the Revolution from the beginning.

Within months of France's awarding itself a new constitution that renounced wars of conquest, its revolutionary factions started maneuvering toward war. However, when the French declaration of war against the Habsburg Emperor finally came in April 1792, it was couched in language that would rather have confirmed the optimists' hope that a new, more benign spirit did indeed inhabit the corridors of power in Paris. The French, the declaration promised, would "never confound their brothers with their real enemies" and would "neglect nothing in order to alleviate the scourge of war."[11] Given that in its initial stages the War of the First Coalition was fought on home soil, against a foreign invader, the French had every interest in minimizing collateral damage. They were best placed to exploit the politics of moral outrage and to preach the righteousness of liberation. However, after Valmy and Jemappes, it was the French armies that surged forward in a two-pronged thrust that resulted in their occupation of the Austrian Netherlands and the Rhineland. The rhetoric emanating from Paris started to change. Georges-Jacques Danton expounded on the shift in a typically flamboyant speech to the National Convention on January 31, 1793: "The limits of France are marked by nature and we will reach them on the four corners of the horizon: the banks of the Rhine, the shores of the ocean, the line of the Alps. To there must extend the boundaries of our Republic."[12] A new episode in the relationship between the French Revolution and the rest of Europe had begun.

FROM LIBERATORS TO OCCUPIERS: THE EVOLUTION OF FRENCH OCCUPATION POLICY

The French army that occupied the Austrian Netherlands and parts of the Rhineland in the autumn of 1792 preached liberation, something that may have strengthened the conviction that this was no traditional occupation. General Adam Philippe Comte de Custine proclaimed to his troops as they entered the Rhineland in late 1792 that they should offer the people one hand in peace and use the other to drive off their oppressors. The French National Convention joined in enthusiastically with its famous decree of November 19, 1792, promising fraternity and assistance to all people wishing liberty and pledging protection from retribution. Typical also of this optimistic phase was the French foreign minister's letter of February 24, 1793, to Dutch revolutionaries, promising that the French Republic had "no other interest than to re-establish you in your rights. . . . The Republic demands as the price of its numerous sacrifices only the establishment of a free Constitution."[13] Implicit from the beginning, of course, was the assumption that Belgians and Rhinelanders would receive fraternity on the condition that they accept liberty, but the French believed this to be inevitable. Initial signs from the Palatinate, for example, where peasant discontent at the Old Regime was apparent, were encouraging. The new slogan, "peace to the cottages, war to the palaces", seemed to strike a chord amid reports of peasants plundering noble fields and wine cellars, expelling Old-Regime officials, and spontaneously planting "liberty trees."[14]

For their part, French generals made real efforts to prevent excesses by their troops against the civilian population. Charles François Dumouriez, who led the thrust into the Austrian Netherlands, instructed his soldiers to have the strictest regard for civilians and their property and made arrangements for supplies to be paid for in hard cash raised in loans according to the proper form. Custine, a stricter disciplinarian than Dumouriez, was prepared to resort to harsh measures against his troops to maintain discipline. When, for example, his troops entered the Rhenish city of Speyer and started to engage in looting, he summarily executed the ringleaders. "Order is restored," he wrote the minister, "the pillage stopped, the pillaged belongings restored to their owners. There was no other way to arrest the disorder and to save the honor of the name of France. This severe example has won the approval of the entire army. . . . My soul is torn by this; but I owed it to the glory of the name of France and I would rather die than see that suffer."[15]

Nonetheless, quickly—within weeks—the French discovered that native discontent with the Old Regime did not necessarily mean adherence to the Revolution. Disappointed, the French engaged more actively in propaganda provided mainly by local radicals known misleadingly as "Jacobins." When this failed, they blamed Old-Regime officials whom they had initially kept on but whom they now replaced as local administrations were "municipalized."[16]

The French persisted in their attempts to win political commitment to the Revolution. They and their allies among the local population flooded the countryside with propaganda, transmitted through flysheets, pamphlets, and revolutionary theater directed against the Old Regime. Attacks against the profligate princely governments touched a raw nerve in the countryside, where suspicion of urban culture ran deep.[17] The propaganda also sought to exploit conflicts over common rights, such as access to wood, which were rife and on the increase. More alarmingly for the civilian population, the French also attempted to flush out counterrevolutionaries by forcing people to make a public declaration of their allegiances. In Mainz, this exercise involved compelling all adult males to sign one of two registers: a black one, decorated with chains representing slavery, and a red one denoting freedom. In the region beyond Mainz, the French and their local allies gathered signatures in favor of "reunion" with France, and on December 15, 1792, the Convention in Paris decreed that elections be held in the occupied Rhineland. Males over 21 years of age could vote provided they swore to be "faithful to the people and the principles of liberty and equality." The authorities regarded those who abstained as counter revolutionaries.[18]

Few natives were prepared to commit themselves, even under pressure. The final realization by the French that they were dealing with a hostile population beyond their frontiers came in early December 1792, when occupied Frankfurt was liberated by the Coalition with the *active assistance* of the civilian population. This event was as important as the French victory at Valmy, which had exploded the myth that the Revolution would collapse in the face of invasion. Events in Frankfurt disabused the French of the notion that they would be welcomed as liberators. Nor were the tumults in Frankfurt unique, for they were replicated in Aachen and Mainz in early 1793.[19]

Jacques Godechot is essentially correct in dividing French occupation policy into two phases: the first, described earlier, lasted but a few months, from the breakthrough of the French armies into the Austrian Netherlands and Rhineland to their expulsion in the spring of 1793. It was characterized by idealism. The second, which lasted from France's military recovery in autumn 1794 all the way up to Waterloo, was characterized by unrestrained exploitation.[20] The French army that reoccupied the Low Countries and the Rhineland in 1794 had changed from that which had left 18 or so months earlier. Not only had it grown considerably, something with obvious implications for supply. Also of significance was the evolution of military discipline in this period. Thanks to the Revolution, reforms were undertaken in the French army to improve the lot of the ordinary rank-and-file soldier. In 1790, a new military code was introduced. This accorded soldiers the right to be tried by a properly constituted court-martial that included provision for a jury composed of at least some members who shared the rank of the accused. The code also abolished the harshest sentences.[21]

GREAT BRITAIN

NETHERLANDS

English Channel

Extent of French Expansion, 1793

Rhine River

Le Havre   Amiens
Roen

Metz

Paris

Normandy

Versailles   *Seine River*   Nancy

Brittany

Orléans

Nantes   Angers

Cholet   Dijon

SWISS CONF.

Vendée   Poitiers

Loire River

Bay of Biscay   FRANCE   Lyons

Grenoble

Bordeaux   *Rhône River*   Valence

Gironde   *Garonne River*

Avignon

Marseilles

SPAIN

REVOLUTIONARY FRANCE

Miles
0   100   200

100   200
Kilometers

David S. Heidler

Map of Revolutionary France. Courtesy of David S. Heidler.

While the framers of the code took considerable care to protect soldiers from "aristocratic" officers, they expended less effort on foreign civilians under French military occupation.[22] Much therefore depended upon the determination of individual officers to impose a degree of summary justice in order to deter mistreatment of civilians. Those of Custine's stamp had the inclination to do so but in the process exposed themselves to charges of being "aristocrats" and of harboring contempt for the common soldierly.

Under the Jacobin Republic (June 1793 to July 1794), this was potentially fatal: Custine, for example, fell to the guillotine on August 28, 1793. Not that the Jacobin regime favored indiscipline. On the contrary, it associated discipline with republican virtue and imposed it with its customary fanaticism. The mechanism for doing so was not the generals, who had all fallen under suspicion following Dumouriez's defection to the Austrians in April 1793, but civilian officials known as representatives on mission, who were first sent to the armies that same month. However, the overthrow of the Jacobin regime in July 1794 coincided with a diminution in the standing of the representatives. These lingered on until 1796, but long before then disciplinary power had reverted to the generals whom Jacobin propaganda had taught ordinary soldiers to distrust. Whether or not an officer managed to overcome these problems depended upon his character and leadership skills. Many fell far short of what was required for the good of the civilian population.

WAR FEEDING WAR: CIVILIANS AND THE SUPPLY OF THE FRENCH REVOLUTIONARY ARMIES

Discipline and leadership were vital during the Revolutionary Wars, given the mismatch between the demands of France's newly enlarged forces and the available supplies. This dimension—the competition between soldiers and civilians for scarce resources—is rightly seen as crucial in determining relations between civilians and the military during the Revolutionary Wars.

The requirements of the French armies of the 1790s were colossal. An individual soldier, according to the regulations, could expect a daily ration of 24 ounces of bread (three-quarters wheat and one-quarter rye), 8 ounces of meat, plus vegetables, rice, salt, vinegar, and wine. If received, this represented more nutritional value than most civilians might expect to receive.[23] When multiplied by the size of the French field armies in the 1790s—their collective strength peaked at about 750,000 men in late summer-autumn 1794—the resulting figures are impressive indeed.[24] In 1794, the average daily consumption of the Army of the North—then the largest of the field armies—was 2,210 quintals of wheat and rye.[25] The Sambre-Meuse army consumed 182 head of cattle, 850 sheep, 210,000 pounds of bread, and 400,000 pounds of fodder *per day*. In any three-month period, it required 250,000 quintals of wheat, 250,000 quintals of rye, 11,250 quintals of rice, 1.2 million pints of brandy, 300,000 pints of vinegar, 1.5 million pounds of salt, 1.62 million quintals of hay, 1.8 million quintals of straw for fodder, 720,000 quintals of straw for bedding, 1,080,000 bushels of oats, and 50,000 head of cattle.[26]

Revolutionary enthusiasm and the empowering legitimacy of *la Nation* might produce an unprecedented amount of manpower. However, it could not solve the technical problem of supplying these vastly expanded forces. How could it, when financial bankruptcy remained fundamental to France's problems? Raising supplies from the rich and privileged alone, as promised in slogans, was quickly recognized as insufficient. Requisitioning—in effect, ordered pillage—from the civilian population was the only answer. This was nothing new, but as old as warfare itself. One of the great seventeenth-century practitioners and theorists of war, Raimondo Prince Montecuccoli, had gone so far as to praise pillage as a great motivator for heroic actions.[27] At the same time, early modern generals recognized the practical dangers of uncontrolled pillage, including the ruination of an area to the extent that it became impossible to operate in. This understand led to efforts in the century preceding the French Revolution to bring the system of supply under central direction. A proliferation of disciplinary codes that proscribed draconian punishment for unauthorized looting accompanied this development.[28]

The French Revolution saw the abolition of such punishment. Jacobin moral purity in turn reversed this: the new military penal code was set aside, and those convicted of even minor pillaging could expect severe treatment at the hands of special revolutionary tribunals.[29] Research on the Sambre-Meuse army indicates these tribunals deserve their reputation for rigor: from June 27 to September 19, 1794, the Sambre-Meuse's tribunal tried 52 soldiers for pillaging. Of these, it acquitted nine. Of the rest adjudged guilty, it sentenced 30 to death, 4 to two years in irons, and 9 to shorter periods of detention.[30] Nor was freelance looting necessarily tolerated under the Directory, though much depended on individual generals. Bonaparte, in the Italian campaign, was quite tough on this issue: on April 22, 1796, he authorized his divisional generals to shoot, summarily, any officers and soldiers engaged in unauthorized pillage. Many were shot, with Bonaparte reporting back to the Directory that he had made "terrible examples" and that he would restore order and "cease to be a commander of brigands."[31]

Of course, all that Bonaparte was punishing was unauthorized looting and pillage, not requisitioning per se. He, and other generals, were simply determined to seize control over the process, not abolish it. This decision was made for at least three reasons: to prevent the army from disintegrating into an undisciplined band; to prevent the exhaustion of local supplies; and in order to monopolize power. Set against Bonaparte's statement on unauthorized pillage is the infamous declaration he supposedly made to the Army of Italy on the eve of its descent into the Po valley in 1796:

Soldiers, you are naked and ill-fed; the government owes you much, and can give you nothing. The patience and courage you have shown in the midst of these rocks is admirable, but they gain you no renown, no glory results to you from your endurance. It is my intention to lead you into the most fertile plains in the world. Rich provinces and great cities will be in your power; there you will find honour, glory and wealth. Soldiers of Italy, will you be wanting in courage and perseverance?[32]

This declaration is probably a fabrication, and yet it well reveals the mood of the army of the time, and of its generals.

A fourth reason for generals like Bonaparte to seize control of the requisitioning process is made explicit in the preceding declaration: the French government had let the armies down in this respect. At the beginning of the Revolutionary Wars, the organization of supply and logistics was largely in the hands of private contractors. The Committee of Public Safety attempted to place the system on a new footing, by pushing toward both greater centralization and accountability under a monolithic commission. However, this body proved overly complicated, and after Thermidor the trend was back toward decentralization.[33] There was a plethora of organizational problems associated with the restructuring of the French army that made it impossible for those responsible for supply to keep track of particular units.[34]

Given the chaos, the French were fortunate that campaigning in the 1790s took place in regions—the Low Countries, the Rhineland, and the Po valley—blessed with agricultural prosperity. These seemingly untapped riches contrasted with the poverty of an exhausted France that was having to import wheat from abroad in order to survive. The northeastern departments, ravaged by war, were drained, and subsequent troop deployments, including the move forward into the Austrian Netherlands in summer 1794, were in part determined by the need to discover new supplies. A similar dynamic helped project French forces stationed in the Austrian Netherlands into the neighboring Rhineland in the autumn. The Rhineland now needed to provide for the army, while Belgian supplies were redirected to supply the needy French market. In the space of one month—September 22 to October 21, 1794—the French army extracted from the Lower Rhine 154,405 quintals of wheat, 145,827 quintals of rye, 8,461 head of cattle, and 9,778 sheep. Official estimates for the first 10 months of occupation calculated that the region north of the Moselle provided supplies amounting to 227,030,000 *livres*. Depressingly, much produce never even reached the army but perished in depots because of mismanagement. Competition for scarce food supplies led to a tripling of the price of bread, with soldiers and civilians alike teetering on the edge of starvation during the terrible "hunger winter" of 1794–95.[35]

The French acted out of necessity rather than malice. Naturally, they sought to justify their actions by claiming it was only fair that those who were being given their freedom should pay. Given that no one could sensibly place a price on "liberty," this logic justified boundless extortion. This was not limited to supplies in kind, for the French also demanded vast amounts of hard cash from towns, cities, and entire regions: from Tournai, 10 million *livres* in 1794; in 1796, from Lodi, 20,000 *livres*, from Frankfurt 6 million *livres*, from Nuremberg 2.5 million *livres*, from Würzburg 5 million *livres*, and from the lands between the rivers Sieg and Rhine 5.6 million *livres*; in 1798, 16 million *livres* from the Swiss cantons of Bern, Zurich, Soleure, and Fribourg.[36] The French seized local notables as hostages to ensure that their demands were met. They also took over feudal dues and tithes, which they extracted more rigorously than before. Local communities, crushed by the burden, took out loans at disadvantageous interest rates, shifting a proportion of the costs onto future generations. As if this were not enough, additional burdens included forced billeting, which was aggravated by the lack of an equitable system, while towns unfortunate enough to contain French general officers needed to provide generous table money. The French also requisitioned labor for work on fortifications and logistics.

Necessity might excuse the requisitioning of essential supplies and services for the army. However, there was a gradual extension of what was meant by this. Paris dispatched special extraction committees to requisition strategic raw materials to augment the Republic's resources. This eventually not only included items of importance to the war economy but encompassed even art treasures. In June 1794, the Committee for Public Education in Paris ordered the attachment of "experts" to the army responsible for identifying valuable cultural objects in occupied territories. The painter Jacques-Louis David was initially earmarked for such a post in the Austrian Netherlands and the Rhineland but then was dropped following Thermidor. His replacements proved thorough enough: from Aachen alone the cultural "extraction" mission bagged more than 50,000 volumes of books and numerous other objects before it was wound down in spring 1795.[37] And even this achievement paled compared to the quantity and quality of artistic material looted by Bonaparte from Italy during his campaign of 1796–97.[38]

IDEALISM OR PRAGMATISM? FRENCH MILITARY ADMINISTRATION IN OCCUPIED EUROPE

The need for more efficient resource extraction prompted an administrative reordering in the occupied territories. In November 1794, the French set up new administrative structures in the Austrian Netherlands and the Rhineland north of the Moselle. For the Austrian Netherlands, this included a central administration in Brussels and eight subordinate districts. Overall, about one-third of officials staffing both the central and district administrations were native Frenchmen, and two-thirds were Belgians. In the Rhineland, the French established a central administration in Aachen together with seven districts. As in Belgium, this new structure at the central and district levels supervised the Old-Regime local authorities that remained intact. In practice, the new arrangements failed. The central and district administrations continued without much authority and were bypassed by other French agencies. Relations between the civilian administrations and the French army were generally abysmal and on occasion descended into physical violence. This was of course a time—post-Thermidor—when the army was beginning to show alarming signs of feeling superior to all civilians, irrespective of whether they were

Belgian, Rhenish, or French. The earlier revolutionary ideal of the ordinary soldier as essentially a citizen-in-arms was being superseded by a new image of the professional warrior who had his own superior virtues that would one day regenerate society as a whole.[39]

Local administration in the occupied territories remained in indigenous hands. However, here, too, French resource extraction made an impact. This included the marginalization, in most areas, of radicals. This occurred for several reasons. Events in Frankfurt, Mainz, and Aachen at the turn of 1792–93 seemed to prove Robespierre's point about soldiers being poor missionaries. If foreign civilians could not be won over, why bother making the effort? Voices like that of the *montagnard* deputy in the National Convention Jean Lambert Tallien began to be raised. "Belgium [the Austrian Netherlands]," he wrote, "like all our conquests, must be treated like a conquered land. Why seek out allies in a land where we have never found a friend."[40] Second, it soon became apparent that local "Jacobins" constituted an unrepresentative and indeed hated minority. In Mainz, they were never more than about 6 percent of the population, and that percentage assumes that all who joined the local Club in 1792–93 did so out of political conviction.[41] Membership figures for the Club alone reveal little as to why Rhinelanders joined. A better source is the electoral investigation into collaboration that followed Mainz's recapture in early 1793. This reveals that, for many, Club membership stemmed less from ideological than from pragmatic considerations.[42] The public fury, which was as much directed at local radicals as toward the French upon their withdrawal from the city in 1793, confirmed the isolation of this group.

The new chauvinistic mood in Paris spelt disaster for foreign "patriots" and "Jacobins." They had burnt their bridges with the Old Regime in supporting the French invasion. There was no going back, despite the degeneration of French rule into brutal exploitation. Some bravely attempted to intercede on behalf of the civilian population. However, while in 1792–93 they might have expected a polite hearing, now they were met with contempt. The trouble was that neither they nor the rest of the civilian population had done anything to earn French gratitude. They had done nothing to assist in their own "liberation." Even the Dutch "Patriots," the best-organized group of radicals in the territories occupied by the Republic, had failed to make any contribution to the French invasion. Instead, their own rising in October 1794 had gone off half-cocked, something that earned them the kind of contempt expressed by General Joseph-Alexandre Sauviac to the Committee of Public Safety:

Holland has done nothing to avoid being classed among the general order of our conquests. It was the ice, the indefatigable courage of our troops and the talents of the generals which delivered her and not any revolution. It follows from this that there can be no reason to treat her any differently from a conquered country. With a very few exceptions the patriots of this country are all timid adventurers led by ambitious intriguers, avid speculators who never dared take up arms in our favour.[43]

When the Dutch "Patriots" persisted in their delusion that they might somehow negotiate terms with the French as if they represented a sovereign and allied people, they simply encountered crushing comments like that of Emmanuel Joseph Sieyès: "It is not for you to cede; it is for us to take."[44]

Like all revolutionary regimes, the French now confronted a basic choice between ideological purity and technical ability. Like all regimes, they eventually opted for technical ability. Upon reoccupying the Rhineland in 1794, the French ruled that locals make up three-quarters of local government. The Republic needed talent. Hence, it "requisitioned" it like everything else. Such talent was especially vital in the judiciary, where established local lawyers alone could make sense of the numerous local customs and laws.[45] As the Revolutionary Wars progressed, the immediate requirements of resource extraction eclipsed totally any idea of reordering society or local government according to some ideological template. Instead, generals like Lazare Hoche and Napoleon Bonaparte behaved pragmatically. When Hoche took over in the Rhineland, in 1797, for example, he abolished the various central and intermediate structures set up under the occupation and instead reintroduced those of the Old Regime. His only concern was the extraction of supplies and money. Hoche died before his scheme was realized, and the Rhineland soon followed along the path already trod by the Austrian Netherlands: administrative integration with France. However, even then the French relied upon predominantly old-regime native talent: a survey conducted in the four new Rhenish departments in 1800 indicated that more than 60 percent of the 900 officials employed there were natives of the region. Most came from the university-educated elite, and a majority had previously served in the administration or judiciary. Continuity with the Old Regime was especially pronounced in the latter.[46]

Accounts of the 1790s are often couched in terms of a titanic clash between revolution and counterrevolution. No room is left for those who may have preferred to occupy a space between these extremes. Historians are not entirely to blame for this, as contemporaries themselves freely bandied about labels such as "Jacobin" and "aristocrat" in order to smear opponents. A closer look at the French-occupied territories reveals a host of essentially nonideological reasons for either supporting or opposing the French.

Minorities that had previously suffered discrimination tended, on balance, to support the French. Catholics in the United Provinces, Protestants in parts of the Rhineland, and Jews almost everywhere potentially stood to gain from the new order and initially at least tended to be more positive towards the French.[47] For example, Jews in the Rhineland were twice as likely to sign the petitions in 1798 in favor of "reunion" with the Republic as their Christian neighbors, even though the French continued to exploit "feudal" impositions, including discriminatory taxes.[48] This in turn caused resentment among the dominant confessional communities. The French occupation's disruption of the delicate religious balance established by the Westphalian settlement of 1648 threatened to reignite sectarian feuds in large parts of Europe. Catholic communities forced to take out loans to meet French demands found themselves dependent upon Protestant and Jewish creditors and became resentful. Jealousies arose where religious minorities found their public status radically improved under the occupation. Such was the case in Aachen, where the Protestants' rise to prominence created resentment among Catholics, and in Worms, where Lutherans complained as previously excluded Calvinists and Catholics entered high office.[49] Religious minorities needed to be careful, lest they become too much associated with an occupation that was not guaranteed to last. Nor were the French rank-and-file necessarily sympathetic to religious minorities, especially Jews. In the Army of the Rhine, for example, anti-Semitism was quite common. Some commanders too, including Hoche, were personally ill disposed toward Jews.[50] The French failed to pass any general measure sweeping away anti-Jewish discrimination in the occupied territories, though they closed the ghettos and allowed Jews to settle in places from which they had previously been excluded. Of course, less could be done to extirpate popular anti-Semitism, which remained a fact of life in much of Europe. Indeed, the general breakdown of order and banditry that accompanied the Revolutionary Wars threatened vulnerable groups like the Jews more than most.

The majority of civilians living in territories occupied by the French army during the Revolutionary Wars were neither Protestant nor Jewish but Roman Catholic. It was for the French an unfortunate accident of fate that the regions neighboring them included some of the most religiously devout parts of Catholic Europe: Spain, the Rhineland, the Austrian Netherlands, and Italy. Neither here nor in France itself was the French Revolution initially viewed as fundamentally anticlerical. This changed with Pope Pius VI's condemnation of the Civil Constitution of the Clergy in 1791 and the increasing vociferousness of revolutionary anticlericalism under the Jacobin Republic. By 1794, devout Catholics in occupied Europe clearly confronted a choice between their faith and the new ideology. Inevitably, the vast majority opted for the former. By then the first wave of intense anticlericalism—at least, at the official level—had given way to a more tolerant approach. However, a second wave in 1798–99 hit the Austrian Netherlands with full force, resulting in the arrest and deportation of 8,000 priests.[51] The Catholic Church in the neighboring Rhineland escaped anything like this but nonetheless experienced persecution in the form of anticlerical measures such as a ban on monasteries taking novices, the abolition of the tithe and the sequestration of church property, suppression of public religious processions and their replacement with the revolutionary fest-cycle, and the abolition of religious education in the newly established central schools. The French army of the 1790s remained consistently anticlerical, even when its nominal masters in Paris were adopting a softly-softly approach. On the ground, the Catholic Church presented too tempting a target to ignore, and reports abound of the desecration of churches, the requisitioning of ecclesiastical buildings and their conversion to profane use, the harassment or suppression of religious services and processions, and, not least, the prominence of radical ex-priests among native collaborators. All this offended Catholic sensibilities and turned most clergymen into proponents of counterrevolution.[52]

The French army's anti-clericalism antagonized, above all, the urban and rural masses. The Catholic elite had a more ambiguous relationship with religion and Church. While recent historiography has played down anticlericalism as a defining feature of the Enlightenment, elite Catholic opinion in the second half of the eighteenth century was undoubtedly turning against the baroque flamboyance of the Counter-Reformation in favor of a simpler, more austere form of worship. Hence, French attacks against popular shrines and pilgrimages, though not necessarily welcome, were nonetheless not as shocking to members of the elite as to the rest of the population.

Ironically, given slogans about "war to the châteaux, peace to the cottages," it was also the elite rather than the masses that stood to gain from other aspects of the French occupation. This was especially so for the rising class of lawyers, merchants, and entrepreneurs, whose newly acquired professional and economic status had, in many places, not yet translated into political influence due to ossified structures that enshrined the continuing dominance of patricians and guilds. Within France itself, the revolutionary government abolished the latter with the so-called Le Chapelier Law of June 14, 1791. This was quickly introduced into the occupied territories— for example, Mainz on February 25, 1793—and earned for the French the unerring hostility of yet another sizable constituency. In much of Europe, old craft guilds were already losing ground as wealthier elements such as the growing class of merchant-manufacturers bypassed their restrictions and excluded them from urban government. The guilds were also threatened by the new elitist culture of enlightened sociability that bridged confessional and territorial barriers while it widened social ones.[53]

Despite some of the positive aspects of French occupation, potential collaborators among the native elite needed to tread warily. It was not only that they exposed themselves to popular vengeance, like that inflicted upon the Mainz "Jacobins" when the French abandoned the city in 1793, but also that they were vulnerable to retribution from their sovereigns to whom they legally remained bound until the treaties of Campo Formio (for the Austrian Netherlands) and Lunéville (for the Rhineland). These sovereigns generally distinguished between two forms of collaboration:

ideological commitment to the invading French, which was unacceptable, and the disinterested continued discharge of public administrative responsibilities to prevent anarchy, which was encouraged. Ideological commitment amounted to treason, against which the Habsburg emperor Francis II issued several warnings.[54] Such threats carried weight following the reversal of French military fortunes in late 1792 and at various times in 1795, 1796 and 1799, when it appeared they might be expelled from their conquests. When it came to the second form of collaboration—one that did not imply ideological attachment—the princes were initially more pragmatic. The Elector of Cologne, whose territory was occupied in the autumn of 1794, stated: "It is far better [that the administration] should be in the hands of old established families than *sans-culottes*," while his colleagues in Trier and Mainz allowed officials to stay behind and promised not to punish individuals compelled to take a French oath so long as they remained loyal "in their hearts." The Palatine government even threatened to discipline officials who abandoned their posts.[55]

The French may have been unfortunate in occupying areas distinguished by religious devotion. They were fortunate, however, in that those same areas for the most part—the Austrian Netherlands, the left bank of the Rhine, parts of the Catalan and Basque lands—fell into one of two territorial classifications: they were either peripheral territories ruled by a distant prince, as in the case of the Austrian Netherlands, northern Rhenish Prussian territories, and Catalan and Basque territories, governed respectively from Vienna, Berlin, and Madrid, or they were church states run by prince-bishops or prince-archbishops, as was the case in the greater part of the Rhineland. This had important implications for the French occupation and for the relationship between the military and civilian populations. The inhabitants of both types of territory lacked the kind of focus that could have provoked greater resistance to the French: by definition, the church states could not be dynastic, so the kind of bonds that developed, for example, between the Austrian Habsburgs, the Prussian Hohenzollerns, and the Spanish Bourbons and their subjects in their core possessions over many generations could not develop. Dynastic loyalties were similarly absent in the peripheral territories, with which the Habsburgs, Hohenzollerns, Bourbons, and other princely families enjoyed relations analogous to those entertained between nineteenth-century absentee British landlords and their Irish estates.

Instead, the inhabitants of both type of territory owed their earthly allegiance to either their region or their city. They put the interests of their city and region before that of Spain, Prussia, or Austria. These interests might dictate engagement with the French, not outright opposition. Such was the conclusion reached by Spain's Basques, as represented in the junta of Guetaria, who during the brief French occupation of 1794 negotiated directly with the invaders in order to gain the concessions important to them, namely respect for religion and local privileges and freedom from military obligations.

The interests of Spain as a whole did not figure.[56] Something analogous occurred in the Rhenish church states, whose rulers had only reinforced their status as outsiders by fleeing across the Rhine in the face of the French invasion, abandoning their subjects to their fate. From safety, they issued warnings against local attempts to negotiate neutrality agreements with the French occupation authorities or to enter into other special arrangements that would undermine their own sovereignty.[57] Yet, such negotiations went ahead. In Trier, the estates feared French retribution for the Elector's earlier hospitality to the *émigrés* and sought to make amends by openly calling for neutrality following the outbreak of the First Revolutionary War. Despite the Elector's rejection of this, representatives of the estates nonetheless opened negotiations with the French that were, arguably, treasonable. This raised fundamental constitutional questions over who ultimately enjoyed sovereignty, the prince or the estates. The same happened elsewhere in Germany, where the estates increasingly saw themselves as popular representatives and, in a few instances—as, for example, when Bavaria's estates entered into independent peace negotiations with the French general Jean Victor Moreau in 1796—acted on that basis.[58]

Revolutionary ideology, which treated all institutions of the Old Regime with contempt, prevented the French from fully exploiting the tensions between princes with absolutist pretensions and estates that was a feature of much of Europe. It was only from about 1796, when a new generation of political generals such as Hoche and Bonaparte finally threw off the shackles of civilian tutelage, that a pragmatic policy of working through existing institutions and elites and dividing these from their ruling dynasties was seriously attempted in the occupied territories. Hoche pursued such a policy when he took charge in the Rhineland in 1797. He blamed "misguided extremism" and "false political and administrative principles" for all ills in the occupied territories and recommended the return not only of the personnel but also the institutions of the Old Regime as alone possessing legitimacy and popular confidence. "Experience should have corrected our mania of wanting to municipalise Europe," he concluded, noting that it was pointless trying to reconcile natives to the Revolution.[59] Paris accepted Hoche's recommendations and, on March 12, 1797, reintroduced the old structures. Hoche's policy eventually collapsed with his death, on September 19, 1797, and the simultaneous decision by the new regime brought in by the Fructidorian coup (September 4) to proceed with the region's full administrative integration into France as a prelude to de jure annexation. However, before it did collapse, Hoche's new pragmatism threatened to drive a wedge between the local estates and the princes and also between those groups—the nobility and the clergy—that enjoyed fiscal privileges and those that did not. The shedding of ideological inhibitions allowed for a classic policy of divide-and-rule.[60]

Generals like Hoche and Bonaparte recognized the importance of attracting local men of standing to serve as interlocutors between the

French army and the civilian population. Such men emerged throughout the occupied territories. They organized petitions and managed the distribution of the burdens of occupation, often acting without reference to the exiled princes. The chronicler of the small Rhenish town of Dormagen recorded how the local mayor, on his own authority, managed demands from the French army, organized patrols to counter plundering by isolated bands of soldiers, ensured the town's provision of firewood in winter, dealt with outbreaks of disease caused by troop movements, bribed key French officers to lighten requisitioning, and traveled to the French army headquarters at his own expense to negotiate reductions in Dormagen's quota of men to be requisitioned for work on fortifications, fix the price of supplies, and reroute two army columns. Such activity preserved Dormagen from the worst effects of the Revolutionary Wars, and, as the chronicler shrewdly observed, it was useful for the French themselves to have influential natives as intermediaries.[61] In many areas, local businessmen achieved greater prominence, as they possessed the resources and connections to meet the army's demands while alleviating the burden on the general population. This was the case with the von der Leyens, who dominated another Rhenish town, Krefeld: it was they who ensured the supply of bread, not only to their own workers but also initially to the whole community, and who imported coal from the right bank to guarantee fuel supplies over winter. Their efforts were facilitated by easy access to senior French officers billeted on their luxurious mansions, which served as headquarters of the Sambre-Meuse army.[62] In this way, the Revolutionary Wars directly helped catapult into prominence a new figure—the businessman—who, despite his wealth, had, in many parts of French-occupied Europe, previously occupied a relatively marginal social and political position.[63]

COMBATANTS AND CIVILIANS IN THE VENDÉE

This chapter so far has focused on the impact of the Revolutionary Wars in those *foreign* areas operated in and occupied by the French army. However, a component of these continent-wide conflicts were civil wars that flared along the Atlantic fringe of Europe: in the Vendée in 1793–94 and in Ireland in 1798. No account of civilians and warfare would be complete without analysis of this dimension.

Of all the conflicts of the 1790s, whether civil or international, none was so distinguished by its brutality than that which erupted in the Vendée in 1793. Historians extremely critical of the French army's actions in the Low Countries, the Rhineland, and Italy nonetheless stop well short of accusing it of genocide in those regions. In the Vendée, in contrast, the charge of genocide is compelling. Genocide was not an invention of the French Revolution. It was, however, closely associated with the rise of the state, with its absolute claims to sovereignty, and even more so with the rise of states that legitimized themselves by latching on to the concept of the nation, with all that is implied in that term with respect to cultural uniformity and intolerance for difference.[64] The French Revolution added to this the idea that it was possible to renew everything, replacing provinces with departments and ancient units of measurement with the metric system and revolutionary calendar. Why should this "sweeping away" not be applied to whole populations, especially if this also served the practical military function of creating a landscape devoid of civilians and thus facilitating the destruction of the rebels?

Chronologically, the events in the Vendée[65] lend themselves to a four-fold division: phase one, from the outbreak of the French Revolution in 1789 to mid-March 1793; phase two, from March 1793 to December 24, 1793; phase three, from January 1794 to July 1794; and finally, the fourth phase, from July 1794 until the Napoleonic period. The first phase was marked by a general estrangement of the region from the new regime in Paris. Religion, and especially the trouble sparked by the Civil Constitution of the Clergy (July 12, 1790), served to create a gulf between most of the region's devout inhabitants and a center bent on the subordination of the Church to the nation. This essentially ideological conflict exacerbated existing sociological tensions in the Vendée caused by an emerging commercial elite that was challenging an old-established incumbent. At a practical level, government persecution of priests who refused to swear loyalty to the new order, and their protection by the rest of the community, familiarized ordinary Vendeans with the clandestine techniques necessary to oppose a powerful state. This learning process, to which pilgrimages—involving the coordination of the movement of large numbers of people over considerable distances—also contributed, was arguably a precondition for successful guerrilla warfare later on. To sociological conflict and the religious issue were added, increasingly from about 1792, the policy of terrorism employed by the government in response to growing rural discontent. The paramilitary National Guard, recruited locally from the mainly urban pro-revolutionary community, was responsible for what was in reality sectarian violence rather than impartial policing. It established for itself an evil reputation among large segments of the population, and even with the authorities. A sense of its style can be discerned from an account of its behavior following its defeat of a minor peasant uprising in August 1792: the National Guards engaged in a general massacre and returned home with noses, ears, and shreds of human flesh stuck to their bayonets as trophies. Even government commissioners were shocked at the site strewn with bodies, including those of women and children.[66]

Seething discontent and violence between "blues" (republicans) and "whites" (royalist Catholics) exploded into a full-scale regional insurrection against the central government with the *levée* of 300,000 new recruits nationwide ordered by the Convention on February 24, 1793, in response to the deteriorating military situation during the War of the First Coalition. The majority of Vendeans had no interest in being conscripted to fight for a hated regime, especially when pro-republican elements within the region tended to fall within those categories that enjoyed exemption from the levy. This started to be implemented on the ground in the following month and sparked spontaneous uprisings throughout the region. The most dramatic events occurred in Machecoul on March 11, when 3,000 to 4,000 men took over the town to cries of "No lottery, and give us our priests!" The rebels then proceeded to massacre local patriots: local officials, the constitutional priest, and National Guard officers—500 or so in all. The rout of a 2,000-strong government column by rebels just over a week later, at Pont Charrault, indicated that Paris faced full-scale civil war in the west.

Both sides in the conflict contributed to the spiral of violence and retribution that marked the conflict that would rage for the rest of 1793. Reports and rumors of rebel atrocities, including the implication of Vendean women as well as men in these, reached the policymakers in Paris and helped shape future government actions.[67] Yet, by all accounts, the insurgents were not especially bloodthirsty—at least, not compared to their opponents—and also distinguished themselves with acts of humanitarianism, such as the release of republican prisoners. The National Convention, in contrast, responded to news of the rising and to republican defeats with predictably draconian laws. However, initially these were aimed at the usual suspects: priests, *ci-devant* nobles and seigneurs, and foreigners, rather than the population as a whole. When, in May 1793, Armand Louis Duc de Biron took up the command of Army of the West and asked the Minister of War how prisoners should be treated, he was told that only the leaders and instigators should be put to death.[68] Jean-Paul Marat urged that only the clergy and aristocrats who were behind the rising should suffer retribution, not the ordinary people who had been led astray.

Following further setbacks in the Vendée, the tone in Paris started to change. Increasingly, the entire region was portrayed as being infested with "brigands," and place of residence alone, rather than ideological affiliation or class, rendered people suspect.[69] On August 1, Barère de Vieuzac, deputy of Haute-Pyrénées, in the name of the Committee of Public Safety, declared to the Convention that the only way the government could bring the war to an end was through a scorched-earth policy. Indeed, he described the Vendée as the "Palatinate of the Republic," thereby implying that it deserved the same treatment as had been inflicted on the Palatinate by Louis XIV. Only such methods would "exterminate this race of rebels." He suggested that a corps of pioneers should "burn down woods, flatten the land and drive the brigands from their lairs in copses, woods and ravines."[70] The Convention took little persuading and passed a decree approving the destruction of the Vendée:

while old men and women would be deported to the interior, pioneer companies, equipped with combustible materials, would systematically destroy everything necessary to sustain human life.

It was difficult to see how pioneers might methodically engage in environmental destruction in the context of Vendean successes in beating off "blue" forces. However, the republican victory at Cholet on October 17 broke the back of the rising. This now degenerated into a two-month long retreat by the remnants of the rebel column, which headed north, reaching the coast at Grandville before heading south again to final defeat at Savenay on December 23 by a government army under Brigadier General François Joseph Westermann. Savenay was less a battle between evenly matched armed forces than a large-scale massacre of a refugee column, composed of women and children as well as men, by regular soldiers. Westermann's subsequent report to the Committee of Public Safety has become notorious:

There is no more Vendée, citizens, it has perished under our free sword along with its women and children. I have just buried it in the marshes and mud of Savenay. Following the orders that you gave me I have crushed children under the feet of horses, massacred women who at least . . . will engender no more brigands. I have no prisoners with which to reproach myself.[71]

Horrible though all this was, it might be observed that states on numerous other occasions have responded to the acts of domestic rebels with a harshness that would be unthinkable when dealing with foreigners, whether combatants or not, in the context of international war. However, what sets the Vendée apart is less the second stage of the conflict, which ended at Savenay, than the third stage. Significantly, this started only in January 1794, after a time lag of several weeks after the final suppression of the rebellion and months after the Vendeans had ceased to constitute a serious threat to the Republic; hence the impression of cold-blooded calculation that was absent before. Two additional characteristics associated with this third stage of the conflict justify labeling it as genocidal: the lack of even a pretense that the retribution was restricted only to those guilty of participation in the rising, as opposed to the entire population, and the sheer ambition of the authorities to kill as many as possible of both sexes and all age groups.

An almost unhealthy interest in some of the more novel forms of mass murder proposed (for example, mass asphyxiation) and in some cases implemented (including mass drowning) by the Republican forces has overshadowed the fact that most of the victims were killed by more tried-and-tested methods: bayoneted, bludgeoned, shot, herded into buildings where they were burnt alive, or else confined and condemned to die of starvation, exposure, and disease. The machinery for all this was provided by the regular army. It deployed 100,000 troops for the exercise and divided these into a dozen flying columns, dubbed *colonnes infernalles*, that crisscrossed the countryside killing all they encountered, regardless of age or gender. That these forces ultimately proved unequal to the task put forward by their commander, General Louis Marie Turreau, on January 17, 1794—the elimination of the entire population within six days—was the result not of a lack of intent or determination but of the sheer logistical magnitude of the task. The genocidal campaign continued well beyond the six days initially envisaged and ended only with the overthrow of the Jacobin regime in July 1794. By then, a minimum of 130,000 had been killed, out of a total population of just over 800,000.[72]

Peace did not yet return to the Vendée, even after Thermidor. The rebel armies had been smashed, but banditry and violence plagued the region for the rest of the decade. Only a substantial investment of military manpower, combined with the cunning of General Hoche, appointed to the west in autumn 1794, kept such aggression within bounds. Hoche, despite the progress he made on the narrow militarily front, nonetheless also urged a policy of conciliation on the government. He had no faith in the ability of the local republican elite to govern in the Vendée, as its members were consumed by the spirit of vengeance. Instead, he advised his superiors:

give, as far as possible, patriots the least amount of authority. Inspire confidence in the Vendeans by measures that are even a little counter-revolutionary; flatter their religious ideas, make concessions to their fanatical monarchism. . . . One day the Republic will harvest the good fruit of what will be sown; the Vendée, do not deceive yourselves, is a good land. There is honor and courage within its children. The Revolution was in error in denying this.[73]

It would take another general, Napoleon Bonaparte, to complete the pacification of the Vendée beyond the military level. His solution involved the construction of strategic roads in the region, the foundation of a new provincial capital (La Roche-sur-Yon, with 15,000 inhabitants), improvements in the relations between civilians and military, the negotiation of the Concordat, the appeasement of all but the most intransigent clergy, vigilance over the civil administration, the placement of all fanatics, whether on the left or the right under police surveillance, and the issuance of an amnesty for former rebels.[74]

THE TREATMENT OF CIVILIANS BY THE SOLDIERS OF OLD-REGIME EUROPE

Analysis of the civilian experience under the armies of the other Great Powers in the 1790s dispels the notion that the prospect faced by Belgians, Rhinelanders, and Italians (though not Vendeans) under the French Republican army was uniquely unpleasant. The Russian occupation of

Poland during the War of 1792 throws up some interesting parallels with experiences in the Austrian Netherlands and the Rhineland that same year. Russian soldiers, like the French, presented themselves as liberators with instructions to treat the Poles in a friendly manner and to act only against the "enemies of the Commonwealth" (supporters of reform). Like the French, the Russians—Catherine the Great included—soon admitted that the Poles were not flocking to join them. They now recognized that the minority of Poles who had encouraged their intervention were an unrepresentative, isolated, and hated minority. Acts of violence by Polish civilians against the Russian army multiplied. Bodies of Russian soldiers appeared in alleyways and out-of-the-way spots, and even officers were abused and assaulted on the streets. The Russian forces responded with forced billeting, arbitrary arrests and interrogations, and press censorship. Catherine fumed, "now I see that I shall have to do everything myself with the bayonet."[75]

The Russian army easily won the War of 1792 and imposed a puppet regime on the country. Seething Polish resentment against the Russian occupiers and their collaborators flared, in spring 1794, into a revolution, known as the "Kosciuszko uprising" after the most prominent personality on the Polish side of the conflict. Given the balance of forces in Poland in 1794, and the balance of power in Europe as a whole, there was never any doubt as to the ultimate fate of the Polish revolution. Russian armies closed in on Warsaw. The climax came on November 4, 1794, when Russian forces commanded by Alexander Suvorov attacked the suburb of Praga and, after three hours of fighting, breached the defenses. There followed a massacre that left thousands dead after a few hours. The Russian general Grigorii Engelhardt wrote: "Right up to the banks of the Vistula one found only dead and dying people of all estates; and the banks themselves were heaped with the bodies of soldiers, civilians, Jews, priests, monks, women and children. My heart froze at the sight of all this, and the loathsome picture revolted my soul."[76] Suvorov warned that the same fate would befall Warsaw if it failed to capitulate. The strategy succeeded, as the population inside the city pressured the leadership into surrendering. Suvorov then entered Warsaw unopposed on November 9 and occupied the whole city without any more slaughter. Far from being reprimanded for his actions in Praga, which shocked even contemporaries, Suvorov was instead promoted by Catherine to the rank of field marshal as a reward for his actions.[77] Conflicts involving the Russians and Ottoman Turks in southeastern Europe tended to be even more brutal. Four years before the massacre in Praga, another Russian army under Suvorov butchered up to 40,000 Turks after storming Ismail in December 1790. Warfare on Europe's eastern fringes had traditionally exhibited greater savagery than conflicts fought in western theaters.[78]

Not that the actions of the Duke of York's British army on campaign in the United Provinces in 1794 represented a proud chapter insofar as the experience of civilians at the hands of the military was concerned. By all accounts, the conduct of British troops in the towns on which they were billeted was appalling and became even worse during their retreat in the face of the advancing French. The evacuation of Nijmegen in particular was accompanied by pillage, violence, and rapine on such a scale that the Dutch were goaded into defending themselves against their supposed allies. An employee of the States-General complained to his superior:

It would be impossible to convey to you any idea of the universal indignation which the circumstances of this disastrous evacuation have excited . . . a person of distinction, until now known as a partisan of England, told me in so many words that only a traitor to the Fatherland could possibly at this moment find anything to say in favor of the English.[79]

As morale collapsed following defeat and the cutting off of supplies and pay, the retreating British took with them almost anything that could be moved. Arguably, one reason the Dutch were not ready to rise against the French, either then or in the War of the Second Coalition, was the actions of British troops. Most Dutch were happy to see the backs of them, and of their Prussian allies.[80]

Britons prided themselves on their freedom from military-style government, and a lingering suspicion of standing armies endured into the 1790s. Many in England believed that martial law had been made illegal with the Petition of Right under Charles I. The British practice in Ireland, however, was less restrained.[81] Here, from late May to the end of June 1798, the British army confronted a spontaneous popular rising that in certain respects bears comparison with what happened in the Vendée. As in the Vendée, Ireland in the 1790s was confronted by an ever-deepening agrarian crisis that reinforced sectarian hatreds.[82] A growing level of violence *preceded* the main outbreak. Under pressure from the Protestant gentry to act against growing Catholic unrest and evidence of an imminent general revolt, the British viceroy, John Earl of Camden, gave in to the hawks and ordered extreme measures to force the disarmament of the potential rebels. Generals like Gerard Lake—"a run-of-the-mill general, of little intellect or military skill, who believed in the reckless exercise of military power" and who became commander-in-chief in Ireland on April 25, 1798—found themselves off the leash. They responded with policies that one visiting British peer described as comparable only to those of the French in the Vendée. The British forces set up special portable triangular flogging frames as they scoured the countryside. Suspects would be tied to the frames and then whipped until they confessed the location of stashed pikes. Other favored measures included "half-hanging," in which the victim would be repeatedly suspended from a mobile gallows, and pitch-capping, where a mixture of pitch and gunpowder was rubbed onto the victim's scalp and then set alight. As in the Vendée, some of the worst atrocities were committed not by regulars but by local militia forces motivated by sectarianism.[83]

CAP^TN. SWAYNE
Pitch Capping the People of Prosperous

"Captn. Swayne pitch capping the people of prosperous." From *The Irish Magazine or Monthly Asylum for
Neglected Biography* (1810). © Copyright the Trustees of
the British Museum.

Again, as in the Vendée so in Ireland, the mass rising occurred only after
considerable provocation and out of desperation. Something akin to the
"Great Fear" that had swept France at the beginning of the French Revolution engulfed Ireland in the first months of 1798. Protestants feared they
would be massacred by Catholics, and Catholics by Protestants. Nor were
these fears restricted to the poor and uneducated.[84] The atmosphere of the
time is well captured by a contemporary, Thomas Cloney of Honeymore:
"No one slept in their homes, the very whistling of the birds seemed to
report the approach of the enemy."[85]

Government forces reacted to the uprising proper, which started in the province of Leinster on May 23–24, 1798, with ferocity. Viceroy Camden declared martial law on May 24, and this gave the government forces wide legal cover to summarily execute not only rebels but a potentially much broader category of those "in any manner assisting the rebellion." In Dublin, rebel suspects were executed and their bodies hung from lamp-posts. The rebels also committed atrocities: the start of the rising in County Wexford was marked by the murder of Protestants, though women and children were, despite the events at Scullabogue on June 5, on the whole spared.[86] The evidence indicates that the majority of the atrocities were committed by government forces, not by the rebels. This in turn provoked reprisals and counterreprisals. However, unlike in the Vendée, this vicious cycle of terror developed not so much from the deliberate actions of a central authority—not that this can serve as exoneration—but because of a vacuum on both sides: on the one side an ineffectual viceroy and on the other the absence of any central revolutionary leadership because of its decapitation by the British in the months before the rising. Local forces bent on settling scores thus wreaked havoc unhindered. A few commanders, like the generals Ralph Dundas and John Moore (of later Peninsular War fame) recognized that the population was caught in a hopeless situation and wherever possible allowed rebels to surrender on generous terms. When Moore captured the rebel stronghold of Wexford on June 21, he sensibly ordered his militia units to remain encamped outside the town and allowed only regular British troops to patrol its streets.[87]

Most areas were less fortunate, and in all thousands died in the blaze of retribution in the aftermath of the uprising, which, in effect, ended with the defeat of United Irish forces at Ballynahinch and Vinegar Hill in June.[88] Some within the Protestant elite now thought in terms of genocide: Robert, Earl of Roden, described as a more "high-minded" member of the Ascendancy—the local Protestant elite—pondered the annihilation of one or two million inhabitants "who are a disgrace to humanity". The new viceroy, Charles Marquess Cornwallis, nonetheless did his best to stop indiscriminate murders and pushed an amnesty through the Dublin Parliament despite pressure from the Ascendancy for bloody retribution. Nevertheless, local paramilitary units remained a force unto themselves as they went about settling old scores. By the time the violence fizzled out, 20,000 had been killed in the rising and its aftermath, the large majority on the rebel side.[89]

No army in the 1790s accorded the same rights to civilians who engaged in armed conflict as were generally afforded to uniformed soldiers under the command of an officer. This was irrespective of whether those armed civilians were engaged in rebellion, as in the Vendée and in Ireland, or in resistance against an army of a foreign state that had invaded and occupied their country. Nothing distinguished the French from their enemies in this respect. All would have subscribed to the views expressed by the general commanding the Spanish army during its brief foray across the Pyrenees in 1793, in a communication transmitted to his French counterpart:

The rules of war not permitting peasants or bourgeois to have, use, or carry arms,—something neither you nor I would approve, since it would bring about the devastation and the ruin of the land—I declare, and I hope that your excellency's humanity will lead you to declare with me, that any peasant or bourgeois who is found to have arms upon his person or hidden on his premises, and above all, if he uses the same against my troops or any villages which I have occupied, whether he calls himself a "miquelet" or anything else, and if he is not serving in some company of which he is wearing the uniform, badges and equipment (or if, being an officer, he is wearing anything other than his officer's uniform and decorations) I shall immediately hang him, and shall be justified in doing so. On the other hand, my troops, far from engaging in murder and rapine, will respect the property, goods, liberty and personal safety of all peaceful peasants, no matter what their politics recently have been, provided they remain at home in their villages and houses, carrying on in their normal way.[90]

TOWARD TOTAL WAR IN THE 1790S

The Spanish general's statement contained a number of assumptions. One was that civilians had a duty to refrain from attacking his troops because these in turn were committed to leave them in peace, irrespective of their politics. Within the context of the 1790s, and with signs that war was becoming more total, this sounded like a cry from the past. Of course, the chances of civilians actually being killed by direct enemy military action remained slight when compared to the situation in the twentieth century. Only a tiny number of civilians were directly caught up in set-piece battles. Civilians who lived in fortified cities of strategic importance were most exposed, as they had always been. The rules and customs of war as practiced in the revolutionary period saw no modification regarding the treatment civilians might expect. Besieging forces retained the right to block the escape of civilians who wished to leave following the declaration of a state of siege in order to hasten the moment when the defenders' food supplies would run out. Death through enemy bombardment remained a real possibility. The Dutch town of Grave, besieged by the French in 1794, was hit by an estimated 3,000 shells within the space of 10 weeks—a rate of about one every half an hour—reducing it to rubble.[91] On other occasions, the threat of the deliberate destruction of civilian housing was used to hasten the enemy's surrender and to avoid a long, drawn-out siege. This was done not only by the French but also by the Austrians (notably at their siege of Lille) and the Prussians (at Mainz).[92] Cities taken by storm, such as Praga by the Russians or Pavia by the French in May 1796, could expect to be sacked.

At a strategic level, one might argue that most Europeans experienced a form of siege warfare in this period, in the shape of the naval blockade imposed on the Continent by the British and the countermeasures adopted by the French. Though refined during the Napoleonic wars, this form of strategic warfare was already a feature of the Revolutionary Wars.[93] On March 25, 1793, the British and Russian governments agreed to stop the export of foodstuffs to France from their own ports. The French foreign minister denounced the enemy policy to the American representative in Paris as something "disapproved by laws of humanity and by those of war. . . . You will see on the one hand, the firm determination of destroying several millions of victims, merely to satisfy a spirit of vengeance or of ambition."[94] The justification for blockade was an obvious one: the destruction of the enemy's war-making potential. However, the French and indeed some on the British side accused London of deliberately attempting to starve an entire nation into submission. This accusation was unjustified—the blockade was aimed chiefly at French naval power—but the possibility had now entered public discourse.[95]

Nonetheless, blockade resulted in the premature deaths of thousands of European civilians. Coastal regions dependent upon oceanic trade were especially vulnerable. Barcelona, for example, saw the doubling of the price of grain from 1792 to 1795 because of the disruption of war, and the number of deaths in the city rose from 3,702 in 1792 to 6,686 in 1795. Though it remained unoccupied by the enemy, it can hardly be said to have been untouched.[96] In northern Europe, the victims included the Dutch fishing fleets and communities, which suffered devastation by blockade in the 1790s. In the coastal fishing community of Vlaardingen, one contemporary witnessed "the most distressing symptoms of impoverishment and decay. The harbor was crowded with fishing vessels no longer employed and many of them unserviceable through neglect or the absolute inability of their owners to keep them in repair . . . the quay was covered in long grass and a melancholy assemblage of beggars importuned us for relief wherever we walked."[97]

The impact of warfare on civilians extended wider still. The economic effects were fiscal as well as commercial. Expenditure on war forced the reform of tax structures in Europe's states. Such was the case in the United Provinces, for example, which saw the creation of its first national tax system, including the introduction of an income tax, in order to finance a large French army of occupation.[98] Pitt the Younger's government introduced the first income tax in Britain, in the budget presented in December 1798, again in direct response to the Revolutionary Wars. The Jacobin Republic embarked upon a degree of resource mobilization within its own frontiers that prefigured the total wars of the twentieth century. The National Convention's decree of August 23, 1793, is often reproduced to signify the Republic's intent on this front:

From this moment on, until the enemies have been chased from the territory of the Republic, all Frenchmen are in permanent requisition for the service of the armies. The young men will go to combat; married men will forge weapons and transport food; women will make tents and uniforms and will serve in the hospitals;

children will make bandages from old linen; old men will present themselves at public places to excite the courage of the warriors, to preach hatred of kings and the unity of the Republic.[99]

Rhetorical generalities were turned into precise measures in subsequent legislation that redirected the output of whole economic sectors toward the armed forces. The decree of October 25, 1793, for example, ordered every shoemaker in the Republic to produce five pairs of shoes every 10 days for the army for a period of three months.

The armies fighting the Revolutionary Wars consumed men as well as money. It was in this aspect of resource extraction that the French proved truly innovative in the 1790s, with the introduction of military conscription. This was a process, rather than an event. It started in May 1792, when the Legislative Assembly in practice resorted to the use of a ballot in those departments that had failed to meet their quota of "volunteers" for the national levy of 74,000. The same method was employed for the levy of 300,000 in the following spring, by which time it was clear that the voluntary system was inadequate. The end of the process came with the *Loi Jourdan-Debrel* of September 5, 1798, which essentially rationalized the rules and practices already in force. Unparalleled French mobilization forced the Coalition powers to consider adopting similar measures. The Habsburg emperor, Francis II, proposed a *levée en masse* within the Holy Roman Empire, though this faltered in the face of decisive Prussian-led opposition. Part of this opposition was based on conservative fears of the revolutionary implications of arming the people. Certainly, this weighed even on those Rhenish princes who were arguably the most exposed to French aggression. Nor were these fears completely unfounded: in the Palatinate, peasants responded to the call to arms with demands for the abolition of noble and clerical privilege, demands echoed also in Electoral Cologne. The princes suspended mobilization rather than make concessions.[100] Because of this failure on the part of their opponents, the French maintained their numerical advantage throughout the Revolutionary Wars, despite fighting against coalitions whose total demographic weight exceeded their own.

Heightened resource mobilization changed the relationship between the individual and the state. It brought the relationship closer, both in France and within its enemies. Conscription and new forms of taxation required larger bureaucracies that relied upon statistical information in the form of censuses and cadastres to raise money and men; it is no accident that the first modern censuses in both Britain and France occurred in 1801. This expansion of the state generally came at the expense of intermediate corporate bodies such as provincial estates, trade guilds, and the churches. Indeed the latter, and especially the Catholic Church, emerged as one of the great losers of the Revolutionary Wars. It was to its wealth that governments turned to cover much of the cost of the fighting in the 1790s.

Monasticism, which had flourished in large parts of Europe for centuries, virtually disappeared as a result. This, in turn, had effects in a wide variety of areas beyond the spiritual, including the provision of poor relief, upon which many thousands depended and which the state in this period was ill equipped to supply, either materially or philosophically.[101]

HOW REVOLUTIONARY WERE THE REVOLUTIONARY WARS?

What was revolutionary about the impact on civilians of the wars of the 1790s? In many respects, not that much. Though the wars were fought on a large scale, the number of combatants on each side was not of a different order of magnitude than had characterized previous wars, such as the War of the Spanish Succession at the beginning of the century. Certainly, the French army briefly attained a size—750,000 men—well in excess of anything achieved by Louis XIV, whose own land forces peaked at about 400,000. Nevertheless, Louis XIV's armies were recruited from a smaller population, and the revolutionary army quickly shrank from its maximum strength, reached in the autumn of 1794. The armies of the coalition powers were not significantly above—if at all—their greatest strengths attained in the pre-1792 period.

If the wars were not fundamentally different in quantitative terms, were the protagonists in the Revolutionary Wars any different in qualitative terms from their predecessors? In particular, to what extent was the army of the French Republic a fundamentally different force? Here again, the most recent research tends to play down the differences. Far from being a disorganized horde, it seems that the revolutionary army quickly reached a level of technical proficiency that allowed it to adequately perform difficult maneuvers, such as forming defensive squares under fire. Nor can it be assumed, as we have seen, that military justice simply evaporated. Certainly, the French logistical organization left much to be desired, but the notion that Old-Regime armies had supplied all their needs through depots and trains as opposed to local requisitioning is also erroneous. The most that might be conceded is that requisitioning occurred on a larger scale in the 1790s than previously. It was only in the systematic extension of requisitioning to include items that were not of immediate use to the army, such as artistic objects for the Louvre or industrial objects, that the French were innovators in the 1790s.

What about the French army's treatment of foreign civilians? Here again, there was no sea change from previous practice. Burke's dire predictions of an apocalyptic war, resembling perhaps the Eastern Front during World War II, failed to materialize. Certainly, things did not improve much, either: cities taken by storm were still sacked, civilians who took it upon themselves to offer physical resistance were killed and punishment against entire communities on occasion meted out, and isolated bands of soldiers still engaged in a variety of crimes, including rape, serious physical assault, pillage, and murder. None of this was new.

However, in at least two areas, there was novelty: in the unprecedented importance of ideology in the conflict, which was reflected in the initial attempts by the French army at revolutionary proselytizing in collaboration with native radicals and in the assault against established religion, and in the reporting of war by the press. With respect to the first element, it might be commented that what really antagonized so many Europeans was not merely the material depravation caused by the revolutionary French army but also that the destruction was accompanied by self-righteous preaching about liberty, fraternity, and equality. Ideology got in the way of understanding between occupier and occupied, at least until a new generation of generals emerged of which Bonaparte was the most prominent representative. As for the second, one could of course claim that previous wars had been reported in the press and that the expansion of the public sphere and the creation of public opinion predated the 1790s. However, the wars of the 1790s were reported to a greater extent than any previous conflict. More than that, the conduct of war, including the treatment of civilians, was analyzed and subject to debate and scrutiny. Belligerents needed to justify their conduct as never before. As one Rhinelander put it, the wars of the 1790s were, to an extent, an "*Opinionenkrieg*": a war in which public opinion was an important component.[102]

In what other ways were the wars of 1790 new with respect to the experience of civilians? In general terms, they saw a further extension of the power of the state, and not only in France. Income tax and conscription serve as indicators of this. States not only became better at the technicalities of resource extraction. They—and this point concerns Britain as much as France—also became better at retaining the support of their populations for the vast effort through their appeals to national, patriotic, and loyalist sentiment. However, even when it comes to this area, one can only conclude that the wars of the 1790s marked the continuation of an ongoing process, rather than a departure.

All of this suggests that the Revolutionary Wars were less significant than once thought. In one particular respect, they were of great importance. For the commanders of the French armies that fanned out across parts of western, central, and southern Europe, they provided an education not only in leading soldiers in battle but in how to administer civilian populations in a time of crisis. Two generals in particular have figured prominently in this chapter, though they were merely the two most prominent of their class: Lazare Hoche and Napoleon Bonaparte. Neither shrank from the use of extreme force when necessary. Both, nonetheless, also recognized the importance of a degree of civilian consent for administration to function and understood that this could be attained only through a pragmatic policy that recognized sociological and ideological reality. In many places, this meant ditching much of the revolutionary project. Hoche, of course, did not survive the Revolutionary Wars and hence is remembered simply as one among France's promising new crop of military talent of the 1790s. Napoleon, in contrast, went on to reshape the government of France and of a large part of Europe, drawing on lessons he had learned as a general of the Revolutionary Wars with responsibility for the government of millions of civilians in his care. And much of his legacy still lives on today.

NOTES

1. See, for example, T.C.W. Blanning, *The French Revolutionary Wars 1787–1802* (London: Arnold, 1996).

2. The outbreak of the War of the Second Coalition should be dated to the Anglo-Russian military alliance concluded on December 29, 1798, though Austria entered only in March 1799. The second coalition finally fell apart with the conclusion of a separate peace by Austria at Lunéville. Britain, of course, fought on alone among the Great Powers, until March 1802.

3. Angus Heriot, *The French in Italy 1796–1799* (London: Chatto and Windus, 1957), 10, 56.

4. Paddy Griffith, *The Art of War of Revolutionary France 1789–1802* (London: Greenhill Books; Mechanicsburg, PA: Stackpole Books, 1998), 130.

5. Geoffrey Best, *Humanity in Warfare. The Modern History of International Law of Armed Conflicts* (London: Weidenfeld and Nicolson, 1980), 54–55, 65–66. Also, Richard Shelly Hartigan, *The Forgotten Victim: A History of the Civilian* (Chicago: Precedent, 1982), 107–108, 119. Vattel nevertheless qualified his acceptance of scorched-earth tactics: it must be conducted only with moderation and when absolutely necessary. Louis XIV's infamous devastation of the Palatinate in the 1680s did not meet these criteria, according to Vattel.

6. Hartigan, *Forgotten Victim*, 109.

7. Jacques Godechot, "Les Variations de la politique française à l'égard des pays occupés 1792–1815," in *Occupants-Occupés, 1792–1815. Actes du Colloque qui s'est tenu à Bruxelles, les 29 et 30 janvier 1968* (Brussels: Université libre de Bruxelles, Institut de sociologie, 1969), 17.

8. My translation of part of titre VI, "Des Rapports de la nation française avec les nations étrangères," quoted from Charles Debbasch and Jean-Marie (eds.), *Les Constitutions de la France*, 2nd ed. (Paris: Dalloz, 1989), 37.

9. See book 1, chapter 4, of Jean-Jacques Rousseau, *The Social Contract and Discourses*, translated and introduced by G.D.H. Cole, revised and augmented by J. H. Brumfitt and John C. Hall (London and Melbourn: Dent, 1973), 185–189.

10. Edmund Burke, "Letter to a Member of the National Assembly (1791)," quoted from Conor Cruise O'Brien, "Introduction," in Edmund Burke, *Reflections on the Revolution in France and on the Proceedings in Certain Societies in London relative to that Event*, edited and with an introduction by Conor Cruise O'Brien (Harmondsworth: Penguin, 1969), 61–62.

11. Best, *Humanity*, 78.

12. My translation of original French, quoted in T.C.W. Blanning, *The French Revolution in Germany. Occupation and Resistance in the Rhineland 1792–1802* (Oxford: Clarendon Press, 1983), 2.

13. Simon Schama, *Patriots and Liberators. Revolution in the Netherlands 1780–1813* (London: Collins, 1977), 161.

14. Joseph Hansen (ed.), *Quellen zur Geschichte des Rheinlandes im Zeitalter der französischen Revolution 1780–1801*, 4 vols. (Bonn: P. Hanstein, 1931–38), 1: 414; 2: 562–564, 785–786.

15. Custine's report to the minister of war is dated October 1, 1792. Quoted from Best, *Humanity*, 80.

16. For the French occupation of Speyer in 1792, see Jürgen Müller, *Von der alten Stadt zur neuen Munizipalität. Die Auswirkungen der Französischen Revolution in den linksrheinischen Städten Speyer und Koblenz* (Koblenz: Görres-Verlag, 1990), 104.

17. Almost all of the radical propaganda publications are printed in Heinrich Scheel (ed.), *Die Mainzer Republik*, 3 vols. (Berlin: Akademie-Verlag, 1975–89).

18. T.C.W. Blanning, *Reform and Revolution in Mainz 1743–1803* (Cambridge: Cambridge University Press, 1974), 280.

19. For the debate that the events in Frankfurt sparked in the French National Convention, see the *Archives parlementaires de 1787 à 1860. Recueil complet des débats législatifs et politiques des chambres françaises imprimé par ordre du Sénat et de la Chambre des députés* (1st series [1787–1799], vols. 54–57, originally published Paris, 1898–1900, and reprinted in Neudeln Liechtenstein: Kraus, 1969). In particular see 54: 717; 55: 16–17; 56: 139ff., 163ff., 256. In the debate of January 22, 1793, a certain deputy Bourdon, who represented the Oise, demanded that Frankfurt be razed to the ground in the next campaign. This met with outraged opposition from the rest of the Convention, and the proposed motion was rejected. For this, see 57: 543. Also, for Frankfurt, see Hansen, *Quellen*, 2: 621–622. For Aachen, see ibid., 775–777. In contrast to Frankfurt, the French Convention, acting on Robespierre's initiative, decreed on September 25, 1793, that Aachen would be torched when recaptured.

20. Godechot, "Variations," 19.

21. Jean-Paul Bertaud, *The Army of the French Revolution. From Citizen-Soldiers to Instrument of Power*, translated by R. R. Palmer (Princeton: Princeton University Press, 1988), 48.

22. Not that the French were alone in being neglectful of this aspect of military justice; the first concise handbook accessible in the field and designed to make explicit the rules for the treatment of civilians, the so-called Lieber code, was produced only in 1863, during the American Civil War.

23. Peter Wetzler, *War and Subsistence. The Sambre and Meuse Army in 1794* (New York: Lang, 1985), 94–95.

24. Bertaud supplies the following figures for the overall size of the French army: August 1794: 732,474; August 1795: 484,363; August 1796: 396,016; 1797: 381,909. Bertaud, *Army*, 272.

25. Ibid., 248.

26. Wetzler, *War*, 33–35, 93–95, 117–118, 136. One bushel in this context equals 13 litres dry, the equivalent of 0.358 of an English bushel; a French pound, as used here, is equivalent to 489.5 grams, or 1.08 English pounds.

27. Frank Tallett, *War and Society in Early-Modern Europe, 1495–1715* (London: Routledge, 1992), 49.

28. Ibid., 123.

29. Bertaud, *Army*, 195, 202.

30. Wetzler, *War*, 243–255. To put these figures into perspective, the strength of the Sambre-Meuse at this time was about 140,000. For the representatives-on-mission, see also Griffith, *Art of War*, 88–106.

31. Godechot, "Variations," 26–27.

32. Heriot, *French in Italy*, 86–87.

33. Griffith, *Art of War*, 73–74.

34. Bertaud, *Army*, 82.

35. Hansen, *Quellen*, 3: 771–772, 762.

36. Godechot, "Variations," 272–278.

37. For the extraction commission, see Ferdinand Boyer, "Les Conquêtes scientifiques de la Convention en Belgique et dans les Pays Rhénans (1794–1795)," *Revue d'Histoire Moderne et Contemporaine* 18 (1971): 355–357, 366–367, 373.

38. Blanning, *French Revolutionary Wars*, 162–163.

39. Bertaud, *Army*, 219, 316.

40. Godechot, "Variations," 24–25.

41. For profiles of the leading Clubbists, see Franz Dumont, *Die Mainzer Republik von 1792/93: Stuien zur Revolutionierung in Rheinhessischen und der Pfalz* (Alzey: Verlag der Rheinhessischen Druckwerkstätte, 1982),130–135, 205–209; Blanning, *Mainz*, 283, 291, 295–296. Also, Hansen, *Quellen*, 2: 499.

42. Karl H. Wegert, *German Radicals Confront the Common People: Revolutionary Politics and Popular Politics, 1789–1849* (Mainz: von Zabern, 1992), 26–37.

43. Schama, *Patriots*, 201.

44. Ibid., 204.

45. For the requisitioning of native administrative talent, see Hansen, *Quellen*, 3: 4, 230, and Archives Nationales, Paris (AN), D. XLII, 7, fo. 380. For the dependence of the French on local lawyers, see Marcel Erkens, *Die französische Friedensgerichtsbarkeit 1789–1814 unter besonderer Berücksichtigung der vier rheinischen Departements* (Cologne: Böhlau 1994), 137–139. For French administrative policy in general in the occupied Rhineland, see Jörg Engelbrecht, "Grundzüge der französischen Verwaltungspolitik auf dem linken Rheinufer (1794–1814)," in Christof Dipper, Wolfgang Schieder, and Reiner Schulze (eds.), *Napoleonische Herrschaft in Deutschland und Italien—Verwaltung und Justiz* (Berlin: Duncker and Humblot, 1995), 79–91.

46. Karl-Georg Faber, "Verwaltungs- und Justizbeamte auf dem linken Rheinufer während der französischen Herrschaft. Eine personengeschichtliche Studie," in *Aus Geschichte und Landeskunde; Forschungen und Darstellungen. Franz Steinbach zum 65. Geburtstag gewidmet von seinen Freunden und Schülern* (Bonn: L. Röhrscheid, 1960), 350–388. See also Sabine Graumann, *Französische Verwaltung am Niederrhein. Das Roërdepartement 1798–1814* (Essen: Klartext, 1990), 156–160, 164, 166, 176–177; Erkens, *Friedensgerichtsbarkeit*, 149–151.

47. Hansen, *Quellen*, 1: 774 n.1, 784, 786, 804–805.

48. Hansgeorg Molitor, "Die Juden im französischen Rheinland," in Jutta Bohnke-Kollwitz et al. (eds.), *Köln und das rheinische Judentum. Festschrift Germania Judaica 1959–1984* (Cologne: Bachem, 1984), 87–94.

49. For Catholic resentment of Protestants in 1790s Aachen, see Albert Huyskens, 'Die Aachener Annalen aus der Zeit von 1770 bis 1803," *Zeitschrift des Aachener Geschichtsvereins* 59 (1939): 10, 51, 62.

50. Bertaud, *Army*, 226.

51. Martyn Lyons, *France under the Directory* (Cambridge and New York: Cambridge University Press, 1975), 107.

52. Blanning, *French Revolution in Germany*, 207–247.

53. Joachim Kermann, *Die Manufakturen im Rheinland 1750–1833* (Bonn: L. Röhrscheid, 1972), 118–160.

54. Hansen, *Quellen*, 2: 668–669, 728–732, 848–850.

55. For Cologne, see Max Braubach, *Max Franz von Österreich, letzter Kurfürst von Köln und Fürstbischof von Münster* (Münster: Aschendorff, 1925), 308, 311, 385–387, and Hansen, *Quellen*, 2: 618–621. For Trier, see Hansen, *Quellen*, 3: 280–282, 295 n. 2. For the Palatine government, see the electoral order no. 2398 of July 14, 1794. Johann Josef Scotti, *Sammlung der Gesetze und Verordnungen, welche in den ehemaligen Herzogthümern Jülich, Cleve und Berg und in dem vormaligen Herzogthum Berg über Gegenstände der Landeshoheit, Verfassung, Verwaltung und Rechtspflege ergangen sind. Vom Jahr 1475 bis zu der am 15. April 1815 eingetretenen Königlich Preußischen Landes-Regierung* (Düsseldorf, 1821), part 2, 742.

56. Pierre Vilar, "Quelques aspects de l'occupation et de la résistance en Espagne en 1794 et au temps de Napoléon," in *Occupants-Occupés*, 227, 235.

57. Those issued by the Elector of Trier were especially threatening and provoked resentment. Hansen, *Quellen*, 3: 280–282.

58. For Germany generally and Bavaria in particular, see Eberhard Weis, "Kontinuität und Diskontinuität zwischen den Ständen des 18. Jahrhunderts und den frühkonstitionellen Parlamenten von 1818/1819 in Bayern und Württemberg," in idem, *Deutschland und Frankreich um 1800. Aufklärung—Revolution—Reform* (Munich: Beck, 1990), 222. The conflict between the elector and estates of Trier can best be followed in the documents published by Hansen. Hansen, *Quellen*, 2: 166–1668, 424–427, 446–469, 454, 481–491, 529 n. 1, 627, 664 n. 1, 721–722, 786–798, 875–876. In Cologne, the Elector suspected the estates were prepared to exploit the threatened French invasion to strengthen their political position, and took care to dissolve them before evacuating Bonn because it would be "extremely dangerous" to have them assembled under enemy occupation. Hansen, *Quellen*, 3: 79–80, 255; Braubach, *Max Franz*, 286, 389.

59. Hoche to the Executive Directory, February 2, 1797. Louis Fernand René Joseph Longy, *La Campagne de 1797 sur le Rhin* (Paris: Librairie militaire R. Chapelot, 1909), p. 462. Hansen, *Quellen*, 3: 878–879.

60. For Hoche's policy with respect to Electoral Cologne see Hansen, *Quellen*, 3: 935–942. HStAD, Kurköln II, 3254, nos. 13–16, 37–40. Also, Braubach, *Max Franz*, 386–390. Hoche's divide-and-rule strategy provoked similar tensions between the local estates and government in the Prussian duchies of the Lower Rhine. Wilhelm Steffens, "Die linksrheinischen Provinzen Preußens unter französischer Herrschaft 1794–1802," *Rheinische Vierteljahrsblätter* 19 (1954): 422–425, 438.

61. H. Cardauns and R. Müller (eds.), *Die rheinische Dorfchronik des Johann Peter Delhoven aus Dormagen, 1783–1823* (Neuss: Gesellschaft f. Buchdruckerei, 1926), 92, 97–99, 117, 128, 131–132, 134–135, 140, 145, 159–160, 165, 168. For a recent study that looks at this more generally, see Uwe Andrae, *Die Rheinländer, der Revolution und der Krieg 1794–1798* (Essen: Klartext-Verlag, 1994), 21–25, 28, 31–33, 36–41, 45–46.

62. Wilhelm Kurschat, *Das Haus Friedrich unt Heinrich von der Leyen in Krefeld. Zur Geschichte der Rheinlande in der Zeit der Fremdherrschaft 1794–1814* (Frankfurt a. M: Klostermann, 1933), 33, 45–52, 58–59, 77–81.

63. Jeffry M. Diefendorf, *Businessmen and Politics in the Rhineland, 1789–1834* (Princeton: Princeton University Press, 1980), passim.

64. For a sophisticated, up-to-date analysis of genocide, see Mark Levene, *Genocide in the Age of the Nation-State*, Vol. 1, *The Meaning of Genocide*, and Vol. 2, *The Rise of the West and the Coming of Genocide* (London and New York: I. B. Tauris, 2005).

Of genocide, Levene writes the following: "Genocide occurs when a state, perceiving the integrity of its agenda to be threatened by an aggregate population—defined by the state as an organic collectivity, or series of collectivities—seeks to remedy the situation by the systematic, *en masse* physical elimination of that aggregate, *in toto,* or until it is no longer perceived to represent a threat." Levene, *Meaning of Genocide,* 35.

65. Vendée here, and in the following paragraphs, is taken to mean *Vendée militaire.* This encompassed the area north of the departments Deux-Sèvres and Vendée and south of Maine-et-Loire and Loire-Inférieure.

66. Tilly, *Vendée,* 227, 254–255, 263–304; R. Secher, "Introduction," in Gracchus Babeuf, *La Guerre de la Vendée et le système de dépopulation,* edited by R. Secher and J. J. Brégeon (Paris: Tallandier, 1987), 15; Michael Ross, *Banners of the King: The War of the Vendée 1793–4* (London: Seeley, 1975), 222.

67. Ross, *Banners of the King,* 81.

68. Ibid., 135–136.

69. Claude Mazauric, "Quelques Réflexions sur les relations entre occupants et occupés dans les pays vendéen et chouan pendant la Révolution française," in *Occupants-Occupés,* 291–304.

70. *Archives Parlementaires,* 70: 101–102, 108.

71. Simon Schama, *Citizens. A Chronicle of the French Revolution* (1989; London: The Folio Society, 2004), 2: 760.

72. This is the estimate provided by Peter Paret, *Internal War and Pacification: The Vendée, 1789–1796* (Ann Arbor, 1979: photocopy of original publication, Princeton, 1961), 68. Substantially higher estimates are supported by other scholars. Blanning suggests "400,000 for both sides" as the "most authoritative estimate." Blanning, *Revolutionary Wars* 98.

73. My translation. Quotation taken from Marcel Faucheux, "Le Cas de la Vendée militaire," in *Occupants-Occupés,* 349.

74. Ibid., 348–52. Also, Paret, *Internal War,* 63–64, 67.

75. Adam Zamoyski, *The Last King of Poland* (London: Cape, 1992), 382, 389.

76. Ibid., 429.

77. Ibid., 429–430.

78. Tallett, *War and Society,* 129.

79. Schama, *Patriots,* 672 endnote 133.

80. Ibid., 176, 183.

81. Frederick Bernays Wiener, *Civilians under Military Justice. The British Practice since 1689 Especially in North America* (Chicago: University of Chicago Press, 1967), 219–221.

82. Thomas Pakenham, *The Year of Liberty. The Story of the Great Irish Rebellion of 1798* (Hodder and Stoughton: London, 1969), 34–35. More recent publications tend to play down the socioeconomic context and instead focus more on the ideological and political origins of the 1798 rising. Certainly, Pakenham's dismissal of the disaffected Irish as having "had no serious political aims" appears unsustainable in the light of more recent research.

83. Pakenham, *Year of Liberty,* 66–73, 97–98.

84. Ibid., 139, 143–144. Brian Cleary, "The Battle of Oulart Hill: Context and Strategy," in Dáire Keogh and Nicholas Furlong (eds.), *The Mighty Wave. The 1798 Rebellion in Wexford* (Dublin: Four Courts Press, 1996), 82. This fear of massacre, as perceived by the Protestant side, is revealed in the collection of letters of Protestant women in 1798; John D. Beatty (ed.), *Protestant Women's Narratives of the Irish Rebellion of 1798* (Dublin: Four Courts Press, 2001), 32, 44–45, 90–116.

85. Pakenham, *Year of Liberty,* 147.

86. At Scullabogue more than 100 prisoners of the rebels, including 20 women and children, were locked in a barn, which was then set on fire.

87. Pakenham, *Year of Liberty,* 127, 135, 161–167, 170, 180–184, 192, 197–199, 207–208, 240, 251, 255, 258–260.

88. Pakenham writes of probably between 2,000 and 4,000 deaths. Ibid., 266.

89. Whelan estimates that 17,000 deaths were inflicted by the government side and 3,000 by the rebels. Kevin Whelan, "Reinterpreting the 1798 Rebellion in County Wexford," in Dáire Keogh and Nicholas Furlong (eds.), *The Mighty Wave. The 1798 Rebellion in Wexford* (Four Courts Press: Dublin, 1996), 27–28.

90. Best, *Humanity,* 118–119.

91. Schama, *Patriots,* 186.

92. Griffith, *Art of War,* 105, 243.

93. Indeed, naval blockade had been practised as a strategic weapon in earlier wars, including the War of the Spanish Succession.

94. Desforgues to Morris, October 14, 1793, quoted in Best, *Humanity,* 99.

95. Charles, 3rd Earl Stanhope, accused the British government of attempting to starve France, when speaking in January 1795 in the House of Lords in favor of his motion against interference in the internal affairs of France. William Cobbett, *The Parliamentary History of England, from the Earliest Period to the Year 1803. From Which Last-mentioned Epoch It Is Continued Downwards in the Work Entitled, "The Parliamentary Debates"* (vols. 13–36, edited by John Wright. London: Longman, 1812–20), 31: 1132.

96. Vilar, "Quelques aspects de l'occupation et de la résistance en Espagne," 233.

97. Schama, *Patriots,* 370–372.

98. Ibid., 374, 384–387.

99. Schama, *Citizens,* 2: 736.

100. Roger Dufraisse, "Les Populations de la rive gauche du Rhin et le service militaire à la fin de l'Ancien Régime et à l'époque révolutionnaire," *Revue Historique* 231 (1964): 117–119.

101. Derek Beales, *Prosperity and Plunder. European Catholic Monasteries in the Age of Revolution, 1650–1815* (Cambridge and New York: Cambridge University Press, 2003).

102. Michael Rowe, *From Reich to State. The Rhineland in the Revolutionary Age, 1780–1830* (Cambridge: Cambridge University Press, 2003), 80.

FURTHER READING

The so-called revolutionary wars of the 1790s have attracted much scholarly attention, though the experience of civilians has tended to be neglected in favor of other aspects.

The general foreign-policy context is well represented by Paul W. Schroeder, *The Transformation of European Politics 1763–1848* (Oxford: Clarendon Press, 1994). More focused, but with some interesting comments on the outbreak of wars generally, is T.C.W. Blanning, *The Origins of the French Revolutionary Wars* (London and New York: Longman, 1986). The same author is responsible for the best general survey of this conflict: T.C.W. Blanning, *The French Revolutionary Wars 1787–1802* (London: Arnold, 1996).

The main protagonist in these wars—the French army—has been the subject of a number of studies accessible to readers of English. These include Jean-Paul Bertaud, *The Army of the French Revolution. From Citizen-Soldiers to Instrument of*

Power, translated by R. R. Palmer (Princeton, NJ: Princeton University Press, 1988); John A. Lynn, *The Bayonets of the Republic: Motivation and Ttactics in the Army of Revolutionary France, 1791–94* (Urbana: University of Illinois Press, 1984); and Alan Forrest, *The Soldiers of the French Revolution* (Durham and London: Duke University Press, 1990). All three shed much light on the experience of the ordinary soldier and the extent to which he was motivated by revolutionary propaganda. More recently, Rafe Blaufarb, *The French Army, 1750–1820: Careers, Talent, Merit* (Manchester: Manchester University Press, 2002), focuses on the social composition of the French army over a period that encompasses the Revolutionary and Napoleonic eras.

   Recent research on the army of the French Republic questions the extent to which it really was "revolutionary." Paddy Griffith, *The Art of War of Revolutionary France 1789–1802* (London: Greenhill Books; Mechanicsburg, PA: Stackpole Books, 1998) in particular stresses how the French army quickly returned to more traditional techniques of making war after discovering that these alone succeeded, given the technological constraints of the 1790s, which placed massive practical constraints on what could be achieved, irrespective of revolutionary enthusiasm. This was especially evident in the area of logistics, the subject of Peter Wetzler, *War and Subsistence. The Sambre and Meuse Army in 1794* (New York: Lang, 1985).

   French armies surged forward in the 1790s, occupying the Low Countries, the Rhineland, and of course Italy, whose experience is made famous by the activities of Napoleon Bonaparte. However, despite (or perhaps because) of this association, relatively little has been written on the experience of ordinary civilians in the peninsula. Angus Heriot, *The French in Italy 1796–1799* (London: Chatto and Windus, 1957), remains the basic text but is now showing its age. The Rhineland, in comparison, is much better served. For an extremely critical appraisal of the behavior of the French army in this region, see T.C.W. Blanning, *The French Revolution in Germany. Occupation and Resistance in the Rhineland 1792–1802* (Oxford: Clarendon Press, 1983). Not only does this study conclusively demonstrate the brutal nature of French occupation, but it also documents the widespread resistance that this engendered among the vast majority of Rhinelanders. More recently, Karl H. Wegert, *German Radicals Confront the Common People: Revolutionary Politics and Popular Politics, 1789–1849* (Mainz: von Zabern, 1992). and Michael Rowe, *From Reich to State. The Rhineland in the Revolutionary Age, 1780–1830* (Cambridge: Cambridge University Press, 2003), investigate the complex motives behind collaboration and resistance in the occupied Rhineland. As bleak in its appraisal of the French as Blanning is Simon Schama, *Patriots and Liberators. Revolution in the Netherlands 1780–1813* (London: Collins, 1977), which is especially revealing of the dilemma faced by so-called Dutch patriots—radicals sympathetic to the French Revolution—when confronted with the rapacity of their supposed "liberators."

   French military success in the Revolutionary Wars ensured that their armies came into contact with foreign civilians to a greater extent than did the armies of the Coalition with the inhabitants of the Republic, and this is reflected in the literature. Nonetheless, some insights into the behavior of the British army are provided by Schama, *Patriots and Liberators.* Civilian-military relations from the perspective of the Austrian and Prussian armies, in contrast, remain underresearched. The same can be said of Russia, whose forces arguably committed some of the worst atrocities in this period, notably against the inhabitants of the Ottoman Empire and Poland. The latter are referred to briefly in Adam Zamoyski, *The Last King of Poland* (London: Cape, 1992).

The ferocity of the Russians was, mercifully, not equaled by the armies of either revolutionary France or its opponents when it came to the treatment of foreign civilians. However, it was exceeded, at least in the case of the Vendée, when it came to conflict between the armed forces of the state and domestic insurgents. To this day, the Vendée arouses passions that are not equaled in analysis of the international conflict of the 1790s. Controversy rages in particular around the final body count and around whether the repression meted out by the French Republican government against the population of the western departments qualifies as genocide. A powerful recent case for viewing it as genocide is put forward in Mark Levene, *Genocide in the Age of the Nation-State,* Vol. 1: *The Meaning of Genocide,* and Vol. 2: *The Rise of the West and the Coming of Genocide* (London and New York: I. B. Tauris, 2005).

The number of deaths that resulted from the Irish rebellion of 1798 was far smaller than even the lowest estimate made for the Vendée. Nonetheless, similarities exist between these two uprisings that occurred on Europe's Atlantic seaboard. The classic account of the Irish uprising remains Thomas Pakenham, *The Year of Liberty. The Story of the Great Irish Rebellion of 1798* (Hodder and Stoughton: London, 1969). More recent publications, including some of the chapters in Dáire Keogh and Nicholas Furlong (eds.), *The Mighty Wave. The 1798 Rebellion in Wexford* (Dublin: Four Courts Press, 1996), which challenge Pakenham's stress on the socioeconomic (as opposed to ideological) origins of the rising and the notion that the rebels were a disorganized rabble. A reader who wishes to discover the sheer terror that confronts civilians in an environment of civil war is referred to John D. Beatty (ed.), *Protestant Women's Narratives of the Irish Rebellion of 1798* (Dublin: Four Courts Press, 2001).

FIVE

Civilians in the Napoleonic Wars

Michael Broers

The past century was a time of unprecedented horrors on a planetary scale. Its two massive conflicts have driven a wedge between ourselves and previous generations, for we are in need of well-honed historical imagination to grasp how those who lived and died before 1914, without knowledge of the Great War and its still more hideous successor, could conceive of war and its consequences on scales comparable to our own. That is the hurdle we must attempt to cross, when approaching the Revolutionary and Napoleonic wars in any and all of their manifestations, military or civilian, direct or indirect. The past ten decades have set new standards in slaughter, mayhem, trauma, and dislocation for the human race where the impact of war is concerned, and this has, in its turn, made the past—even the relatively recent past of the early nineteenth century— truly "another country" for the honest inquirer. This makes the history of the years 1792–1815 all the more important to study, for the profound ramifications this conflict produced remain with us; they are of enduring consequence for successor generations, as are the deep scars these wars left on the European psyche, both individual and collective.

The Revolutionary and Napoleonic wars were the largest, most widespread, and most savage conflicts Europeans had yet experienced; they touched more people, in and out of uniform, than anything known or imagined hitherto. That, in time, European society got over them sufficiently to embark on a new cycle of carnage is perhaps the clearest indication that they were not of the scale or intensity of the two world wars of the next century. Nevertheless, the wars waged between Revolutionary France and the rest of Europe lasted more than 20 years; they transformed states and societies and touched hundreds of millions of lives, simply because they went on so long. That they did not become the watershed in human perceptions of horror reached in the aftermath of the two world wars owed more to the lack of technology at the disposal of the protagonists than to any sense of cultural or moral superiority to later warlords. The turn of the eighteenth and nineteenth centuries was a curious time. It was an age when the mental furniture of modernity was being set in place, often forcibly as a motive for conflict; certain perceptions of the Enlightenment—whether perverted or pure hardly matters—were carried on the points of the bayonets of armies of unprecedented size across vast tracts of the European continent. These were new ideas: liberty, equality, fraternity in one interpretation; authoritarianism, cultural arrogance, bullying conformism, in another. For most educated people, the wars became a crusade between light and darkness, between good and evil, between superstition and reason, between God and the Devil. Darrin McMahon has puts it perfectly in defining the whole era of revolutions as the "charged, developmental struggle (of the Enlightenment) with the oppositional movements it brought into being. This dialectical process would then be seen, collectively, as constitutive of modernity."[1] It was a battle of ideas, but one that enveloped hundreds of millions of ordinary people and took place in the real world. That ideologues sought to penetrate the life of all humanity meant that the political aspirations that drove the hordes of campaigning soldiers were those of total war in the sense that the next century would come to understand it. The Napoleonic wars took place to change the world and to stop it from being changed, to reshape humanity and to hold back its evolution. In the minds of their elite protagonists, the fate of civilization hung on victory or defeat. Fortunately for all concerned, reality intervened.

The discourses generated by the wars and the concepts behind them are very modern, insofar as they resemble—if not quite foreshadow—the ideas that dominate the contemporary world. They were read by few, for few could read. Ironically, though, the theories of the Enlightenment were recorded on parchment and written with quill pens by candlelight; they were carried by sailing ships and by pack animals along unpaved roads or mud tracks. There was only one road in the Kingdom of Naples in 1799, and that led out of it, to Rome; in its central province of the Basilicata, there were no roads at all.[2] The armies sent forth to uphold and diffuse these ideas, or to turn them back, marched or rode into battle; they fought with muskets loaded laboriously with balls and powder horns, not even breached-loaded with bullets. Indeed, many commanders still felt that the bayonet—little different in its use or conception from the short stabbing spear used by the Roman legions—was by far the more effective weapon. "With the bayonet the individual soldier can spear two or three of his enemy, while 99 bullets out of a hundred hit nothing but air," the great Russian general Suvorov concluded in the last months of the eighteenth century.[3] Napoleon, like most of his contemporaries, considered the muskets at his disposal so rudimentary and their accuracy so poor, even in expert hands, that he preferred to concentrate his infantry training on mass fire and mass bayonet charges.[4] It all came down to discipline and training, to human qualities. As Rory Muir has put it, for military men of the time, "the musket mattered far less than the quality of the troops who wielded it."[5] This is not to say that technical advances or advantages were unknown. The French under Napoleon did achieve a level of superiority over other armies in the quality of their field artillery, but even the best guns were accurate, at best, up to only 100 yards.[6] Not surprisingly, the Royal Navy developed ships with hulls far more maneuverable than those of the French and Spanish, but even this did not prove quite as decisive at the key battle of Trafalgar as the ability of British seamen to refit their ships in storm conditions, on the open sea, the result of intensive training.[7] Wars could not yet be won by technology, and even important advances in military technology could seldom do real damage beyond the field of battle itself.

The Revolutionary-Napoleonic wars truly marked an era when the refinement of theories, of ideas, was approaching that of our own and when ideas were being established through struggle, for this was the root of the conflict. Later generations, our own as vehemently as its predecessors, espouse or decry the concepts the Enlightenment. These wars were their forge. Yet, if we are, indeed, all children of that Enlightenment—rebellious or dutiful—these very modern ideas were born of a world whose technology was little changed from that of an early modern world of very different intellectual horizons. If we see ourselves in their writings, much earlier generations would have been at home in the surroundings of the *philosophes.* Napoleon and Nelson were men with a disturbingly contemporary sense of "fame," of celebrity, but they had only paintings and hand-driven printing presses to propagate their highly "spun" images. They had only crude weaponry and cruder transport to build their reputations, just as Adam Smith had to propagate global capitalism, or Voltaire the liberty of expression, by the same primitive means. This, then, was the world of the wars, of modern political theory amid subsistence agriculture, of Hegel's world vision among isolated peasant communities. The battle for modernity was fought out hand-to-hand, its wounded cared for by primitive medical science.

Contemporaries were profoundly aware of this. They knew that the scope of their ideas and the magnitude of the conflict they had engendered were beyond the scope of their technology, and they strove to expand it. The means to allow them to do so were almost upon them, but not quite. The steam engine, the repeating rifle, electric power were all on the cusp on their world but just beyond their grasp. The Committee of Public Safety,

Napoleon, Castlereagh, Metternich, and Tsar Alexander did not dispose of the technology of Lincoln, Bismarck, or Cavour only a few decades later. That was just as well for the peoples of Europe, for the warlords and statesmen at the helm of the wars strained every sinew their countrymen possessed in the pursuit of victory. It was by chance, not design, that the material havoc they wreaked was not usually long lived. Conversely, the most serious economic crises of the period 1810–1811 were not wholly or directly caused by the Napoleonic blockade but rather were the result of perennial problems of too little demand for industrial capacity to supply. Many fragile industries, particularly textiles, benefited from the fleeting protection from British competition offered by Napoleonic hegemony, at least if they fell on the right side of the arbitrary and unequal tariff borders Napoleon drew within his empire. However, no act of political will, even if supported by the *Grande Armée*, could stem the tide of British economic and industrial superiority built on its financial and industrial power and on the nation's unique weapon of mass destruction, the Royal Navy. The technological constraints of the era made Napoleon's vision of an all-encompassing blockade impossible to realize.[8] His pursuit of comprehensive, water-tight control of the entire coastline of western Europe was unenforceable. The same proved true of his vision of a "Continental System"—a European economic order predicated on and arranged for French prosperity at the expense of all industrial competitors, real or potential, under his hegemony. In different ways, the blockade and the Continental System represent, perhaps, the most striking examples of the gap between the propensity to conceive and the ability to achieve that characterize the intellectual world of the Enlightenment. Russell Weigley is on firm ground when he contends that the French approach to the Revolutionary-Napoleonic wars "was the first forging of the thunderbolt of a new kind of war—the total war of nations pitting against each other all their resources and passion." Weigley sees its birth in the *levée en masse;*[9] its culmination might well be defined as the Continental System. The principle of total war was established in the course of these conflicts, "the moral and ideological foundations of total war," as Roger Chickering has called them.[10] The vision outstripped the capabilities, however. The men of the age could not do the harm they set out to do, in the measure they desired.

They left their mark, nonetheless. If the wars did little permanent damage to Europe, it was not for want of trying, as the cost in lives attests. In his lucid study of the military aspect of the Napoleonic wars, David Gates has drawn together the stark casualty figures in telling comparative context: "Overall, the Napoleonic Wars resulted in some five million dead, the same proportion of Europe's population as was to be claimed by the conflict of 1914–18." France may have lost close to one million combatants in the wars, a national mortality rate of 38 percent, exceeding that of 1914–18; British losses of approximately 225,000 were comparable to those of the Great War, as a percentage of its population.[11] It took the governments of the early nineteenth century more than five times as long to achieve this parity in carnage as it took in the early twentieth, but the raw figures are instructive, just the same. Mass slaughter took time, however, because it was achieved with relatively primitive technology.

If "tribute" is the right word, then it was a tribute to the organizational skills of the first post-Enlightenment generation of European soldiers, politicians, and administrators of Europe that so many men were mobilized, deployed, and engaged at all. This process involved millions of people, both running the war efforts and being run by them; the huge casualty rates touched even more lives indirectly than they did in direct combat, for this was still a world of extended peasant households and tightly knit rural communities. The state expanded apace; the numbers of those it affected did so in tandem. This is the core of the historical experience of the noncombatant peoples of Europe who lived in the shadow of the Napoleonic wars.

TIME AND PLACE: A GEOGRAPHY AND CHRONOLOGY OF WAR

Even so gargantuan a conflict as the Napoleonic wars could not, given the constraints of technology, impose itself everywhere in comparable measure, nor did the fighting really encompass the whole period between 1792 and 1815. War zones shifted, as did political boundaries, through conquest, reconquest, and the resultant peace treaties. Indeed, a salient feature of the Napoleonic wars, in contrast to the immediate wartime impact of the First World War, for example, is the degree to which they changed the map of Europe as the conflict went on. Whereas the great redrawing of European borders followed World War I, Napoleonic expansion went hand-in-hand with reorderings of states. Much of this work survived, and the Congress of Vienna created far fewer new states and altered fewer borders than did the Versailles conferences a century later, however often Vienna changed the rulers. In this respect, civilian populations were left undisturbed.

Thus, there are several different processes at work in the configuration of Napoleonic Europe. As much of what follows is predicated on the assumption that the Napoleonic empire can be divided into different zones, it is probably wise to outline the shifts in territory, less in the spirit of diplomatic history than to give a sense of the magnitude of the upheaval civilian populations endured and to explore the new regional configurations within Europe, that Napoleonic expansion engendered. There was the process of "carve-up," of the creation of new states and borders, together with the shifting of the war zones, moving conflict away from some regions and into others, over the period. Finally, there was the question of how the peoples of Europe responded to the new conditions imposed on them by all these changes.

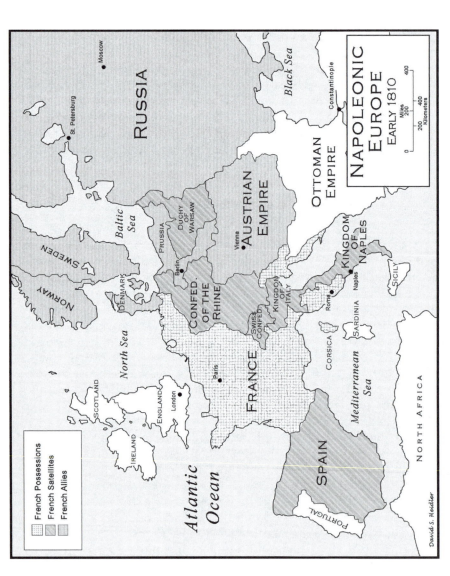

Map of Napoleonic Europe, early 1810. Courtesy of David S. Heidler.

The Napoleonic Empire itself was of short duration, but it expanded rapidly from the traditional borders of France as the wars progressed. The French Republic had already seized modern Belgium and the left bank of the Rhine by the time Napoleon took power in 1799, but, by 1811, the official frontiers of the French Empire included about 45 million people, more than half of whom had recently been ruled by someone else, and were different from the political borders of only a few years before. The "Grand Empire," defined widely to include not only the satellite states but also the allied territories of the Confederations of Switzerland and the Rhine, embraced 80 million people, although Spain and much of southern Italy, and even parts of western France, were barely under its control. Political borders did not correspond neatly to the geography of effective control by governments, as shall be seen. Nevertheless, from the perspective of civilian populations, upheaval was the hallmark of the era. Napoleonic expansion into Spain and Italy was achieved with blood and gore; in Spain, it never changed, while, in Italy, the north was quickly removed from the war zones, whereas the far south—the Kingdom of Naples— remained convulsed throughout the period. When the means needed to assert control over these polities are compared to their diplomatic fates, however, the irony is evident. Neither Spain nor the Kingdom of Naples underwent any territorial alterations; upheaval came through changes of dynasty and the need to enforce them. By contrast, northern Italy's political landscape was utterly altered. Some of the oldest, most deeply rooted states in Europe simply disappeared: the core of the Savoyard monarchy and the two ancient city republics of Genoa and Venice, the last two never to resurface. An entirely new polity, the Republic, later Kingdom, of Italy (1800–1814) was carved out of Austrian-ruled Lombardy and parts of the Papal state; it would vanish in 1814 but was arguably one of the most influential political creations of the revolutionary era, giving example, as well as impetus, to later plans for Italian unity. The Grand Duchy of Warsaw had an even shorter life than the Republic/Kingdom of Italy, lasting from 1807 to 1814, but it played a comparable role in the rebirth of Polish nationalism, and its importance was recognized immediately by its new ruler, Tsar Alexander I, when he prolonged its life as the Congress Kingdom of Poland, which was suppressed after the 1831 revolution. Indeed, the most lasting and important changes to the political map were achieved without a shot being fired. A combination of skillful diplomacy—the wooing of the princes of the middle-size German states—and the threat of military pressure on Austria brought about a thoroughgoing redrawing of the map of Germany. In 1803, the Holy Roman Empire—soon to dissolve itself as a result of the changes—agreed to the absorption and disappearance of 112 small states, mainly free cities and the fiefs of the Imperial Knights. Almost all of them passed to the middle states, rather than to the French Empire, and, as a result, Bavaria, Baden, Württemberg, Nassau, and Hesse-Darmstadt emerged as stronger, more viable polities, ever loyal to Napoleon for his influence in the process. The settlement of Germany, the *Hauptschluss,* was as enduring as it was fundamental, ending only with unification in 1871. In simple human terms, tens of millions of Europeans saw their formal allegiances change in these years. For many, things would never be the same again, as new states adopted new ways of ruling.

There is another aspect about the process of Napoleonic state-building that is highly unusual and that relates directly to the course of the wars. As has been noted, Napoleon created and helped to reshape a host of new states in western and central Europe; this process occurred not after the wars but during their course. Thus, when a new state emerged, such as the Republic/Kingdom of Italy or Westphalia or the Grand Duchy of Berg, in Germany, their institutions were molded directly in response to the needs of the war effort. The deeper ramifications of this pattern will be discussed in the course of this essay, but the central point should be made immediately, that the needs of war became the raison d'être of the new states; they were the motors of the wars, not their end result. This could lead to variations, as well as attempts to "clone" the model of Napoleonic France onto foreign bodies. Within the compass of the "inner empire"—broadly, the lands under French control before 1807—the "cloning" model prevailed. The new Italian state, as well as Berg, in Germany, and, at one remove, the allied states of the Confederation of the Rhine, simply adopted as much of the Napoleonic state structure as they could usefully absorb. Further east, however, the model began to break down, and pragmatism, based on the exigencies of war, ruthlessly brushed aside initial plans to push the Napoleonic blueprint still further afield. When, in 1807, Napoleon carved out the entirely unprecedented Kingdom of Westphalia from Hesse-Kassel and parts of Prussia and Hanover, he enjoined its new ruler, his youngest brother, Jerome, to create there "a wise and liberal administration" that would make the prospect of renewed Prussian rule there anathema to its people. This plan soon collapsed, as did similar plans for the Grand Duchy of Warsaw, when Napoleon realized that, by maintaining the power of the feudal baronage, he could recruit hordes of serf conscripts on the traditional pattern. Pragmatism induced by war prevailed the further the Napoleonic state system spread from its west European core.

As the political map shifted, so did the war zones, but, at their extremes, some parts of Europe knew intense suffering, while others escaped direct involvement altogether. However, even here there is a vital caveat. Napoleon's initial claim to political success was his ability to forge peace with the allied coalition by 1801. This began with the armistice with the Habsburg monarchy following the campaigns of 1800–1801 in Italy and on the Rhine and culminated in the Peace of Amiens in 1802, which even brought an 18-month respite in the war with Britain. Much is made of the brevity of the peace between Britain and France, but this is somewhat misleading, at least on the level of formal military hostilities. When hostilities resumed between them, they were confined to the colonies and naval warfare. All of continental Europe knew real, if very uneasy, peace between 1801 and November 1805. There were also significant periods when open warfare was confined to the Iberian peninsula, notably in 1808 and in 1810–1811. Similarly, large areas of eastern Europe and, perhaps most significant, mainland Britain avoided direct involvement in the fighting. Jane Austen could never have written of her society as she did in any circumstances other than those of peace. Her women look for suitable spouses among the unusually high numbers of officers they meet at fashionable spas. They are neither swept off their feet by all-conquering foreigners, as were the Italian heroines of Stendhal's *The Charterhouse of Parma* or real-life Berliners in 1807, if the memoirs of Norvins de Montbretonne are to be believed. The French officers found theaters full of society women, but virtually no men; a French victory as degrading as Jena ensued:

At the end of the performance, as I watched our officers offer their arms to the ladies as they left their boxes and went down the staircases, and saw them accompanied to their carriages or to their doorsteps, I learned just how Prussian hatred, once as vibrant as a bobbin, came to lose some of its severity. The fact is that the Prussian women believed our troops would stay there, as a garrison, and they can be pardoned for that.[12]

Superficially, this may resonate of the impact of the Meryton militia on the settled society observed warmly in Jane Austen's *Pride and Prejudice;* there may, indeed, be an argument that the juxtaposition of Hampshire and Berlin reveals human nature to be universal. However, the Meryton militia had not just butchered and humiliated the husbands, beaus, and brothers of the well-heeled denizens of the exclusive boxes. The scenes and exchanges Norvins painted in his memoirs smack more of occupied Paris a century and a half later than of contemporaneous England.

Nor, if Austen's determined subjects were successful in their tender conquests, would their fate as the wives of officers become that of George Sand's mother, whose husband fought all over Europe for Napoleon. Together with her young daughter, she followed him to Spain, the forefront of what was then the hottest battle. Sand's mother had decided to join her officer husband in Spain, "from a sense of jealous suspicion," and it was no light undertaking. Sand remembered vividly passing through a village that had been burned down the day before and finding only raw onions to eat. Despite the lack of all furnishings and comforts, her mother and her friend spent the night there, fearing to travel after dark:

We reached Madrid in the course of May (1808); we had suffered greatly on route, and I remember nothing of the last days of the journey. That we reached our goal without catastrophe was almost a miracle, for Spain had risen in several places, and everywhere, the storm was ready to break. We followed the lines protected by French troops, it is true, but the French were safe nowhere, against these new

Sicilian Vespers; and my mother, carrying one child within her and another in her arms, had only too many things to fear.[13]

The business of husband-hunting in Napoleonic Spain involved terrifying ordeals and the risk of life and limb, not just a touch of the social embarrassment or emotional uncertainty so dreaded by Austen's heroines.

In terms of intensity, the brunt of the Napoleonic wars fell on certain people, in certain parts of Europe, more than on others. Nowhere else in Europe experienced fighting as prolonged and intense as the Iberian peninsula, and the area's life and character were changed by it, almost forever. The ebb and flow of the French occupation ensured that every part of Spain was touched directly by hostilities at some time or other. The material ruin and emotional trauma of the Peninsula War is graphically, indeed gruesomely recorded for posterity in the paintings of Goya.[14] The horrors he immortalized are enunciated in the devastating honesty of a report of a pro-French Spanish official in Ronda, in Andalucia, an area caught between the rebel stronghold of Cadiz and French-held Seville, where the French army, local bandits, and the pro-Cadiz guerrillas were at odds and where, in the midst of the conflict, the noble landlords still sought to exact rents from a peasantry beset on all sides by rapacious soldiers, regular and irregular alike:

The farm workers of this area have been the primary victims of the war and the calamities and the misery that goes with it. Caught between the requisitions of the French and the banditry of the rebels, normal agricultural cultivation is impossible here. They have reached breaking point; the people have become a skeleton, and must be seen as an object of compassion.[15]

Suffering of this kind blighted the lives of peasants all over Europe, as the fighting and the war zones ebbed and flowed, but in Spain and other areas of continual hostilities, such as Calabria, they never abated.

Just as Jane Austen's novels could pertain only to England, so even as troubled a soul as Wordsworth could only imagine the dread across the Channel. His 1808 poem "To the Clouds" traced the movements of imagined armies, presumably those newly locked in combat in Spain. "To the Clouds" interprets the war as a recurring, daily phenomenon, but, as Mary Favret has astutely commented, few poems express how difficult it actually was for Britons at home to grasp the reality of war, so reduced were they to abstractions.[16] Wordsworth's metamorphosis of his impressions of clouds as armies makes a contrast charged with ironies when set beside the innocent recollections of the four-year-old George Sand of her retreat with her mother and officer father from Madrid in 1808:

Being at a window one evening with my mother, we saw the sky, still lit by the setting sun, but full of criss-crossing fires, and my mother said to me, "There, look, it's a battle, and your father is probably in it." I had no idea what a real battle was. What I saw looked like a gigantic fireworks display, something funny and wonderful, a party or a tournament. The noise of the cannons and the great columns of fire made me happy. I was like a spectator at a show, all while eating a green apple. I don't remember to whom my mother said, "Happy are the children, for they understand nothing."[17]

In the same year, Goya needed to look no further than his own window to be scarred forever. Indeed, there are few better emotional charts of the impact of the wars on Spain than Goya's oeuvre as a whole. Even in 1808, he depicted a ramshackle, often archaic, but essentially stable world. After that, he changed utterly, becoming the weathervane of the collective nightmare of the War of Independence, from which Spain emerged into a century and a half of politics dominated by a military establishment that had scarcely existed before 1808. Indeed, had the military establishments of Spain and Portugal been even remotely effective in 1808, Napoleon would not have intervened directly in their affairs. He occupied Spain and Portugal not because they posed a military threat to him but, rather, because they were ineffectual allies, unable to repulse British encroachments. When the dust finally settled on Iberia, in 1814, both states were left with swollen armies that would dominate their politics until the last quarter of the twentieth century. In stark contrast, Britain—although having created a vast military machine from an even smaller base than Spain's—systematically dismantled its armies after 1814. Britain's greatest commander, Wellington, did, indeed, become Prime Minister briefly in the late 1820s, but of little more than a caretaker government; he left office in 1830 on the heels of a crushing electoral defeat. The contrast with the succession of generals, of both Left and Right, whose names and military coups—*pronunciamentos*—trail across the history of modern Spain could not be more different. Franco was but the end of a long process. No more profound transformation of whole societies by war could be found than took place south of the Pyrenees.

However, when assessing the impact of the wars on civilian populations, it would be wrong to assume that their most lasting effects correspond symmetrically to the most intense fighting. France was the cockpit of the conflict. Its revolutionary governments and, even more, Napoleon were indisputably the most consistent and ferocious aggressors of the era; the wars came to dominate French government and society at every level and in every respect. Yet the hallmark of the campaigning was the removal of France from the war zones. François Furet made the acute observation that "the war ran the revolution more than the revolution ran the war."[18] It was even more the case under Napoleon. Only at the war's inception, 1792–1793, and at its end, in 1814, was French territory the theater of the great international conflict. Indeed, the very threat of allied invasion was enough to bring down the Directory and to make way for Bonaparte in 1799, and then to spell his own end, in 1814 and again in 1815. Even Waterloo had to be fought in Belgium for any victory to be credible. Likewise, the bulk of the Napoleonic armies were usually garrisoned beyond the borders of France, in northern Italy and in the states of the Confederation of the Rhine, as well as being on constant active service in Spain, from 1808 on. Prior to the outbreak of the Peninsular War, Spain—as a French ally—had been "host" to a French army of 180,000 men. Only between 1801 and 1805, the years of general peace, did Napoleon maintain a huge military presence in France proper, and that was the Army of England, based in the Channel ports in the far northeast of the country. Thus, although the Napoleonic state and French society were increasingly organized to support the military machine, neither was truly militarized, certainly not to the degree of Spain or Portugal. The same was broadly true of the other parts of Europe longest under Napoleon's hegemony: the Low Countries, northern Italy, and the states of the Confederation of the Rhine, in western and southern Germany. The experience of these regions differed from that of France in that they had to support the bulk of the armies in peacetime and when the armies were not on active service but, like France, they were seldom in the war zones between 1800 and 1814. They had been the main theaters of the wars of the 1790s, but the consolidation of Napoleon's grip on western Europe at Amiens in 1802 ensured that their position altered completely until his fall, and then only briefly in 1813–1814.

None of this is to imply that the impact of the Napoleonic wars on western Europe north of the Pyrenees was neither lasting nor profound. It was both. Rather, it should indicate that their influence was all the more powerful for being felt at one remove. The very prevalence of peace meant that the whole process of reform and change—cultural as well as institutional, social as well as political—that Napoleonic rule entailed could be wrought more thoroughly in this part of Europe than elsewhere, where French rule was transient, if traumatic, and where the fighting was fierce but transient. Much, if not all, of France itself, the Low Countries, northern Italy, and the Confederation of the Rhine were Napoleon's "inner empire," his power base and the core of his empire. This was so because there he could make his rule stick, his writs run, and his system work. Consequently, these regions bore then, and still bears, his mark. This was not just an inner but an indelible empire. It should in no way be assumed from this that Napoleonic rule was easily or willingly received in these places or that it was established without struggle, for neither of these was the case. It is to say, however, that the often ruthless campaigns of internal "pacification" Napoleon waged against these civilian populations proved far more successful than his great military adventures. Their success assured the longevity of his true legacy to posterity, the modern European state.

The impact of war was less diffuse but more direct elsewhere. It would be wrong to assume that, because French rule was brief in a given region, it left no lasting traces. Rather, the pattern that emerges on the margins of the "Grand Empire"—in places like Spain, the Illyrian Provinces (mainly

"Il 18 brumale, anno VIII." Italian print published on the occasion of Napoleon's coming to power in France, November 9, 1799, following his successful campaign in Egypt. Image depicts France as a giant sphinx wearing the cap of Liberty and lying on architectural ruins and bodies. Behind the sphinx, Napoleon is unfurling a flag with his emblem of bees. The background shows a military camp within a fort, ships at sea, and four balloons flying in the distance. Courtesy of the Library of Congress Prints and Photographs Division, Washington, DC.

present Croatia and Slovenia), central Italy, and the North Sea coast of Germany—is one of the most enduring memories of dislocation and resentment. These regions felt the full impact of conscription, military occupation, and, in most cases, prolonged, full-scale war, but they were under Napoleonic hegemony too fleetingly to acquire any real inkling of the benefits of its system of government, at least outside the propertied elites. Trauma engulfed these regions, as an alien political order swept into them on the tide of military violence and disruption. This was their baptism into the ways of the modern state, and it was seldom, if ever, perceived as benevolent. There are many revealing signs of this: to this day, Slovenian dialect has preserved the word *fronki* as a term for taxes,[19] while, since its creation in 1844, the Spanish *Guardia Civil* has hidden its institutional origins in the Napoleonic gendarmerie, claiming as its true ancestor the *Santa Hermandad* of the sixteenth century. Indeed, resistance to the whole concept of a Napoleonic-style police force in Spain throughout the early nineteenth century, at a time when other states in less obvious need of one were embracing it, was in large part the result of the trauma of the occupation.[20] In this "outer empire," Napoleonic rule was characterized by unabated resistance, not a gradual process of embedding institutions and norms. In the north, from the Netherlands to Denmark, it was symbolized by the burning customs house, as maritime communities fought the decimation of the blockade in the south, and by the defiance shown in the staging of religious processions on banned holy days as archaic Catholicism emerged as a vibrant collective manifestation of defiance to the new order. The new state was, on first acquaintance, fought tooth and nail, by any and all means; it would continue to be loathed and feared, however briefly and imperfectly it had been experienced.

All this amounts to a "hidden history" of the Revolutionary-Napoleonic wars that historians in many countries have been unearthing from many different perspectives in recent years, to shape something akin to a victims' perspective of the conflict. Undeniably, this was the real experience of the mass of European people, of all classes and many regions. Beside it, however, must also be set the fundamental contribution of Napoleonic expansion to the creation of modern European political culture, particularly in the lands of the "inner empire." There is still another element to the impact of the wars on the civilian population of Europe, however, and of France, in particular. The wars, and especially the unheralded imperial expansion of Napoleonic France, opened unprecedented career paths, wells of opportunity, for a generation of Frenchmen. Beside those who seized the wars as an opportunity, were also those, mainly the French counterrevolutionaries but not them alone, who perceived the conflicts in terms of loss, both personal and cultural. Their experience created, possibly for the first time in European history, a sense of a scission with the past.

INTRUSION: THE WARS AND THE EXPANSION OF THE STATE

Ironically, it was during the years of general peace, between 1800 and 1805, that most of the peoples of western Europe, now under the control of the Napoleonic hegemony, most felt the impact of reform. This was when the newly established Consular regime consolidated itself in a number of ways that would fundamentally alter the nature of the state and its relationship to civil society. It would be wrong to characterize either the Consulate (1799–1804) or its successor regime, the First Empire (1804–1814), as military dictatorships, and this is even less true of the satellite and client states allied to it, in Italy, western Germany, or the Low Countries. Napoleon did not rule through the army; none of his generals was ever given a major ministry, except that of War, and the only one of his Marshals to rule a satellite state—Murat, in Naples, from 1808 to 1815—did so because he was Napoleon's brother-in-law, not through his role as his cavalry commander. Indeed, the real hallmark of the regime and all its imitators was to firmly establish a professional civil service as the core of government and to implant it geographically, both on a macro level, across western Europe, and in localized form, from the center of power to the remote peripheries. Napoleonic hegemony meant the forging and embedding of a professional bureaucracy and its increased ability to direct civil society and the wheels of the state. The clearest proof of its unshakable power and efficiency was, perhaps, revealed in 1812 when a rumor spread in Paris that Napoleon had been killed in Russia. The rumor was widely believed, and, when General Malet tried to stage a coup to restore the republic, he was quickly arrested without fanfare. No one thought to proclaim a regency for Napoleon's son or to take any action related to the role of head of state. No one in the heart of the administration panicked, and the wheels of government rolled normally. Napoleon quickly drew the lesson that the state he had created did not actually need him; it was not an autocracy, still less a military dictatorship. The Napoleonic state bore no resemblance, in a crisis, to the kind of charismatic, military-backed regimes that came to dominate Latin America and Spain in the nineteenth and twentieth centuries, which are so often thought of as manifestations of his political legacy. By 1812 the Napoleonic state was nothing of the kind. Its essence was the professional bureaucracy, and that edifice would survive the military collapse of 1814, not just in France but in almost every country under the influence of the Napoleonic model of the state. No one recognized this faster than Napoleon himself. When he did surface, alive and livid—less at Malet's coup than at the official reaction to it—Napoleon redrew the constitution to ensure that his wife and a small regency council drawn from his family would run the empire should he be captured or killed. Only in its last two years did the First Empire really become a true dynastic monarchy, and it took this extraordinary event to expose the fact that it had not been one. Even at this point, however, it did not occur to Napoleon to bring the army or its generals into politics. The year 1812 represented a shift from one form of civilian regime to another. This new system was not put to the test. Neither the Bonapartes nor most of Napoleon's marshals survived his fall; the Senate and his closest ministers engineered his deposition in 1814, when the fighting had reached a virtual stalemate. Nor did full-scale regime change alter the continuance of civilian rule. The civil servants and their ministerial superiors continued to rule France under Louis XVIII. The *Grande Armée* was dismantled; the prefects continued to rule the departments, and the leading ministers of state remained to direct their work. The robotic "man-in-the-gray-suit" is the true heir of Napoleon, not the likes of Juan Perón or Franco.

That the Napoleonic regime was not a military dictatorship is not at all to say that it was not shaped in great part by the needs of the army and the wars it fought, however. No single factor drove the growth and impelled the effectiveness of the Napoleonic bureaucracy more than the war effort. These exigencies would thrust its presence and power into the heart of every village and, indeed, into the lives of every family under its sway. The wars intensified and accelerated trends of centralization and professionalization within the French state that predated the Revolution and whose aims were not solely the product of a military Leviathan. Nevertheless, this was the side of the state's activities that most people would see and feel with most force in the years it first gained ascendancy over civil society. Between 1800 and 1805, Napoleon set about pacifying France and the adjacent regions under his control, establishing the machinery of the state and then using it to forge a new and unheralded military establishment. The process began just before Napoleon's seizure of power in 1799 and, indeed, was a cause of it. As the French armies reeled from a series of crushing military defeats in 1798, the Directory, in its last days, enacted one of the most fundamental and enduring pieces of legislation in modern European history, the Jourdan Law (September 5, 1798), named after the deputy, himself a general, who introduced it. The Jourdan Law systematized conscription for the first time. Hitherto, the revolutionary regimes had called intermittently for huge levies of men on an ad hoc basis; henceforth, there would be regular levies on a smaller scale. Each department of France—which by now included all of present-day Belgium and much of the west bank of the Rhine—was assigned an annual quota of conscripts, based on its population, who would be chosen three times a year, according to the needs of the army. The whole process was to be administered by the civil service. Needless to say, in 1798, the numbers demanded were huge.

The reaction was massive and ferocious, if predictable. Peasant rebellions on a scale not seen since the first levies of 1793 swept across the Belgian departments and the southwest of France. In the west—the Vendée region and the Brittany-Normandy border, the scene of the first mass revolts against the Revolution—the guerrilla bands known as *chouans* ("sparrow hawks," from their warning signals) and many of the larger formations in the Vendée—found new energy, swelled by the ranks of deserters. The southeast and the Rhone valley, always troubled areas, also saw a resurgence of violence, now fueled by new recruits fleeing conscription to join the well-established counterrevolutionary bands. Over vast tracts of France, local authorities either caved in to the rebels or ran for cover; convoys carrying tax revenues and supplies destined for the armies were ambushed by guerrilla bands, whose hard cores may have been genuine royalists, political opponents of the Revolution, but whose bedrock of local support was now founded—and strengthened—by the imperative of resisting conscription. The net result was the collapse of the fragile law and order the Directory had come close to building in the late 1790s. This was the hard reality Napoleon faced over much of his state in 1799.

The rhetoric of the regime trumpeted peace and reconciliation among the warring factions of the Revolution, and, within the confines of the propertied and political elites, support for the regime soon became considerable. In the first years of its rule, aided by the achievement of international peace, the Consulate made real progress in making a reality of its twin policies of *ralliement*—the creation of a widespread consensus of passive support for the new government around the protection of property and the restoration of order—and *amalgame*—the bringing together of the various political factions in the service of the Consulate. Royalists found shelter under it, as well as former revolutionaries; men of both backgrounds worked loyally in its ranks, and these years were marked by a series of amnesties, especially directed at royalists who had emigrated during the Revolution. The Concordat reached with the Papacy reestablished a degree of normalcy in religious life, however circumscribed by the reforms of the Revolution or in comparison to the prominence of the Church under the old order. The regime's success in winning elite support has been seen in isolation, however. Its official polices of *ralliement* and *amalgame* won rapid support.[21] However, the success the regime enjoyed among the French elites masked the hard realities of provincial unrest, as Howard Brown has pointed out in a study destined to become seminal for our understanding of the period. Writing with immediate reference to southern France, he offers an analysis that has, in fact, a European dimension of applicability:

The war added a ready supply of accomplices in the form of draft dodgers, deserters, and escaped prisoners of war [to preexisting provincial disorder]. . . . However, it was not a removal of Jacobins from positions of power after Brumaire . . . or the defeat of royalist elsewhere in France, notably in the west, nor even the Concordat or the Peace of Amiens in 1802 that ended the cycle of violence . . . it was sustained, ruthless military repression.[22]

In truth, the desperate need of myriad communities to resist the application of the Jourdan Law eclipsed the other efforts of the new government to end the unrest of the revolutionary decade. Napoleon, having first had to fight a conventional war to establish his regime, now had to fight a series of civil wars to consolidate it. Napoleonic rule began with a concerted, ruthless "dirty war" to end the disorder rampant in most of revolutionary Europe, encompassing both politically inspired disorder and the common crime engendered by the breakdown of effective government inside and outside France in the course of the 1790s. The Consulate proclaimed social peace and political reconciliation repeatedly and profusely; it acted very differently, but its actions were decisive.

What was euphemistically called the process of pacification—then and since—was, in reality, a series of sustained and brutal paramilitary campaigns waged against recalcitrant civilian populations to secure the countryside. They were largely successful and were soon followed by the effective imposition of conscription and taxation, and thus the rebuilding of the exhausted French war machine. The Consulate quickly deployed the troops, now no longer needed for war service, to sweep the most recalcitrant parts of France. Mobile columns descended on the western departments, on the Rhone valley, and on most of southern France, executing far larger numbers of people than had been the case during the notorious "Terror" period of 1792–1794; they harried brigands and rounded up conscripts, and they usually did so in brutal fashion, which is hardly surprising. However, the Consulate matched this by its recourse to military justice to back the military process of repression. Civilian tribunals were, at least momentarily, set aside in Belgium and most of southern and western France, to be replaced by military commissions. Effectively, many regions were, temporarily, under martial law. Most commissions consisted of seven officers, many without any legal training or backgrounds; if limited in geographic scope, they had few other restraints upon their actions. At times, they adopted a policy of executing offenders on the spot, rather than in the urban centers like Avignon, where they were based, as a way of instilling terror into the populations of the areas known most for trouble. As Brown has put it, "Bonaparte reached for the military commissions to cut the Gordian knot," but the cumulative consequence of military repression "reduced relations between the new regime and (these) communities . . . to two factors: force and fear."[23] The most peaceful years of the Napoleonic regime were, in reality, a living hell for vast numbers of those who lived under it.

The pattern of repression carefully constructed by Howard Brown for southern and western France was replicated wherever the French advanced in the course of Napoleonic expansion. Effectively, that meant the whole of western Europe. In the same years that the military commissions of Nice, Avignon, and other centers in France set about their work, identical operations took place in the newly acquired departments of Piedmont, in northwestern Italy. French occupation was met by large-scale revolts in its northern province of Aosta, in 1801 and again in 1802, which were dealt with by military commissions, at a point when Piedmont was not yet formally a part of France; like their counterparts in the interior, the military commissions were short lived. At annexation, however, two new military commissions were established, in Turin and in Alessandria, and, in 1804, the military governor of the region, General Menou, prolonged their life indefinitely. They began to be wound down only in 1808, after the defeat of the two major brigand bands of southern Piedmont. Across the Alps, in regions "hit," as it were, by the Jourdan Law at the same time as France, Menou kept the aggressive spirit of the early Consulate alive for far longer than in France.[24] Moreover, this pattern was repeated on the annexation of Parma and Piacenza, in 1805, and of Tuscany, in 1808, when the introduction of conscription helped to trigger large, if short-lived, peasant revolts in the valley communities of the Apennines.[25] On each occasion, the French dealt with them by military justice, mobile guillotines, and the ruthless methods of "pacification" first deployed on their own territory in the early years of Consular rule.[26] When the French pushed further afield and met even fiercer, more sustained resistance, especially in the Kingdom of Naples and in parts of Spain like Aragón and Navarre, where they established a precarious hold, the policies and patterns of official behavior detected by Howard Brown in "the interior" were perpetuated yet again.[27]

It is little wonder that "pacification" behind the lines—indeed, in time of peace, technically defined—generated responses and folk memories as vivid and bitter as anything wrought by conventional military conflict. It was probably in Navarre, on her way to her father in Madrid in 1808, that the young George Sand met a tame magpie, trained by her innkeeper owner to shout at the little girl over and over, "Death to the French!" while scraping its beak on the bars of its cage.[28] Within France, itself, a study that casts the repression of the Vendée as a deliberate policy of "cleansing" by the revolutionary government and asserts its "will to wipe from the earth all trace of this rebel people . . . constitutes the definition of genocide" was based in part on a local oral tradition that was still alive in the 1960s.[29] The opening chapter—the moment of first contact, to borrow from the discourse of the historiography of colonialism—was usually as bloody and cruel as anything meted out to colonial peoples. Napoleon swept ruthlessly into his own hinterlands and his new territories beyond France, as he tried to do in the Caribbean colony of Saint Domingue (present Haiti) in the same years. Vendéans, Provençales, Belgians, and Piedmontese were dealt the same rough hand as the rebel slaves led by Toussaint L'Ouverture, but without the jungle and malarial swamps to protect them and ensure their victory.[30]

There would be lasting benefits from Napoleonic rule, even if they were occluded by the specter of conscription, "the blood tax," as it was called by contemporaries. The greatest irony of the period, for the vast civilian populations of the inner empire, was to live simultaneously under the new, genuinely egalitarian justice of the Code and the exigencies of conscription. The former would make a wholesale restoration of noble or corporate privilege difficult, and usually impossible, after 1814; the latter, however, engendered a permanent threat of peasant revolt throughout the period in many places. The state, through the prefects, was there to protect the rights of the individual and his property, but he was also there to tax and conscript. It was the process of conscription that brought the state closest to its hinterlands and changed forever its relationship to the peoples of western Europe. The process was ruthless and unrelenting. Isser Woloch has shown in some detail the triumph of the Napoleonic state in imposing itself on the most remote and initially recalcitrant part of France, the departments of the Massif Central. The permanent presence of the prefects to organize and lead tri-annual mobile columns, but backed by an efficient bureaucracy that knew the population profile of each department and its subdivisions, simply wore the peasant villages of the Massif down to the point that, by 1810, they were among the most reliable "suppliers" of conscripts in the Empire.[31] Woloch emphasizes the new relationship this created between the state and the citizen, even on the most remote periphery: conscription, however hateful, came to be seen as an inevitable duty, comparable with taxation. There was another response to its imposition, however, even where it proved successful. Alan Forrest's series of integrated regional studies of resistance to conscription in France would seem to indicate that the relentless tours of gendarmes and mobile columns of troops to wrest conscripts from the countryside often produced an effect in direct contrast to that outlined by Woloch. Resistance might have been largely unsuccessful as the period progressed, and it certainly became more localized, never attaining the widespread proportions of open rebellion as in the early years. Nonetheless, the need to thwart the "blood tax" and its collectors served to perpetuate and intensify many traditions of local solidarity and a collective identity forged in revolt that were anathema to the economic and social individualism embodied in the Code.[32]

Beyond the borders of France proper, Forrest's thesis, rather than Woloch's, seems more the norm, even in areas where conscription soon came to function as smoothly as, if not more smoothly than, in the interior. The Rhineland and the Italian departments of the French Empire are cases in point. The Napoleonic empire moved into a traditional power vacuum in western Europe; in terms of *Realpolitik,* that meant that it simply absorbed the territories of small weak states, and, in direct imitation, the middle German states—Napoleon's most loyal allies and willing clones—did the same in the tiny former states of the Bishop Electors and Imperial Knights. These regions had no prior experience of conscription. Referring to the Rhineland, Michael Rowe has astutely observed how military service actually reversed its normal function in the region through the transition from Reich territory to French departments:

The recruitment by foreign powers of Rhenish troops throughout the eighteenth century represented an economic transaction rather than an act of compulsion. Arguably such recruitment, far from being socially disruptive, smoothed social tension by removing young men living on the fringe of an over-populated region.[33]

No longer. The new regime simply imposed military service as a duty of citizenship; it was part of being a member of the new regime, no more, no less. The region poured out conscripts, as the demands of war mounted: as early as 1804–1805, the first year in which these departments were part of France in wartime, their quotas exceeded the French average by 8 percent; by 1810, they surpassed it by 42 percent. Conscription was resisted, just the same, and in ways that strengthened communal bonds, rather than weakened them. Many deserters and draft dodgers found protection and alternative livelihoods in that other major expression of resistance to Napoleonic rule, smuggling. Indeed, conscription created a world that pitted united communities against increasingly careerist bureaucrats, who saw that advancement depended, above all, on the successful enforcement of the "blood tax." Overt, violent resistance became increasingly rare in the Rhineland, but subtler forms of evasion, such as falsification of records and specious medical exemptions paid for communally, multiplied.[34]

A more poignant example still comes from the experience of the Tyrol, traditionally an Alpine province of the Habsburg monarchy that enjoyed many privileges as a region. The Tyrolese not only enjoyed exemption from numerous taxes and their own customs' regime, which was especially lucrative in an area which commanded mountain passes between Italy and Germany, but also were free from military service. Rather like the Piedmontese peasantry and inhabitants of the provinces of Navarre and Catalonia, in Spain, the Tyrolese voluntarily provided local militias for the Habsburgs, but only for regional service. When Joseph II tried to impinge on these provincial rights in the 1780s, he was met with fierce resistance that should have served as a clear warning to future rulers.[35] Following the war of 1805 against Austria, Napoleon awarded the Tyrol to Bavaria, his loyal German ally. Its ruler, Max Joseph, and his first minister, Montgelas, soon proved how akin their vision of the state was to that of the French, as they forced upon the Tyroleans their version of the Code, their religious reforms modeled on the Concordat, the abolition of all local fiscal privileges in the name of the Continental system, and the introduction of conscription. An area once noted for its dynastic loyalty and the propensity of its men to fight for a distant ruler soon rose in one of the most widespread and serious rebellions the Napoleonic regime would ever face. It took enormous resources, drawn from France and the Kingdom of Italy, to suppress the rebels, under the charismatic leadership of an innkeeper, Andreas Hofer, whom Napoleon ranked with the Vendean leaders and who really bears comparison with the chief of the Navarrese guerrillas, Espoza y Mina.[36] The Tyrolean revolt is illustrative of how the new concept of the state, and particularly the institution of conscription, could drive a civilian population to revolt and thrust relatively humble men like Hofer to the forefront of public life. It was a pattern already present in the Vendée in the mid-1790s, when Jacques Cathlineau, a man whose background and temperament were remarkably similar to those of Hofer, rose to prominence in the "Royal and Catholic Army." This was seen again, in the Spanish guerrilla, or in the far-from-famous leaders of the revolt of 1805–1806 in the Piacentino, the innkeeper and local militia captain Giuliano Brandini and his "chief of staff," Rivar, a local surgeon.[37] All these men were thrust from genuine obscurity to the forefront of history, however briefly, by the need of their communities to resist the Napoleonic "package" of conscription, taxation, and "pacification." Napoleon's quip that there was a Marshal's baton in the knapsack of every common soldier was not without foundation when the composition of his officer corps is examined, but, ironically, it proved even more the case among the men who chose to resist him. The Tyrolean revolt is revealing, in a very different context, of the new order emerging in western Europe, in the lands most firmly under Napoleonic hegemony. Hofer's rebellion was one of the most serious of the period, yet it was provoked not directly by Napoleon or by the presence of the French state but by Bavaria and by Bavarian officials. The Tyrol is, perhaps, the most dramatic illustration of the extent to which Napoleon's allies chose to imitate his model of government, even when not compelled to do so. It was a marker for the future of the continent.

The shock of mass conscription was even greater in the small Italian states, none of which had any prior experience of it, save Piedmont, where it took the form of local militia service, specifically for self-defense. Indeed, the small states of Parma-Piacenza, Tuscany, Liguria, and the Papal states were among the least governed, generally, in Europe. Napoleonic rule, initially and primarily through the process of conscription, brought them, quite literally, kicking, screaming, and fighting into modern political culture. These little states were models of what might be termed "government at one remove." The state had little part to play in the lives of the communities of the Apennine valleys until the arrival of the French under Napoleon. Their links to the nominal capitals of their countries were the clergy and ties of patronage and clientage through noble landowners; justice worked less on the enforcement of laws handed down from the center of power than through the arbitration of magistrates sent from the capital but respected for their sensitivity to local patterns of power, interest, and conflict. As in the patchwork of small German states destroyed by the connivance of Napoleon and the "middle princes" between 1800 and 1805, the Italian states were simply too small to merit standing armies; the absence of any higher allegiance than to their own states—unlike those of the old Reich—removed them still further from the wars of the period and provided no incentive to take foreign service. Only in the late 1790s, following the first French invasions of Italy, did some men from these regions find their way into Austrian service. Those who did were isolated examples, as witnessed in the ferocious and well-supported, if short-lived, rebellions that followed the regions' annexation by France. Few institutions could have been more alien to such communities than conscription, but the matrix of centralized government through prefects and codified law that followed it rammed home the alien nature of the new regime. Tuscany had gone so far as to abolish the death penalty in the 1780s, but the arrival of the French in 1808 brought with it the well-established cycle of conscription, rebellion, military commissions, and mass public executions that established in the minds of all classes, from the most exalted magistrates in Florence to the poorest, most isolated peasant communities, the gulf between the Napoleonic order and their indigenous traditions. Conscription emerges from such relationships as a talisman for an even greater estrangement between political cultures.

The process of conscription brought the state closer to society than would otherwise have been the case. In normal conditions, which never applied in the Napoleonic period, a prefect was obliged to patrol his department once a year; the demands of conscription forced him to do so three times annually and often—especially from 1812 on—four times. Even in the most peaceful parts of Europe, these tours were, essentially, another form of mobile column. The prefect sallied forth from his departmental capital, the *chef lieu,* accompanied by a company of regular troops, to visit each canton, the headquarters of the justices of the peace and the paramilitary police, the Gendarmerie, where the ballot for the draft was held. All the local mayors as well as the conscripts gathered in the cantonal towns for the balloting process, the *tirage.* Along the way, however, and at these meetings, the prefects inspected the local infrastructures; roads, bridges, schools, and hospitals were all assessed, petitions were heard, and a full range of administrative business was discussed with mayors and justices of the peace. Napoleonic prefects, without exception, came to know their people and their territory better than any officials of central government before them. The state came "armed to the teeth" and often in belligerent mood, for the troops and the gendarmes were to seek out and arrest any conscript who failed to report and often to occupy the villages to which they belonged or even to take their relatives hostage. The administrative apparatus of conscription was very sophisticated; the archives it left behind reveal a complex, highly evolved bureaucratic culture, but its edge was, literally, cutting, if it met resistance, and it usually did.

In all of these cases, within France and outside it, perhaps the most important aspect of the impact of conscription is the collective, communal character of resistance to the "blood tax." Some regions actually won the battle: the departments of the Vendée were given deliberately light quotas by Napoleon, and most of the conscripts in western France actually came from the towns, which were largely loyal to the regime; Calabria, in the Kingdom of Naples, was exempted entirely. Joseph did not even try, in his Kingdom of Spain, nor did Napoleon encourage him. These examples represent tributes to collective belligerence on a massive scale. The rest of western Europe was not so fortunate, but it did not stop trying. On one level, the success of conscription marks a triumph of bureaucratic organization, determined policing, and devotion to duty by the prefects and their staffs worthy of any elite unit of the *Grande Armée.* Perhaps its most salient impact on the military history of the period came in 1812, in the immediate aftermath of the slaughter of the Russian campaign. Napoleon knew he would be able to fight on—and did so for another two years—because his system of recruitment ensured that he had more than 100,000 conscripts waiting in the depots when the remains of his army finally reached Poland. It did the same for him, again, in 1814, when he was thrown back over the Rhine. Indeed, part of his rationale for embarking on the 100 Days, the following year, was that the system had not yet been fully wound down by Louis XVIII, and that he could therefore count on a large troop contingent yet again.

The Napoleonic state had, decisively and with deadly consequences, successfully tapped the resources of the French nation, more than any of its predecessors. However, the whole process embittered the relationship between the state and the citizen to a degree that is so fundamental as to be incalculable. In peasant communities, the loss of able-bodied young men was a blow to the economy, not just to the families of those concerned. The balloting system was, by and large, fair, but it was also random. In such circumstance, no one was ever sure if he would escape the draft. Fear was permanent. It was possible to buy replacements for military service; this was not a policy the regime liked, but it gradually gave way to it, and it is, perhaps, in this exception to the general rule that the deepest resentment and dread of conscription can be detected among ordinary people. Replacements were costly, but they were not the preserve of the rich. The prices involved, and the relatively lowly incomes of those often "bought out," reveal collective "clubbing together" by extended families and local communities to preserve their future. Thus, the "blood tax" brought people together, not in service of "the Nation" but in defense of the lifeblood of what they knew best, their own villages and families. The prospect of military service taught them not to love country and crown but to cherish their localities. As the wars dragged on, even those initially favorable to conscription began to sense this. The large landowners of Tuscany at first saw the draft as a useful means of social control; they manipulated it to rid themselves of lazy tenants and rebellious elements in their midst, but, by 1812, they, too were complaining that the incessant drain on manpower was damaging agricultural production.

The upper classes came to detest conscription just as much as the peasantry, for the Napoleonic state devised ways to ensnare them in its service, but conscription's impact was felt most on individual elite families. Napoleon tended to tap the able pupils of the state *lycées* for induction into the military academies, and so many upper- and middle-class families began to avoid them. In the Rhineland, leading families sent their sons away to German universities to avoid what they saw as another form of conscription.[38] Many Italian families detested the virtual conscription of their sons into the elite ranks of the civil service just as much.[39] Quite apart from the threat of conscription, many French royalists and almost all the nobilities of the various Italian states conserved a distaste for their curriculum, not just because of its militarism but for its secular content and its emphasis on science and modern languages at the expense of traditional humanism. Noble reaction to the use of the *lycées* as an ill-disguised vehicle for elite conscription somewhat mirrored that of peasant communities, in that the nobility turned inward, becoming very tightly knit against intrusions by the state into their lives. Its most lasting effect was to distance traditional elites from the militaristic Napoleonic *lycées* and to rekindle clerical influence in the education of their young, usually at home. Napoleon had sought from the beginning to coax the old elites back into public life, but, instead, conscription forced them to the margins. For peasant youth, the margins were literal and geographic; they took to the hills and forests. For the sons of their former masters, the margins were cultural. Conscription helped drive a new generation of the European aristocracy into the waiting arms of the Jesuits.

There was far more to Napoleonic rule than the slaughter of the wars and the terror inspired by conscription, however. French hegemony engendered much that was new and different. What followed pacification was not the traditional brief, transient, if iron-fisted, razing of the countryside for men and supplies by the forces of the central government, who then disappeared. Instead, the Napoleonic state implanted itself in local communities, on the furthest reaches of the periphery, and stayed. This whole process marks a decisive turning point in the history of modern Europe, with consequences far more profound than those of the war effort that first spurred it. Behind the mobile columns and the military commissions with their mobile guillotines came a professional bureaucracy, centered on the prefects, created in 1800, and a civil judiciary that applied the Code Napoleon, finally realized in 1804, a legal order that placed equality before the law and open, public trials at its core. Rulers allied to Napoleon quickly saw the benefits of the Code as a method of undermining powerful noble and clerical interests, as in the German "middle states" of Bavaria, Baden, Württemberg, Hesse-Darmstadt, and Nassau, or in the Kingdom of Naples, where it had much less impact, despite the efforts of zealous reformers like Francesco Ricciardi. In areas that achieved a reasonable degree of pacification, or had never needed it, such as France, itself, the German Rhineland, or Lombardy, the Code often took root and changed the attitudes of all property holders, peasant proprietors, in particular, regarding what they expected from state justice. As peace returned, after however brutal a period of pacification, jury trials under professional magistrates came to replace the military commissions; the logic of the Code took over from "booted justice," and a new social order began to emerge as a result of this thoroughgoing legal revolution. Peasants could now face down their landlords in state courts, rather than manorial ones, on equal terms and assert their rights as owners. In 1814, when they acquired the Rhineland from Napoleon, the Prussians concluded that it was the procedures laid down by the Code, more than the laws themselves, that endeared it to them. Rhinelanders had come to value particularly public trial, trial by jury, and the independence of the judiciary from the administration, the cherished revolutionary axiom of the separation of powers. The Code became a surrogate constitution in the region,[40] and, with the coming of the Code, not only noble privilege but the trade guilds, with their powers of monopoly over professions, ecclesiastical immunities, and all forms of religious discrimination fell away. Almost everywhere, religious minorities rallied to Napoleonic rule: Catholics in the Netherlands and Baden, Protestants in France and Bavaria, Jews everywhere.

The institution of the Gendarmerie encapsulates the balance sheet, and the ironies, of Napoleonic rule in the inner empire, the most securely ruled of its territories. This paramilitary police force was a product of the wars, the cutting edge of the process of conscription, yet it was also the arm of the state that turned pacification from a process of military terror into an established order that paved the way for a genuinely policed, stable, and peaceful European countryside. Its most lasting contribution was not the ruthless enforcement of conscription but the security it brought isolated communities from disorder and violence. The men they rounded up for military service were not transformed into citizen-patriots, but the bandits, criminals, and thugs they apprehended along the way forced even the most reluctant communities to realize that the new state had benefits to offer. There had never been a police like the Gendarmerie before; old-regime France had possessed the *Maréchaussée*, a branch of the army responsible for patrolling the royal highways, but it was in no way comparable to the Gendarmerie, created during the Revolution but invigorated by Napoleon and expanded to every part of Europe annexed to France. The satellite states—the kingdoms of Holland, Naples, Italy, and Westphalia—all received carbon copies of the French force. It was drawn from veterans of the regular army, men normally two meters' in height, with basic literacy, who had served at least three campaigns and had clean records. It was not easy, always, to meet these standards, but the regime usually came very close. The corps was distributed across the countryside, and this, too, made it unique. For the first time in history, a central government had a permanent police presence on the periphery; every canton got a brigade of six men, usually housed in barracks, apart from the community they served, and they were almost always outsiders. Civilian populations everywhere now had a new presence in their midst, and it was to remain there forever. In some respects, the mobile columns of the early years of the Consulate were now made permanent, for the gendarmes were not loved and were a permanent reminder of the coercive power of the state. Yet, this was not the whole story, by any means. Where pacification had been successful, the corps devoted itself to setting new standards of law and order on the periphery.[41] In Piedmont, following the defeat of the great bandit-smuggler bands along the border with Liguria, gendarmes pursued packs of wolves with equal courage and determination in the dreadful winter of 1810–1811. The following year, they finally ended a vicious personal vendetta against the wine growers of the little town of La Rochetta Tanaro, where more than 800 vines had been deliberately vandalized.[42] It is through such seemingly insignificant local happenings that the contours of a new society can been seen emerging in those parts of Europe firmly under Napoleonic control. Where the French state took root, so did the Gendarmerie; a settled, permanent police force, under the tight control of the central government, paid regularly and subject to military discipline, brought new levels of state control over the civilian population but also higher standards of public peace than anything known hitherto.

It would be wrong to paint too glowing a picture of this process of transformation, however. The gendarmes were soldiers, veterans of the most brutal wars Europe had seen up to that time, and peasant communities could have more to complain about regarding the gendarmes than their role in enforcing conscription. Just as the Gendarmerie and the prefects often blurred the line between political rebellion and crime under the depoliticized catch-all of "brigandage,"[43] so the behavior of gendarmes could prove brutal and arbitrary. Nevertheless, the Napoleonic authorities pursued cases of indiscipline seriously, and, in most cases, local communities preferred to see individuals, rather than whole brigades, removed. The Gendarmerie was a Napoleonic institution that, for utterly different reasons, was embraced by rulers and ruled alike after the fall of the Empire in 1814. It offered real, effective protection to ordinary people, especially small-property holders who could not afford the private armies of semibandits common among the great landowners of southern Spain and Italy, while it gave rulers more power over their peripheries than they could ever have envisaged before the Napoleonic occupation. Thus, despite changes of name and uniform, almost all the restored states of western Europe adopted the corps, in some form or other, in the course of the early nineteenth century, and often—as in the cases of Piedmont-Savoy and the Netherlands—immediately.[44]

The gendarmerie, the replacement of military justice by the rule of the Code, jury trial, and the prefectoral system of civil administration marked the "settled" boundaries of Napoleonic hegemony, whether through direct rule from Paris or in the context of a satellite kingdom or allied state. They were the pillars of "the new regime" as first mapped out in Revolutionary France and so of a new society.[45] This all took place around a territorial core, however. The Napoleonic Empire, itself, was a transient affair; it did not last long. Within its secure borders, however, success in war brought the peoples of its core zones a new civic order. In so doing, the wars that forged a short-lived empire also traced subtler but enduring frontiers across Europe in ways that often defied political borders. Apolitical frontiers emerged, defined by the different experiences of civil societies caught up in different stages and degrees of the Napoleonic wars. In the inner empire, the state intruded and came to stay. In the outer lands of the Napoleonic hegemony, the wars swept through, and the collective effect is best subsumed under the condition of trauma. In the outer empire, its impact was seldom institutional or positive, but it was lasting and real, nonetheless.

TRAUMA: THE TIDES OF WAR IN THE
OUTER EMPIRE. TOWARD TWO EUROPES?

When the conditions of the inner and outer empires are taken together, they offer a contrast between the fundamentally different experiences of calm and continued trauma. As a result, new and enduring regions took shape, not marked on a political map but real nonetheless. The process began within France itself. Jean-Clément Martin puts it perfectly, at the start of his seminal study of the Vendée:

It is rare to witness the birth of a region. The origins of such things are generally lost in what it is convenient to call the mists of time. The *Vendée-militaire* is an exception to this. This region, which has never received official recognition, but that still retains a vital reality at the end of the twentieth century, was literally born during the French Revolution, through the convulsions of civil war.[46]

Years of Napoleonic rule and strong doses of "pacification" probably helped to entrench this particularism rather than eradicate it. What marked it out was not its geography or ethnography, but its relationship to the new political culture of the French Revolution; it did not adapt to the new regime. In his study of the Sarthe, Paul Bois traced one of the borders of the Vendée and found it running right through the middle of a French department. Bois certainly found important geographic, social, and economic difference between the pro- and counterrevolutionary parts of the Sarthe, yet they had never marked out stark cultural or political frontiers before the 1790s.[47] The world of western France had changed, and, as the French armies rolled forward, similar reconfigurations would emerge beyond the borders of France, usually on a much vaster scale. The Vendée serves as a good example of the fact that France was not entirely or uniformly part of Napoleon's inner empire. As the empire spread, so did similar cases of regions where pacification failed and French institutions were never absorbed and where the trauma of brutal occupation and fierce resistance were the hallmarks of Napoleonic hegemony.

There were parts of Europe to which the wars and Napoleonic came late and brutally, and there were areas where the wars never really went away, at least not sufficiently for the Napoleonic state to take root. The former regions were, on the one hand, the outposts of the last stages of imperial expansion, such as the North Sea Coast of Germany or the "Illyrian Provinces," modern Croatia and Slovenia, areas seized primarily for their strategic importance and to enforce the blockade. Beside them, but quite different, were areas such as Spain, the Kingdom of Naples—its southern province of Calabria, particularly—and even the Vendée region of France itself, where Napoleonic rule never really progressed beyond the ruthless period of "pacification" dominated by military commissions, mobile columns, and successful local resistance to conscription and taxation. Civil peace, reconstruction, and the rule of law never became the norm in any of these parts of Europe. Their civilian populations experienced a history different from that of the inner empire.

The driving rationale behind the creation of the outer empire was the economic war against Britain. Its two chief components were the blockade, hence the pattern of French expansion along the coastlines of northern Europe and the Mediterranean, and the implementation of the Continental System, first articulated coherently in the Berlin Decrees of 1806 and then through a series of treaties in the following years, all designed to reorient the economies of continental Europe away from maritime commerce and so away from Britain. Both policies ended in disaster, as well as failure, but they had rather different impacts on the inner and outer empires, and on different sectors of the economies of given regions. The impact of both the blockade and the System were largely transient; neither left any real marks on the long-term development of Europe. It looked very different at the time, however. Ports everywhere, inside and outside France, stagnated to the point of collapse. In the Dutch departments, whole communities joined together to thwart the blockade, working together in smuggling operations. Even Napoleon's brother, Louis, the King of Holland, took their side to the point that Napoleon deposed him in 1810 for his failure to crack down on his subjects. Opposition to the blockade could make for strange bedfellows, indeed, in the great ports. At the other end of Europe, in Barcelona, the French tried to "pack" the city's council with six French merchants resident in Barcelona, only to find that they readily took the side of the native commercial classes in such matters.[48] Further inland, the changes were more varied, and they could appear staggering. Napoleon operated a ruthless "one-way Common Market," as Louis Bergeron has put it, or what Geoffrey Ellis has termed, perhaps more correctly, a very "uncommon market."[49] The Continental System sought to eliminate all competitive industries outside a tariff line that embraced all of France, parts of the Rhineland, and modern Belgium but excluded the rest of Europe, even areas like Piedmont and Liguria, which were annexed directly to France. This led to the collapse of silk manufacturing in northern Italy and of metallurgy in Switzerland and in the Grand Duchy of Berg, in western Germany, with the resultant unemployment. It also often led to the simple redeployment of enterprises within the tariff barriers, as many German industrialists moved across the Rhine to Strasbourg. It could also bolster the agricultural sectors of the economy, as they now had the French market to supply, if usually on disadvantageous terms, although the results could vary so much that generalizations remain hard to make. Certain industries in France and the Belgian departments, protected artificially from British competition, enjoyed boom periods, mainly textiles and mining. Even this prosperity was fragile, however, conditioned as it was by the volatile, very limited markets for manufactured goods. The Continental System ruined many contemporary Europeans and helped others; it was a classic case of an innovation that had a spectacular short-term impact but that caused very few ripples once the political conditions that created it changed. At the time, however, it caused trauma.

In terms of the conventional political map of Europe, the zones of the inner and outer Napoleonic empire cut right across the future unified states of Italy and Germany. It is arguable that most of the Italian states of the old order, north and south, had more in common in terms of their political culture—or lack of it—than they had differences. After Napoleonic rule, this was no longer the case. The north, with the important exception of the Veneto, lived under Napoleonic rule for most of the period. Its elites knew the Code; its people, however reluctantly, lived under conscription, regular taxation, a sedentary Gendarmerie diffused over the countryside, and a professional bureaucracy, the essence of which was retained by both the Austrians and the Savoyards after 1814. They had also been freed from banditry and disorder in the same manner, and at the same time, as their French counterparts. Nothing could have been further from the experience of the Kingdom of Naples or the core of the Papal state, where "pacification," rampant brigandage, and failed reforms marked the period of Napoleonic rule. Whereas before 1800, all the Italian states had known recalcitrant peripheries, intrinsic disorder, and an "organic" social order, not dependent on an organized state, after Napoleon the north had changed, but the south had not. The heritage of this would be reaped after unification, in the 1860s, when a north long habituated to the norms of the civil order of what Isser Woloch had termed "the new regime" responded to the southern status quo with military commissions, mobile columns, martial law, and a panoply of "pacification" programs of its own. The frustration felt by the Bolognese, who had been part of the Kingdom of Italy, at their return to the ramshackle rule of the Papacy provides a tangible fault line between the two Italys,[50] much as does Bois's analysis of the Sarthe for France. This is mirrored in Germany by the difficult relationship between Prussia and its new Rhenish province after 1814. The Prussians did much more to ameliorate the integration of a former part of the inner empire with a state beyond the Napoleonic state system by retaining the Code there, but the gap in their respective political cultures was perceived by all. It was also signaled by Metternich's reluctant agreement to retain Napoleonic-derived reforms in the middle states and to their culmination in the granting of limited constitutions in Bavaria, Baden, and Württemberg soon after 1814. Taken together, the lands of the "inner empire"—the Low Countries, western and southern Germany, northern Italy, and northern and eastern France—formed a new macro region in Europe. It lost its political expression in 1814, yet it was here that the Napoleonic system of government took root quite firmly and reemerged after the Second World War as the core of the contemporary European Union.[51] It also marked it out from the rest of Europe.

As a general rule, many factors that helped to shape consensus and to achieve *ralliement* to the regime in the inner empire had precisely the reverse effect in the outer empire. Whereas the campaigns of pacification, however brutal, when followed swiftly by the implementation of the Code and the Concordat, resulted in winning the support of wide sections of the propertied classes for the new regime,[52] in much of central and southern Italy, Spain, and the Illyrian provinces, this tested process engendered not only ferocious initial resistance but also deep-rooted alienation from the institutions and political culture of the new order. The Concordat brought a degree of normalcy to religious life in most of France, the Belgian departments, and the Rhineland, and even to the Piedmontese departments and the Italian Republic, at least until the definitive rift with Rome, in 1809. These areas had witnessed the worst excesses of de-Christianization during the Terror period, and the Directory had done little to reverse policies and conduct by the government that were far from conciliatory to the Catholic Church.

The Concordat should not be overpraised, however. It did not restore the regular orders; it continued to prohibit the most popular and well-supported High Days and their attendant processions; it maintained equality of religion, rather than toleration. Nevertheless, it was generally seen as a blessing, if a mixed one, in most of the inner empire. When Napoleon extended the Concordat beyond these areas, however, it was perceived as an attack on a living organism at the heart of society. In essence, its terms only took away; they gave nothing, and the net result was a cultural trauma that struck every community with the same force, if hardly the same degree of urgency, as the arrival of conscription. Communities saw the French conquest followed by the brutal closure of monasteries and convents, usually by regular troops, together with the mass arrest and deportation of clergy who defied the new regime by refusing the oath of allegiance to the Napoleonic state, a drama played out in France since 1791 and largely resolved after the Concordat. All of this culminated in the deposition, arrest, and incarceration of Pope Pius VII, in 1809, followed by his excommunication of Napoleon.

It was much the same with the Code, for all too often its introduction came on the heels of campaigns of "pacification" that could not hope to win the support they did in areas that had been subject to the political anarchy of the 1790s. In places like Parma-Piacenza, Spain, Tuscany, or the Kingdom of Naples, the revolts had been anti-French, first and foremost, however many local vendettas were incorporated into them; the resultant repression could never realistically be perceived by most communities as anything other than brutal conquest. There were signs, it must be said, that the routine of ruthless pacification followed by impartial centralization was winning the French a limited degree of support in the most unprepossessing of soils of Calabria and even in parts of Spain, notably Valencia and Asturias.[53] In Calabria, the presence of the British and the exiled Bourbons in nearby Sicily ensured that any and all sources of opposition to the Napoleonic regime in Naples were ruthlessly exploited. By and large, this meant supporting brigandage, centered on the bands of retainers in the pay of the barons, who were determined to thwart the implementation of the Code. The result was often a civil war that involved the towns, outside baronial control, and the bandits. In parts of Spain, the exactions of the guerrillas were often as onerous as and more capricious than those of the French.[54] Nevertheless, the general trend always remained one of hostility and withdrawal from cooperation when revolt had ceased to be feasible. The people of the Piacentino valleys, the center of the revolt against the French in Parma, never turned to the new French courts and therefore shunned the Code during the entire period of the postrevolt annexation, 1806–1814.[55] In Tuscany, magistrates and people of all classes alike balked at the sight of the guillotine and the conduct of the military commissions in a state that had abolished capital punishment in the 1780s, as has been seen. They were equally appalled by the concept of open, public trials, however, because the Tuscan consensus, like that in many other Italian states, was that this would prevent fair, dispassionate justice, rather than guarantee it.[56]

Thus, there was nothing to follow pacification and repression but alien occupation. Even in relatively secure areas, such as central Italy, the grip of the new regime could be exposed as tenuous. The year 1809 saw a series of inchoate but massive peasant rebellions against the Kingdom of Italy across central Italy; they were sparked by the imposition of new taxes but quickly developed into assaults on the cities of the region as centers of alien government, and the ranks of the mountain communities that started the revolt were soon swollen by hordes of deserters and draft dodgers. The rebels never achieved a coherent program or leadership, and the revolts dissipated and subsided as much as they were crushed. These events shook the local authorities badly, and they were followed by the pattern of mobile columns and military commissions that many had hoped were now in the past. These revolts did not take place as a response to military advances or the prospect of the liberation of the region; rather, one of their most remarkable characteristics is that they occurred after the 1809 Wagram campaign and bore no relation to it.[57] In many regions of the outer empire, where the administration and the Gendarmerie had little real control, resistance to conscription simply took the form of massive transhumance. French officials in the Illyrian provinces wrung their hands as virtually the entire male population of parts of Dalmatia and Croatia simply crossed into the Ottoman Empire at the very rumor of the draft; the population of the city of Rome fell drastically, if only momentarily, between 1809 and 1814, as its youth did the same, either joining the bandits in the mountains or crossing into the Kingdom of Naples. The overall response of vast tracts of Europe to the new regime was first to oppose it and then to avoid it. Strictly speaking, none of this was a direct consequence of military events, but the course of the Napoleonic wars brought about enormous changes in the political configuration of Europe, with deeply significant ramifications for the future. It is in these wider ripples, perhaps more than in the fighting per se, that the lasting impact of the wars is to be found.

Nowhere is this truer, than on the outer fringes of the empire, especially in a country the French did not annex or even occupy for long, Portugal. Once the British had established a firm defensive base there, they set about transforming a whole society to create a springboard against Napoleon. With the royal family in Brazil, Lord Beresford became the virtual dictator of the country, and he set about turning it into a "barracks state" that far outdid anything seen in Napoleonic France. Portugal under the old order had been a weak, ineffectual state, although not one untouched by ideas of enlightened reform. Under the impact of the unsuccessful French invasion of 1808, Portuguese society had simply slipped into anarchy. Beresford changed this entirely: the resources of the whole country were mobilized for the war effort, and his "Orders of the Day"—ruthlessly enforced first by Wellington's British troops but then by a new Portuguese army—reveal the progressive militarization of a whole society. The result was an army that won sustained victories over the French, and won the confidence and respect of the British, as did no other. It also left a hitherto peaceful country with a swollen, martial officer corps that did not leave politics or cease to dominate political life until the 1970s. In terms of the war's impact on civilians, the Portuguese probably suffered more, proportionately, than any other European society. Its population fell by more than a quarter of a million between 1808 and 1814, dislocation that had less to do with the fighting than with the "scorched-earth" tactics conducted by Wellington and Beresford along its border with Spain, resulting in losses of production and infrastructure that proved impossible to repair after 1814.[58] The Portuguese experience most approximates that of "total war" in the Napoleonic period, and it was the work of the British, who rapidly dismantled their own massive war machine in 1814–1815. It was not the work of the Napoleonic state, nor did it bear many of its characteristics. In 1808, Portugal had been a weak, maritime country, quietly aspiring, intermittently, to a degree of enlightened absolutism. By 1814, it was an economic colony of Britain, a militarized society under the authoritarian rule of a regency that imposed far harsher censorship than had Napoleon. Portugal's metamorphosis was almost accidental, but none was more complete. Such are the hazards of war.

The experience of Portugal was rare, in the comprehensiveness, intensity, and longevity of the changes the country underwent as a result of the wars, but the experience of much of the "outer empire" and the regions it bordered was also, if not equally, one of destabilization and trauma. Spain's suffering was widespread and long outlasted the wars; Calabria underwent a similar, if more localized, upheaval that compounded decades of instability. Indeed, the impact of the Napoleonic wars on the Balkans is often overlooked, but it was seminal in inflaming the region, however indirectly. Quite apart from the dislocations wrought by the French occupation of the Illyrian provinces, all the great powers—Russia, the Habsburgs, Britain, and France—poured arms and aid into the region, sometimes to destabilize the Ottomans, sometimes to prop them up. Both the British and the French courted the renegade warlord Ali Pasha, who controlled much of western Greece and southern Albania. Contemporaries dubbed him "the Lion of Jannina," his capital, and Balzac saw him as the only man of his age who was the equal of Napoleon. The Turks dealt with him only after 1814, when all foreign aid collapsed.[59] Likewise, the Austrians and Russians, often with British help, intermittently fostered a series of Serb revolts. Just as in Spain and Calabria, their interest in the region abated after 1814, but the arms they had flooded into the region, and the unrest they fed, did not. The first bitter harvest of all this was reaped in the revolutions of 1820–1821, which swept through Greece, Spain, Portugal, and the Kingdom of Naples. Whereas these revolts were only the beginning of a new cycle of conflict in these regions, the formerly bandit-infested lands of the north Italian valleys and the Rhine settled down, after years of Napoleonic rule, into one of the most stable borders in Europe. Lines had been drawn of far deeper significance than those consecrated by the powerbrokers of Vienna.

The British experience is a telling counterpoint to that of Portugal. No other European state so immersed itself in the war effort against Napoleon, yet no other emerged from the decades of conflict less altered in its fundamental institutions. Britain was never seriously invaded; it never knew the "new regime" of the Napoleonic state system at first hand, nor did it ever feel the temptation—as did its allies Prussia and Austria or even "patriot" Spain—to copy Napoleonic methods to defeat him. Linda Colley's seminal thesis is that the anti-Napoleonic struggle drew together the disparate parts of the United Kingdom into a "British identity," ending a process that had begun a century earlier with the wars against Louis XIV.[60] If it changed Britain and the British, it did so according to their own, indigenous agendas, not as a direct, conscious reaction to occupation, the loss of traditional institutions and values, or the wholesale imposition of an alien public sphere. Indeed, the British ruling classes consciously turned away from reform in this period, seeing it as a product of foreign, essentially French influences that had pervaded movements for political change far too much in the 1790s.

This not to say that Britain did not change during the course of the wars, for it did. War industries, the emergence of a gigantic naval juggernaut and the creation, virtually from scratch, of a massive land army were cardinal changes from the condition of the country in the 1790s, and the triumph of monstrous effort and organization. The Royal Navy in 1793 could barely man a dozen ships of the line, with its strength of 16,000 men. By 1814, its manpower—raised through press gangs as brutal as, if less organized than, the mechanisms of Napoleonic conscription—was close to 200,000; it had more than 140 ships of the line at sea. The growth of the army is even more remarkable. In 1793, two-thirds of its 45,000 troops were overseas; in 1814, at the conference of Chaumont, Castlereagh could count on 160,000 men in the field and was able to tell his allies that Britain could put a quarter of a million more men in the field and keep them there for ten years, unaided, if it had to. However, in a flash, all this disappeared in 1815—not only because Britain was a victor in the war; this was so for every state except France. It was also reflected the fact that Britain was still a civilian state, run by civilian institutions, accountable to other civilians, the electorate. The British parliamentary system was anything but democratic by modern standards, but responsive enough to public opinion to dismantle a war machine that most people always believed was a temporary expedient. It was too expensive, too open to corruption. The clearest sign of the rise of a new middle class, and of its influence on government, was arguably this process of dismantling the military-fiscal state engendered by the wars, which paved the way for the Victorian model of cheap government. The older elites, centered on the squirarchy and local influence, combined with these newer, more urban and business-based influences to perpetuate the most liberal elements of the old order; parliamentary government and a state that was decentralized and unmilitarized. Britain never resorted to anything resembling the prefectoral system or mass conscription, at least for the army.[61]

OPPORTUNITY AND LOSS

The Revolutionary-Napoleonic wars were of inordinate length, the period of general peace between 1800 and 1805 notwithstanding. They drew in a generation and a half of Europeans and shaped the lives of many more people than those who did the fighting or even those who endured it. Above all, they spawned a huge new European land empire and a new political order to govern it. In the process, new men emerged to run it, and others were pushed aside to make way for them. The wars opened Europe to any Frenchman prepared to "rally" to Napoleon and to "amalgamate" himself with the political culture of the new regime. The "carrot" of the Marshal's baton in the knapsack of the common soldier had its civilian equivalent in the unprecedented opportunities and challenges available in the imperial civil service. The Napoleonic wars produced the Napoleonic empire, which, in turn, begot a thrusting generation of colonial administrators imbued with ambition, if soon thrust into obscurity. War offers prospects to more than those in uniform, if seldom in equal measure to the misery and fear it doles out to the mass of civilians.

France was remarkably well positioned to run a large empire. It enjoyed an enviable set of circumstances, being the most populous state in Europe, with vast reserves of potential conscripts and one of the largest pools of educated people on the continent. The sudden acquisition of vast new territories harnessed both these human resources to imperial expansion: The first gave France its huge armies, while the second provided it with a large pool of able administrators. The French had learned the principles of administrative centralization and organization in the course of the 1790s; its educated classes were well prepared to harness and systematize the resources that military conquest brought into Napoleon's lap. They needed to be, lacking the sophisticated financial infrastructures the British had created in the eighteenth century or the geographical impregnability of their other main rival, Russia, to say nothing of the technologies of transport, communications, and armaments that emerged a few decades later. Napoleon tapped the enthusiasm and loyalty of a significant segment of ambitious, educated Frenchmen, and they discovered Europe on their own terms in his service. They are personified by Norvins, already cited, and—above all—by the great novelist Henri Beyle, known as Stendhal. In his best-known novels, *The Red and the Black* and *The Charterhouse of Parma*, published after the fall of Napoleon, he lamented the lost horizons of that part of his cohort who took up the challenge of empire, and mourned its passing.

Norvins and Stendhal were the spokesmen for a wide constituency, just as their Napoleonic careers had been representative of the experience of a generation. Typical of them, if young men from comfortable backgrounds prepared to go to the jagged edges of empire are ever typical of anything, were Armand Binet and Gilbert Boucher, newly qualified lawyers who served as public prosecutors in the troubled departments of central Italy. They acquired the reputation of "troubleshooters" in bandit-infested regions, and on potentially weak tribunals. They suffered from the local climate but never shirked their duty. Boucher became a "golden boy," eventually sent to deal with the highest court in Rome, where he was disliked by his Italian colleagues but respected by his French superiors. Binet emerged as undisciplined but brave and energetic, a man for a recalcitrant imperial posting, an individualist who would have as much trouble settling in peacetime as any demobilized veteran.[62] They were but two of many, for the imperial service became a haven for the ambitious, the restless, and the unruly, soldiers and civilian officials alike. Stendhal and Norvins were simply the most articulate among them.[63] Looking to the future, and to how these conflicts would be perceived by later generations, it is to Stendhal and his ilk, in fiction, and to Norvins, in historiography, that we owe the birth of the Napoleonic Legend, for few wars have been so draped in romance and glamor as these. They were the first exponents of the legend Sudhir Hazareesingh has eloquently pinpointed as nostalgia for a past of unbridled possibilities in an era of shrinking ones:

To all those individuals who felt trapped by the accidents of birth, the weight of social convention, or the constraints of economic circumstances, the Emperor provided a galvanizing ideal of ambition, emancipation, and achievement through personal effort. . . . And to a nation traumatized by military decline, the fear of "decadence", and the threat of physical annihilation, the Emperor's legend responded with the enduring hope of that most sacred of ideas: the achievement of immortality.[64]

Napoleon incarnated war itself, not just those he happened to fight, and, with that, all the possibilities war opens up for those who survive it. In perhaps the finest irony of all, his life became the chief instrument of coping with defeat for those who rose so high, so fast in his wake.

The nostalgia of Napoleon's supporters for the "glory," excitement, and opportunity of the Napoleonic adventure and for the shadow of their exiled, incarcerated leader bore little resemblance to the nostalgia and sense of loss still felt by their political opponents after 1814, however. Chateaubriand, Napoleon's *bête noire* throughout their shared life, and the most eloquent and complex spokesman for reaction, believed that, like Louis XIV before him, Napoleon had shaped his century. But for Chateaubriand, the new century was not a pretty sight. He thought in other terms of loss:

The glorification of our sovereign cost us a mere two or three hundred thousand men a year; we have paid for it with only three million of our soldiers; our fellow citizens have paid for it the paltry price of their suffering and their freedom for fifteen years: is it worth counting such bagetelles? Are not the generations who will follow us to be resplendent? What a shame for those who have disappeared! . . . Never could any genius, any superior being make me agree to [a regime] where one word could deprive me of my freedom, of my home, of my friends. If I have not mentioned my fortune or my honor, it is because it seems to me that fortune is not worth the price of defending it; as for honor, it eludes tyranny: it concerns the souls of martyrs, and the bonds that bind, rather than enchain; it pierces the walls of prisons and carries with it all that is a man.[65]

Chateaubriand was, supposedly, among the winners in 1814, but his thoughts would never betray this. Read carefully, Chateaubriand came out of the wars with nothing more than his honor, surviving into an alien world, Napoleon having destroyed all that mattered from the past. Peter Fritzsche has seen Chateaubriand, in particular, as emblematic of how people in the nineteenth century understood and interpreted the passage of time: his life was defined by loss and alienation, brought about by the French Revolution and, by extension, Napoleon, from whose armies he continually fled. Chateaubriand and his fellow émigrés, for Fritzsche, "encountered the new century from the perspective of displaced persons."[66] It is a sage judgment, but one that could equally be made of his opponents.

In human terms, whether in the shattered limbs of veterans, the unrecorded grief of families left behind, or the more tangible context of the decay and damage done to whole countries, it was a war no one won, save the British propertied classes that now dominated international trade through the Royal Navy and soon withdrew into isolation behind it. In comparison with the horrors to come, the Napoleonic wars wreaked precious little material damage, given their length and scale. The great ports of Europe soon flourished again, after the end of the blockade; the real threat to most industry and commerce was soon seen to come from Britain, not the Continental System. However brutal it had been during its short life; the fields of the inner empire, at least, were soon tended again, now guarded by proper police forces. "Total war" and its indelible scars were not with the world just yet. These had been wars fought and won through human prowess, through mental skills of organization and raw courage, through tactics and strategy, not through technology. They were the work of humans, and it is somehow fitting that their most lasting marks on humanity should be in the psyche and on the soul.

NOTES

1. Darrin McMahon, *Enemies of the Enlightenment. The French Counter-Enlightenment and the Making of Modernity* (New York: Oxford University Press, New York, 2002), 202.

2. John M. Roberts, "The Italian States," in *The New Cambridge Modern History*, vol. VIII, *The American and French Revolutions 1763–1793* (Cambridge: Cambridge University Press, 1976), 378.

3. Cited in Timothy C. W. Blanning, *The French Revolutionary Wars, 1787–1802* (London: Arnold, 1996), 235.

4. Jean Morvan, *Le Soldat imperial*, 2 vols. (Paris: Plon-Nourrit, 1904), 1: 287–288.

5. Rory Muir, *Tactics and the Experience of Battle in the Age of Napoleon* (New Haven: Yale University Press, 1998), 76.

6. Ibid., 43–44.

7. Nicholas A. M. Rodger, *The Command of the Ocean: A Naval History of Britain, 1649–1815* (London: Allen Lane, 2004).

8. Geoffrey Ellis, *The Napoleonic Empire* (Basingstoke: Palgrave, 2003), 113–120, for a masterly, concise survey of Napoleon's economic policies.

9. Russell F Weigley, *The Age of Battles: The Quest for Decisive Warfare from Breitenfled to Waterloo* (Bloomington and Indianapolis: Indiana University Press, 1991), 290.

10. Roger Chickering, "Total War: Use and Abuse of a Concept," in *Anticipating Total War: The German and American Experiences, 1871–1914*, ed. M. Boemeke, R. Chickering, and S. Föster (Cambridge and New York: Cambridge University Press, 1999), 13–28.

11. David Gates, *The Napoleonic Wars, 1803–1815* (London: Arnold, 1997), 272.

12. Jacques Norvins de Montbretton, *Souvenirs d'un historien de Napoléon*, 3 vols. (Paris: A. Pigoreau, 1896–1897), 3: 159.

13. George Sand, *Histoire de ma vie* (first published Paris, 1855; 2004 Stock edition), 54–55.

14. My views on Goya and the wars are deeply influenced by Gwyn A. Williams, *Goya and the Impossible Revolution* (New York: Pantheon, 1976).

15. Cited in Juan Mercader Riba, *José Bonaparte. Rey de España, 1808–1813*, 2 vols. (Madrid: Consejo Superiora de Investigaciones Cientificas, 1983), 1: 213.

16. Mary A. Favret, "War in the Air," *Modern Language Quarterly* 65 (2005): 531–559.

17. Sand, *Histoire*, 68.

18. François Furet, *Revolutionary France 1770–1880*, trans. Antonia Nevill (Oxford: Blackwells, 1992), 182.

19. Maria Senkowska-Gluck, "Illyrie sous la domination napoléonienne, 1809–1813," *Acta Polonia Historica* 41 (1980): 99–121, esp. 116.

20. Enrique Martinez-Ruiz, *La creación de la Guardia Civil* (Madrid: Editoira Nacional, 1976).

21. Frédéric Bluche, *Le Bonapartisme. Aux origins de la droite autoritaire 1800–1850* (Paris: Flammarion, 1980).

22. Howard G. Brown, *Ending the French Revolution. Violence, Justice and Repression from the Terror to Napoleon* (Charlottesville and London: West Virginia University Press, 2006), 300.

23. Ibid., 308, 318.

24. Michael Broers, *Napoleonic Imperialism and the Savoyard Monarchy, 1773–1821. State Building in Piedmont* (Lampeter and Lewiston: Edwin Mellen, 1997), 370–382.

25. It is well worth noting that conscription was equally unpopular when it was mooted as a means of resisting the French. Charles Esdaile has proved this conclusively in the case of Spain in *Fighting Napoleon. Guerrillas, Bandits and Adventurers in Spain, 1808–1814* (New Haven and London: Yale University Press, 2004), 73–82, 100–111.

26. On the revolts of Parma-Piacenza, Tuscany, and Liguria, see Michael Broers, *The Napoleonic Empire in Italy, 1796–1814. Cultural Imperialism in a European Context?* (Basingstoke: Palgrave, 2005), 72–93.

27. On Spain, see Jon L. Tone, *The Fatal Knot: The Guerrilla War in Navarre and the Defeat of Napoleon in Spain* (Chapel Hill: University of North Carolina Press, 1994); Don Alexander, *Rod of Iron: French Counter-Insurgency Policy in Aragón during the Peninsular War* (Wilmington, DE: Scholarly Resources, 1985); Esdaile, *Fighting Napoleon*. On southern Italy, see John A. Davis, *Conflict and Control: Law and Order in Nineteenth Century Italy* (Basingstoke: Macmillan, 1988).

28. Sand, *Histoire de ma vie*, 51–52.

29. Reynald Secher, *Le Génocide franco-français. La Vendée-Vengée* (Paris: PUF, 1986), 308.

30. Laurent Dubois, *Avengers of the New World: The Story of the Haitian Revolution* (Cambridge, MA: Harvard University Press, 2004).

31. Isser Woloch, "Napoleonic Conscription: State Power and Civil Society," *Past & Present* 111 (1986): 101–129.

32. Alan Forrest, *Conscripts and Deserters. The Army and French Society during the Revolution and Empire* (Oxford: Oxford University Press, 1989).

33. Michael Rowe, *From Reich to State. The Rhineland in the Revolutionary Age, 1780–1830* (Cambridge: Cambridge University Press, 2003), 160.

34. Ibid., 165–183.

35. Laurence Cole, "Nation, Anti-Enlightenment, and Religious Revival in Austria: Tyrol in the 1790s," *Historical Journal* 43 (2000): 475–497.

36. Gunther Eyck, *Loyal Rebels, Andreas Hofer, and the Tyrolean Uprising of 1809* (New York, 1986).

37. Broers, *Napoleonic Empire in Italy,* 85.

38. Rowe, *From Reich to State,* 136.

39. Broers, *Napoleonic Empire in Italy,* 281–282.

40. Rowe, *From Reich to State,* 107–110.

41. Clive Emsley, *Gendarmes and the State in Nineteenth Century Europe* (Oxford: Oxford University Press, 1999).

42. Broers, *Napoleonic Imperialism and the Savoyard Monarchy,* 353–356.

43. Alan Forrest, "The Ubiquitous Brigand: The Politics and Language of Repression," in *Popular Resistance in the French Wars. Patriots, Partisans and Land Pirates,* ed. C. J. Esdaile (Basingstoke: Palgrave, 2005), 25–44.

44. Emsley, *Gendarmes and the State.* See also *Gendarmerie, état et société au XIXe siècle,* ed. Jean-Noël Luc (Paris: Publications de la Sorbonne, 2002).

45. Isser Woloch, *The New Regime. Transformations of the French Civic Order, 1789–1820s* (New York: Norton, 1994). On the spread of the Code, see *Révolutions et justice pénale en Europe: Modèles français et traditions nationales (1780–1830),* ed. X. Rousseau, M-S Dupont-Bochat, and C. Vael (Paris and Montreal: L'Harmattan, 1999).

46. Jean-Clément Martin, *La Vendée et la France* (Paris: Seuil, Paris, 1987), 13.

47. Paul Bois, *Les Paysans de l'Ouest* (Paris: Flammarion, 1960).

48. Joan Mercader i Riba, *Catalunya i l'Imperi Napoleònic* (Monserrat: Publicaciones de l'Ababdia de Monserrat, 1978), 307–308.

49. Louis Bergeron, *France under Napoleon,* trans. Robert R. Palmer (Princeton: Princeton University Press, 1981), 173. See also Ellis, *Napoleonic Empire,* 112.

50. Steven C. Hughes, *Crime, Disorder and the Risorgimento: The Politics of Policing in Bologna* (Cambridge: Cambridge University Press, 1994).

51. Michael Broers, "Napoleon, Charlemagne, and Lotharingia: Acculturation and the Boundaries of Napoleonic Europe," *Historical Journal* 44 (2001): 135–154.

52. For a well-researched analysis of how the tide shifted in southern and eastern France, see Brown, *Ending the French Revolution,* 325–335. For the same process in the Piedmontese departments, see Broers, *Napoleonic Imperialism and the Savoyard Monarchy,* 351–404.

53. On Calabria, see Umberto Caldora, *Calabria Napoleonica* (Naples: F. Fiorentino, 1960). On Asturias, see André Fugier, *La Junte supérieure des Asturias* (Paris: F. Alcan, 1931). On Valencia, see Manuel Ardit, *Història del País Valencià,* vol. 4, *L'Època Borbònica fins a la Crisi de l'Antic Règim* (Barcelona: Ed. 62, 1990), 4: 213–215.

54. The unpopularity of the guerrillas is a central theme of Esdaile, *Fighting Napoleon.*

55. Broers, *Napoleonic Empire in Italy,* 193.

56. Ibid., 182–185.

57. Alex Grab, "Army, State and Society: Conscription and Desertion in Napoleonic Italy (1802–1814)," *Journal of Modern History* 67 (1995): 25–54; Grab, "State Power, Brigandage and Rural Resistance in Napoleonic Italy," *European History Quarterly* 25 (1995): 39–70.

58. The best account is António do Carno Reis, *Invasões Francesas: as revoltas do Porto contra Junot* (Lisbon: Editorial Notícias, 1992), which is much wider-ranging than its title suggests.

59. William Plomer, *Ali the Lion: Ali of Tebeleni, Pasha of Jannina, 1741–1822* (London: Cape, 1936).

60. Linda Colley, *Britons: Forging the Nation 1707–1837* (New Haven: Yale University Press, 1992).

61. For a succinct, well-informed discussion of this, see Clive Emsley, *Britain and the French Revolution* (Harlow: Pearson, 2000), 71–73.

62. Broers, *Napoleonic Empire in Italy*, 110–112.

63. Michael Broers, "Policing the Empire: Napoleon and the Pacification of Europe," in *Napoleon and Europe*, ed. Philip Dwyer (London: Longman, 2001),153–168.

64. Sudhir Hazareesingh, *The Legend of Napoleon* (London: Granta, 2004), 268.

65. Réné de Chateaubriand, *Napoléon* (first published 1830; Paris: Albin Michel, 1969), 411–412.

66. Peter Fritzsche, "Specters of History: On Nostalgia, Exile, and Modernity," *American Historical Review* 106 (2001): 1587–1618, esp. 1609.

FURTHER READING

The experience of civilians in the Napoleonic wars has been a badly neglected subject in the traditional historiography, which has tended to focus almost solely on military and diplomatic history. This began to change in the 1980s, as historians focused more on the development of the modern state in this period and on the powerful influence of Napoleonic rule on the societies of western and central Europe.

The change in emphasis from military to political and social history began with national histories, but the first general book to address the development of the state and its impact on civilians was Stuart Woolf, *Napoleon's Integration of Europe* (London: Routledge, 1991). It was followed by Geoffrey Ellis, *The Napoleonic Empire* (Basingstoke: Palgrave, 1992); Michael Broers, *Europe under Napoleon, 1799–1815* (London: Arnold, 1996); and Alex Grab, *Napoleon and the Transformation of Europe* (Basingstoke: Palgrave, 2003). There have also been several recent collections of essays on the Napoleonic period, all notable for their concentration on civilian experiences. Philip Dwyer, ed., *Napoleon and Europe* (London: Longmans, 2001), and Michael Rowe, ed., *Collaboration and Resistance in Napoleonic Europe. State Formation in an Age of Upheaval, c. 1800–1815* (Basingstoke: Palgrave, 2003), deal with the Napoleonic period itself. David Laven and Lucy Riall, eds., *Napoleon's Legacy. Problems of Government in Restoration Europe* (Oxford and New York: Berg, 2000), deals with the aftermath and the legacy of the Napoleonic occupation of Europe.

National histories that treat in depth the impact of the Napoleonic wars on civilian populations are Stuart Woolf, *A History of Italy, 1700–1860. The Social Constraints of Political Change* (London: Methuen, 1979); Thomas Nipperdey, *Germany from Napoleon to Bismarck, 1800–1860* (English trans. Dublin: Gill and Macmillan, 1996); Simon Schama, *Patriots and Liberators. Revolution in the Netherlands, 1787–1813* (London: Collins, 1977); Gabriel Lovett, *Napoleon and the Birth of Modern Spain*, 2 vols. (New York: New York University Press, 1965); Linda Colley, *Britons. Forging the Nation, 1707–1837* (London and New Haven: Yale University Press, 1992); Clive Emsley, *Britain and the French Revolution* (Harlow: Pearson, 2000).

There is no general history of France in English that covers this specific period, but Louis Bergeron, *France under Napoleon* (English trans. Princeton: Princeton University Press, 1981), is still the best general guide to society and the economy in the period, while Isser Woloch, *The New Regime. Transformations of the French Civic Order, 1789–1820s* (New York: Norton, 1994), includes useful analyses of the structures of the state. Martin Lyons, *Napoleon Bonaparte and the Legacy of the French Revolution* (New York: Longmans, 1994), is a more general account, if now somewhat dated. Isser Woloch, *Napoleon and His Collaborators* (New York: Norton, 2001), is a brilliant analysis of the high politics of the first years of the regime. E. A. Whitcomb, "Napoleon's Prefects," *American Historical Review* 79 (1974), is a good treatment of the single most important civilian official of the Napoleonic state.

Few institutions in the Napoleonic period were more important than conscription. Alan Forrest, *Conscripts and Deserters. The Army and French Society during the Revolution and Empire* (Oxford: Oxford University Press, 1989), is very much a social history of France and many annexed lands in these years. It should be complemented by Isser Woloch, "Napoleonic Conscription: State Power and Civil Society," *Past & Present* 111 (1986), which takes a rather different view of its impact on the civilian population. Alex Grab, "Army, State and Society: Conscription and Desertion in Napoleonic Italy (1802–1814)," *Journal of Modern History* 67 (1995), and the same author's "State Power, Brigandage and Rural Resistance in Napoleonic Italy," *European History Quarterly* 25 (1995), together with Michael Broers, "The Police and the *Padroni:* French Gendarmes and Italian *Notabili* in Napoleonic Italy," *European History Quarterly* 26 (1996), cover the same subject for central and northern Italy. The Gendarmerie was central to conscription and to the advance of the stare into the lives of civilians. Clive Emsley, *Gendarmes and the State in Nineteenth Century Europe* (Oxford: Oxford University Press, 1999), is a very good overview, as it covers almost the whole of Europe. Law and order, in a more general sense, are well served by Howard Brown, *Ending the French Revolution. Violence, Justice and Repression from the Terror to Napoleon* (Charlottesville and London: West Virginia University Press, 2006); John Davis, *Conflict and Control: Law and Order in Nineteenth Century Italy* (London: Methuen, 1988); and, if in a slightly different context, Charles J. Esdaile, *Fighting Napoleon. Bandits and Adventurers in Spain, 1808–1814* (New Haven and London: Yale University Press, 2004).

There are now many regional studies of Napoleonic Europe. Michael Rowe, *From Reich to State. The Rhineland in the Revolutionary Age, 1780–1830* (Cambridge: Cambridge University Press, 2003); Michael Broers, *Napoleonic Imperialism and the Savoyard Monarchy, 1770–1821* (Lewiston and Lampeter: Edwin Mellen Press, 1997); and John Lawrence Tone, *The Fatal Knot: The Guerrilla War and the Defeat of Napoleon in Spain* (Chapel Hill and London: Chapel Hill: University of North Carolina Press, 1994), offer different emphases on civilian experiences but also give full portraits of life in their respective regions. Michael Broers, *The Napoleonic Empire in Italy: Cultural Imperialism in a European Context?* (Basingstoke: Palgrave, 2005), is a study of the annexed departments of northern and central Italy; it is now complemented for the south by John Davis, *Naples and Napoleon: Southern Italy and the European Revolutions, 1780–1860* (Oxford: Oxford University Press, 2006). Geoffrey Ellis, *Napoleon's Continental Blockade. The Case of Alsace* (Oxford: Oxford University Press, 1981), is a far more comprehensive treatment of the area than its title suggests.

SIX

Civilians and War in Europe, 1815–1900

Michael S. Neiberg

A few days spent in Paris might take a tourist down streets like the Boulevard de Sébastopol and the Avenue de Malakoff, or across the River Seine on the Pont de l'Alma. It is unlikely that most tourists (or, for that matter, many Parisians) connect these places with war or, more specifically, with the Crimean War of 1854–1856 that they commemorate. Similarly, catching a train at the Solférino metro station after a visit to the Musée d'Orsay might not evoke in the rider's mind the 1859 battle that gives the station its name. Built by Napoleon III's Second Empire to celebrate presumptive foreign policy and military successes, these symbols are faint echoes of a military past that, stuck between the era of Napoleon Bonaparte and the horrors of the First World War, is now all but forgotten.

Naming bridges and new, wide boulevards for Crimean War battles lent these events a grandeur and dignity they did not merit. The French government hoped to use these grandiloquent gestures to conceal the fact that the war had not gone as well as expected. Although few Parisians could have known it at the time, the bloody realities of the Crimean War did not match the heroic images French civilians had of glorious charges leading to even more glorious victories. Instead, the war was characterized by grim sieges, high rates of infectious disease, and inconclusive battles of entrenchment. Moreover, the French had had to rely heavily on support from their allies. The victory at Alma, although commemorated in a Parisian bridge, was, ironically, due mostly to British, not French, efforts. Indeed, the British largely blamed French commanders for not pursuing the victory at Alma with sufficient ardor; had they done so more aggressively, British officers charged, the war in the Crimea might well have ended much sooner and with much less loss of life and treasure.

The naming of the bridges and boulevards of Paris is symbolic of the ways that war affected European civilians in the years between the end of the Napoleonic era and the start of the twentieth century. Europeans of this relatively pacific period felt far fewer direct disruptions owing to war than did Europeans of the eighteenth and twentieth centuries. Even the dramatic midcentury Wars of German Unification (1864, 1866, and 1870–1871) ended quickly and with little direct impact on the daily lives of civilians. The bloody, internecine Paris Commune that resulted from French defeat in the last of these wars stands out as a glaring exception to the general pattern. Notably, the Commune was a civil war connected to, but ultimately separate from, the Franco-Prussian War, of which it was a part. For most Europeans, however, wars occurred hundreds, or even thousands, of miles from home in exotic places like the Crimea, India, and Africa. Naming roads and bridges thus served two purposes for Napoleon III's government: it allowed the government to celebrate narrow and indecisive battles as great victories worthy of public commemoration, and it depicted those victories as triumphs of the nation and the state, not just the ruling regime.

Moreover, the limited nature of war in the nineteenth century constrained the ability of states to achieve great victories. Four factors explain the general absence of large wars in this period. First, and probably most important, European society was worn out from 25 years of nearly incessant war, from the French Revolution to the downfall of Napoleon. Geoffrey Best describes the period 1790–1815 as being defined by war and war's impacts on the lives of men and women across the continent: "War present, war threatened, war in prospect, war not long past, war in every known shape and form, war happening to someone else even if not just then to you yourself, and talk of war as the ultimate conditioner of your existence."[1] After so much turmoil and strife, Europeans in the immediate post-Napoleon period sought stability, predictability, and, above all, peace.

Second, at the diplomatic and political level, European statesmen imposed a system called the "Concert of Europe" that sought to create both a balance of power and a process for adjudicating international disputes through means other than war. In practice, this system came to be dominated by the great conservative powers of the Restoration period, France, Austria, Britain, and Russia. None of these states sought to disrupt or to threaten the general peace until Prussia's great power grabs of the 1860s and 1870s. Even these Wars of German Unification sought limited goals. Otto von Bismarck and Helmuth von Moltke, the two great architects of these wars, did not wish to send their armies from Portugal to Russia as Napoleon had done. Rather, they sought to use military force to achieve clear and limited political goals.

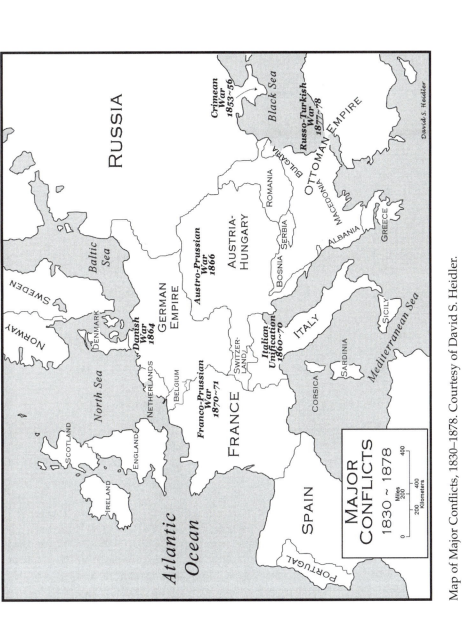

Map of Major Conflicts, 1830–1878. Courtesy of David S. Heidler.

Third, as Europeans became more interested in their overseas empires, they channeled their martial energies away from Europe and toward Africa and Asia. Consequently, while imperial wars devastated indigenous communities, they normally impinged on Europeans lightly and indirectly. Finally, this period was characterized by what F. R. Bridge and Roger Bullen call "international anarchy." Lacking a central authority like the United Nations or a single great power to dominate international affairs, the "European States System" developed a process whereby "a dispute between two states could be settled by the mediation of a third sovereign."[2] This system kept many wars from starting and limited the duration of many others; thus the numerous diplomatic conferences held in European capitals to resolve crises in Europe and Africa. The Franco-Prussian War may be an exception that proves the rule, as French diplomats charged that the British government's reluctance to accept the role of international mediator unduly prolonged that war.

The general absence of war in this period, however, does not mean that war did not affect the lives of European civilians. More than just the names of their streets and bridges changed as a consequence of the wars that states chose to fight. As this chapter shows, war remained a central and dramatic event for Europeans of the nineteenth century. This chapter examines four themes in this vein: the relationship of soldiers to civilians; civilians' reactions to, and support for, wars and imperialism; the impact of war on art, literature, and culture more generally; and, finally, the experience of those civilians unfortunate enough to be caught in the direct path of war's fury.

CIVILIANS, SOLDIERS, AND INDUSTRIAL SOCIETY

Before understanding the relationship of soldiers to civilians, it is important to understand some of the main social, economic, and political patterns that were transforming Europe in the period between the fall of Napoleon and the end of the century. Nineteenth-century Europe underwent a series of tremendous changes associated with what economic historians have come to call the second industrial revolution. Unlike the first industrial revolution, which relied on steam and water power, the second relied on fossil fuels, most notably coal. Industrial goods in this era included chemicals, railroad rolling stock, and specialty metals. Great Britain, France, and the German states led the way, radically transforming the European economic structure through revolutionary increases in the scale and scope of industrial production. This change affected almost every aspect of European life. Three of these changes relate to war and the role of soldiers in European society: the creation of large urban proletariats, the role of armed forces in policing those proletariats, and the reluctance of civilians to embrace soldiers as representatives of the nation and the state.

Industrial Europe was a bleak, dirty, and dangerous place. Low wages, unsafe working environments, and fetid living conditions made working-class life in the nineteenth century extremely unpleasant. The novels of such contemporary European writers as Charles Dickens, Victor Hugo, and Émile Zola brought some of the working class's misery into the comfortable salons of middle-class readers, most of whom empathized but did little to ameliorate the conditions of the workers. Few structures existed to protect workers or to care for them when they became too ill or too old to work. Even workers badly injured on the job had few protections or safety nets beyond those that a rare enlightened factory owner might provide.

Industry also produced periods of cyclical employment and depression. For example, work in the textile mills of Lancashire depended upon the successes or failures of the cotton-growing season in faraway areas like Egypt, India, and the United States South. Economic crises could come seemingly from nowhere and close factories for weeks, months, or even years. Even in good times, the capricious behavior of a factory owner or foreman could lead to a firing and the placing of one's name on a blacklist shared by local employers. Lacking legal protections, government advocates, or labor unions, workers had few choices and little recourse.

These conditions produced the inevitable backlash of working-class activism. The class-based theories of Karl Marx and Friedrich Engels were already well circulated by the time the two men wrote *The Communist Manifesto,* in 1848. The pamphlet's popularity and intellectual importance grew in the wake of a series of revolutions and near-revolutions that shook Europe that year. Although many of the leaders of these revolutions were middle-class liberals hoping to force aristocratic elites to share power, the revolutions gained widespread support in the vast urban slums created by industrialization. Marx and Engels's argument that a general proletarian revolution was not only imminent but inevitable increased tension and middle-class fears about the working classes.

The only instrument of the state that stood in a position to stop revolution and quash working-class movements was the army. Modern police forces were still a novel concept in Europe in the nineteenth century. Even London and Paris, two of the continent's most important metropolises, did not get their first uniformed, professional police forces until 1829; the rest of Britain lacked professional police until 1856. Berlin did not create its first police force until 1848. As cities struggled to build effective, professional police forces, much of the work of controlling domestic dissent fell to the only public institutions capable of doing the job, namely armies.

Consequently, soldiers became the state's strike breakers and enforcers of central authority. Regimes knew they could depend on their armies because military training programs and indoctrination taught soldiers to obey their legal political leaders. The success of these programs became manifest in 1848 when the vast majority of soldiers remained loyal to their governments instead of siding with their "class comrades" among strikers and revolutionaries. In that year, a Cologne representative told his comrades in the Frankfurt Assembly that Germans "have learnt over the last 33 years that the army, instead of protecting them against external enemies, has frequently been employed against the citizens themselves." Although coming from a different perspective, Prussian King Frederick William II agreed, noting with great pride how the army had instilled "total loyalty" to the crown during the crisis of 1848.[3]

The presence of soldiers in garrisons located in or near major cities served as visible reminders of the power of the state to use soldiers to enforce its will on the workers whenever it chose to do so. In the course of putting down the revolution of 1848, for example, French soldiers killed or wounded almost 3,000 French workers and guaranteed that the Second Republic proclaimed in that year would be essentially conservative and more responsive to the wishes of the middle class than to those of the working class.

The wide disparity in power between the army and the protestors contributed to the army's reputation for cruelty. Rather than merely protecting property, soldiers often used their power to attack unarmed demonstrators in the course of restoring order. One of the most famous such incidents in British history occurred at St. Peter's Field, near Manchester, in 1819. A crowd of male and female textile workers had gathered there to debate parliamentary reform; although it was then a city of 200,000 people, Manchester still had no Member of Parliament. As it was a community assembly, many workers had brought their children, and most had dressed in their Sunday best. Led by the pacific Female Reform Societies, the debates were far from the seeds of a revolutionary movement. The noisy gathering nevertheless frightened local leaders enough to ask for military help, which came in the form of local militiamen. The Yeomen Cavalry charged into the meeting, killing 11 people and injuring more than 400 others.

The incident, known to the workers as the "Peterloo Massacre," exposed and exacerbated the great rifts between workers and soldiers. It led to widespread recriminations against soldiers and the government that had employed them in so brutal a fashion. The British media publicized the events at Peterloo, converting the incident into a national scandal. The *Observer*, for example, reported that "defenceless and unoffending individuals were trampled to death while others were cut down in cold blood. It appeared that men, women, and children, unable to escape from their assailants, were destroyed, though innocent of any offence." The newspaper then questioned the constitutionality of using soldiers against an unarmed and legal assembly of British subjects.[4]

This type of anger directed from the working class toward soldiers contributed to a view of men in uniform as tools of the state and, more important, as class traitors. Consequently, many left-leaning republicans and socialists argued for major reforms in the system of recruiting and training soldiers. In lieu of long-term professionals, they advocated a national militia based on short-term service by a larger percentage of men. By reducing the term of service, they hoped to reduce the period of time that men spent under the pernicious influence of the army, thus limiting the power of military indoctrination programs. By increasing the percentage of men who served, they hoped to create an army with closer links to the working class. Such an army, they believed, would be much less likely to side with the elite and more likely to support the workers of the communities from which they came.[5]

Many members of the middle class, most notably professionals and intellectuals, also grew suspicious of the army and its programs of indoctrination. Those programs, critics alleged, transformed men into armed servants of the ruling class, rather than of the nation at large. French military support for the political activity of General Georges Boulanger in 1889 terrified defenders of the Third Republic. Boulanger, they feared, was using military discipline to plan a coup against a democratically constituted government.[6] These tensions exploded in France in 1894 when a French court found Captain Alfred Dreyfus guilty of treason for selling secrets to Germany. Almost all Frenchmen accepted the guilty verdict, and few shed any tears as Dreyfus was ceremoniously stripped of his rank and his sword broken on the parade ground of the *École Militaire,* in the heart of Paris. Dreyfus was then shipped off to the infernal French prison on the appropriately named Devil's Island in French Guyana. Dreyfus soon faded from public view as France focused on new scandals and new crises.

But the popular consensus that a traitor had gotten what he deserved soon turned into one of the most divisive events in French history. Dreyfus's brother managed, in 1897, to convince the journalist and former prime minister Georges Clemenceau that France had condemned the wrong man. Clemenceau, who had turned to journalism after a combative political career that had seemingly ended with an electoral defeat in 1893, made the Dreyfus case his *cause célèbre.* Clemenceau helped to stir up a chorus of angry protests from intellectuals, anticlericals, and Frenchmen suspicious of army authority. In 1898, the French Army responded by placing another officer, Marie Charles Esterhazy, on trial. Despite damning evidence presented at the trial that proved that Esterhazy, not Dreyfus, had been the traitor, Esterhazy was acquitted. Dreyfus, whom a growing number of Frenchmen believed was innocent, continued to languish in prison, not because of his traitorous activity but because of the furtive and conspiratorial actions of the French army and government.

Shortly after Esterhazy's acquittal, the French writer Émile Zola touched off a firestorm in an open letter to the war minister who had overseen Dreyfus's conviction. Clemenceau's newspaper published the letter, known thereafter by its banner headline "J'Accuse" (I accuse). In it, Zola charged the French Army's Catholic leadership of having conspired to convict the Jewish Dreyfus despite knowing that he was innocent of all charges. "J'Accuse" touched a nerve in France because of the already intensely negative reputation of the army, especially its senior officers. Zola's depiction of the army as serving its own interests over those of the French Republic more generally thus rang true to thousands of his countrymen. The government's response to Zola, convicting him of treason and sentencing him to a year in prison, only confirmed those views. Zola's subsequent flight to London guaranteed that the Dreyfus Affair would remain in the public spotlight.[7]

In the end, the Dreyfus Affair was less about the actual guilt or innocence of Alfred Dreyfus (he was finally acquitted, fully rehabilitated, and given the Legion of Honor award in 1906) than the role of the army in French society. To the "Dreyfusards" who supported overturning Dreyfus's conviction, the Affair proved beyond a doubt that the army and its leaders could not be trusted to respect the rights and privileges of citizens in a republican society. The dividing lines in France, according to the historian Douglas Porch, "were clearly drawn between the reactionary France of cutlass and cleric fighting to retain their privileges and the progressive forces of *literati* and representatives of the industrial proletariat."[8] As those progressive forces grew more politically powerful, they came to see reform of the army as critical to domestic liberty. In the years following the Dreyfus Affair, successive French governments worked to open the officer corps to more working-class men, reduce the term of service for French conscripts, and reduce the influence of devout Catholics (whom they saw as agents of conservative rule) at the senior level of the officer corps.

The Dreyfus Affair may have been a quintessentially French phenomenon, but popular notions of the army and the officer corps as agents of the ruling elite were pervasive across Europe. So, too, were negative images of enlisted soldiers. In an effort to keep costs down and ensure that the military did not interfere with the "productive" sectors of society, most military systems enlisted soldiers from the very bottom rungs of society. As a result, daily conditions for soldiers in Europe were abysmal.[9] Pay, low to begin with, was reduced even further by a series of what the British called "stoppages," or charges for uniforms, food, and other necessary items. The British Army set soldiers' pay at one shilling per day in 1797 and did not raise it during the entire nineteenth century. That wage was approximately one-quarter what a bricklayer earned and gave rise to the phrase "taking the King's shilling" as a synonym for enlisting. With wages so low, few men sought to become soldiers if they had any alternatives.

To make matters even worse, war departments often looked the other way as colonels pocketed money designated for the upkeep of the men in their regiments. This method of supplementing officer incomes allowed poorer nobles to become officers and to live the concomitant life of the gentleman expected of them. But as officers skimmed money from their regimental budgets, barracks remained unimproved and living conditions in those barracks often fell below even the primitive standards of the European working class. Needless to say, regular health care for soldiers was virtually nonexistent, and no European army had formal arrangements to pay for the costs of dependents. Most armies even forbade their enlisted men to marry without the permission of the regimental commander, further contributing to the popular image of soldiers as rootless, bacchanalian bachelors. Even in states where working-class men had the franchise, soldiers were often exempted and thus forbidden to vote, underscoring their separation from societal norms; French and Italian soldiers could not vote until after World War I. Worst of all, the discipline in army units was brutal, in part to ensure that soldiers would obey orders and in part to make them too tired to find trouble in their off hours.

In part because of these brutish conditions, soldiers had reputations for both criminality and immorality. Soldiers on leave or passing through towns on maneuvers often sought out alcohol and women. The presence of soldiers attracted prostitutes to towns and led to high rates of sexually transmitted diseases; the abuse of alcohol created all sorts of antisocial behaviors, from petty theft to violence against civilians. Complicating matters further, in most cases civilian authorities could not punish soldiers, who were under the military discipline system. Whether accurate or not, most civilians presumed that military authorities were not interested in punishing their men for transgressions committed away from the barracks. Thus, they believed that most soldiers took excessive liberties with civilians knowing that they would "merely be reprimanded mildly, if at all."[10]

Because of this intensely negative public image and the brutal conditions of daily life, few men joined armies if they had any other options. In Great Britain, which did not use conscription, soldiers tended to come from the most disadvantaged sectors of society. Those made unemployed by the vagaries of industrial economic cycles, criminals, vagrants, and men with a reason for needing to leave their home communities in a hurry formed the backbone of many British units. It is hardly surprising, then, that few civilians had positive images of soldiers or that many tavern owners and innkeepers often refused to serve soldiers.

Most young men did everything they could to avoid the army. Because most continental states practiced some form of conscription, men often had to rely on support from their home communities in evading what the French called the *impôt de sang* (blood tax). Local communities often colluded in protecting their young men (and thus their sources of labor and husbands) by collecting money to hire substitutes, hiding men from government agents, or, in at least a few cases, registering most new births as girls in an effort to trick the army. Some families and communities preempted this decision by purchasing insurance policies from companies that pledged to find substitutes for insured men if they should be chosen for military service.

Civilians were critical to the functioning of the military recruitment system, especially at the local level. The conscription system rarely targeted men as individuals. Most often, central governments told local governments how many conscripts they were to provide. In cases where a mayor simply chose who would go to the army, children of local politicians and middle-class fathers usually had less to fear; many communities, however, selected conscripts and distributed the burden of military service through the choosing of lots. Even then, local politics had much to do with deciding which men were expendable (and thus excellent candidates for the army) and which men were deemed too valuable to ship off to a faraway garrison town, perhaps never to be seen again.

If chosen for military service and not protected by their community, individual men had the option of accepting their fate, hiring a substitute, deserting, or injuring themselves. Deserting was usually the least pleasant of these options, both because of the difficulty of blending in to new communities and the severe punishments for young men if caught. Deserters thus tended to head for frontier communities, where they could slip across international borders for temporary protection from the gendarmes, or for big cities, where they had a better chance of remaining anonymous. Hiring a substitute was for most men far too expensive to contemplate, especially in times of full employment, war, or international crisis, when the cost of such substitutes usually skyrocketed. Many communities had men known as "cripplers," whom young men could hire (illegally, of course) to injure them in a way that would make them unfit for military service. One popular method involved smashing a young man's front teeth, thus rendering him incapable of tearing open the paper cartridges that held powder.

The workings of the conscription system underscored the popular view of the army as an alien institution. Because working-class Europeans seldom felt a direct threat from neighboring nations in this period, they had little reason to see soldiers as protectors. As we have seen, they more often saw soldiers as agents of a repressive state that did not represent their interests. In a Europe where national identities did not always override local and ethnic identities, civilians often regarded the army as an instrument of oppression by a majority (or at least dominant) ethnic group. The Austro-Hungarian Empire's officer corps, for example, was dominated by ethnic Germans and Magyars, yet the army depended upon the active participation of all of its ethnic groups at the enlisted level. While some soldiers may have developed through military service a sense of greater attachment to the empire as a whole, most civilians from minority ethnic groups tended to see the army as a "German" or "Hungarian" institution that neither protected nor represented their own community's interests.[11]

Middle-class reactions to the army were sometimes (although not always) more favorable, because of the army's role in maintaining order against working-class activism. Still, few middle-class families wanted their sons to become common soldiers. One study notes that middle-class men in southern Germany avoided military service as often as possible between 1815 and 1870.[12] Such separation made good economic sense. To middle-class sons, an enlisted career meant downward economic and social mobility. Even a brief period spent in the army or navy meant critical years lost to peers in the professions or in business. Officer careers were much more appealing on both the economic and the social levels, but in most states the aristocracy fought to maintain a tight grip on promotion, especially at the senior levels. The nobility's abiding interest in the officer corps limited the promotion potential for middle-class men, especially in the most prestigious branches, the infantry and the cavalry. In 1860, for example, 70 percent of German cadet school students were from aristocratic backgrounds.[13] Technical services like the navy or the artillery often offered more opportunity for the better-educated sons of the middle classes, but the nobility's hold on the officer corps both underscored its position as an essentially conservative institution and placed ceilings on the advancement of many middle-class men. To many nobles, the army represented the last bastion of conservative values. Keeping middle-class men out of the officer corps thus became a critical means of securing domination of this important institution.

If civilians did not see soldiers as protectors or guarantors of security, they did occasionally see them in other positive lights. The most common benefit soldiers provided to civilian communities was not military but economic. To many civilians, soldiers represented an excellent source of potential customers. Because few armies could regularly supply their soldiers with food from government-controlled storehouses, they had to make deals with local suppliers, especially when they were on the move. Peasants and merchants could therefore profit enormously from contracts to provide food, shelter, and fodder for passing units. Quartermaster officers who lacked the time to learn the ways of local markets were often at the mercy of crafty peasants who knew that officers were under time pressure to get their men fed and housed. Similarly, merchants and industrialists with connections in government could work the system to their great financial advantage, signing lucrative contracts, giving kickbacks to colluding officers, then maximizing profits by supplying soldiers with substandard provisions. In some states, most notably Austria and Russia, the system of bribes and corrupt contracting became so commonplace as to almost become the official means of conducting business.

On a more informal basis, camp followers and officially licensed sutlers were usually near at hand to sell goods to soldiers. Although the men had to pay sutlers and camp followers out of their own pockets, this network allowed soldiers to buy products that they could not otherwise obtain. Food was central to most soldiers; the British Army provided only two meals per day (and those usually of poor quality) until 1840. Camp followers sold a variety of foodstuffs, tobacco, wine, beer, whiskey, coffee, tea, and replacement shoes. They also provided a number of services such as tailoring, laundry, mail, and information about local conditions. Prostitutes and medical services (often provided by the same people) were also often available.

Soldiers fulfilled one other major role for civilians, that of entertainer. Scott Hughes Myerly, in an original and insightful book, argues that the spectacle of military pomp and circumstance had the power to beguile even people who otherwise saw the military as an oppressive and elitist institution. The military played on this allure by staging ostentatious pageants at public gatherings, celebrations, and holidays. In one of the largest such pageants of the nineteenth century, 50,000 soldiers escorted Queen Victoria on her route from Buckingham Palace to St. Paul's Cathedral during the 1897 Diamond Jubilee. Dressed in their finest parade uniforms, with polished weapons glimmering in the sun, soldiers marching in unison did indeed present a spectacle, especially for people in an era with few other distractions that were quite so dazzling. Military bands (paid for with more stoppages from the men's wages), magnificently groomed horses, and an impressive array of gleaming artillery pieces completed the spectacle.

Civilians came out in the tens of thousands to see these pageants. To people of the nineteenth century, these performances represented "a gratis spectacle that involved hundreds or thousands of splendidly dressed performers, complete with 'fireworks.'" This "treat for all," Myerly argues, went a long way toward convincing otherwise wary civilians of the value and majesty of armies.[14] Myerly's depiction of these spectacles as performance is apt, for performances they were, carefully choreographed and bearing very little resemblance to the drudgery of military life. In this way they are analogous to French efforts to name bridges and streets for "glorious battles" that were in actuality anything but glorious.

These spectacles most often occurred as part of a larger local or national celebration, such as a coronation, a local harvest festival, or a carnival associated with a local saint's day. Occasionally, however, the military brought civilians more closely into contact with training and operations. The British Army, for example, invited civilians to observe parts of the four-month-long training camp near Chobham in 1852. Involving 17,000 men training for operations like pontoon river crossings and limbering of artillery caissons, such exercises were a spectacle of a slightly different sort. Possessing less of the pomp and circumstance characteristic of a military band, military maneuvers showed off the military in an idealized form of work in a fashion akin to modern-day air shows.[15] On more than one occasion, crowds of civilian observers grew so large that armies found it difficult to perform their required exercises.

Spectacles and parades were not only a British phenomenon. One study of daily life in France under Napoleon III, which notes the ambivalence many French civilians felt toward the army, nevertheless also stresses the importance of such spectacles in the lives of both rural and urban observers in France:

Seeing soldiers of the Second Empire on parade, marching proudly and nobly, was a must. The crowds pressed in to see them parade past; those in the crowds admired the soldiers. The men paraded accompanied by military music played by a drum and bugle crops, who preceded them, dominating the parade with their size, the dexterity of the drum major, and the ornate instruments. The crowd applauded the variety of soldiers they saw: artillerists in somber uniforms, cavalrymen in splendid uniforms, cuirassiers with shiny metal breastplates, soldiers in dark tunics and red pants with tall shakos.[16]

As in Britain and France, so, too, in Germany. Moritz Bromme, born in 1863, recalled the importance of military influences in his youth. He noted that in his childhood, schools often closed to allow students to see army units on their way to maneuvers. He later remembered that he and his schoolmates "stood gaping open-mouthed, unable to see enough of this resplendent spectacle—after all, we'd never seen anything like it before."[17]

As these examples show, spectacles projected an image of armies as exemplars of order and discipline. If the army could take the dregs of society and turn them into obedient soldiers arrayed in neat lines and squares, then maybe it had some domestic value after all. The army thus represented a sense of stability in an age of great change. Through this "seductive attraction of the martial vision," Myerly argues that the British Army came to be a more popular institution during the course of the nineteenth century.[18] Spectacle and the association of the military with order and discipline also allowed the military to become a more effective and powerful institution, allowing it to emanate an aura of competence. Small numbers of well-drilled and "well turned out" infantry could thus disperse crowds by their mere presence, often without having to fire their weapons. In one famous case, a single soldier in his full dress uniform broke up a demonstration outside Downing Street in 1830 armed with only a single-shot musket.

Spectacles therefore served to paper over civilian discontent through a decorous and majestic performance, but suspicions remained. Some governments realized the problems created by having such intensely unpopular armies. In the 1870s and 1880s, successive French Third Republic governments made reforms intended to make conscription fairer by eliminating many exemptions and making it harder for men to hire substitutes. The result was a conscription system that appeared more equitable and more representative of all social classes. Moreover, as more and more families sent their sons to the army, the institution became a more national one. Civilians thus began to see soldiers less as men unfortunately unable to find a way out of military service and more as young men doing their turn in service to the Fatherland.[19] The growing power and efficiency of the central government's bureaucracy also put an end to much of the local chicanery that had allowed sons of local power brokers to evade service. As more sons from more families served, the army came to be more of a shared experience.

The image of armies also benefited from domestic reforms. By the end of the century, police forces had taken over many of the crowd control and strikebreaking roles formerly assigned to armies, which in turn responded by moving many units out of cities, making them less visible and, thus, less immediately objectionable. Soldiers still broke strikes and quelled disturbances in the countryside, and they could always be called into cities if the need arose, but these episodes became less common as the nineteenth century wore on. Growing international tensions also led to changes in the images of armies, as the same workers who had once cursed soldiers for breaking strikes looked to them for protection in the event that tensions turned to war. Occasional war scares and, of course, wars might lead to a growing popularity of soldiers, though, as we will see, it did not always do so. Common soldiers thus remained outside the mainstream of nineteenth century European society, with important consequences for the relationship among civilians, the army, and war.

CIVILIAN REACTIONS TO WAR

The general European revulsion toward soldiers in this era did not mean that wars themselves were always unpopular. Indeed, the sight of an army marching off to war might be welcomed as underscoring the proper role that civilians expected soldiers to play. Better, many civilians concluded, to see soldiers acting in their intended role as arbiters of international disputes than in their domestic role of strikebreaker and enforcer of elite desires. Wars in defense of home and hearth were understandably the most popular types of wars. Civilians located near frontiers likely to be overrun by enemy soldiers often greeted wars with the most enthusiasm, hoping that a successful mobilization and an early campaign might bring the war to the enemy's towns and farms and thus spare their own homes from destruction.

In an age of developing nationalism, wars provided important moments for domestic opponents to bury hatchets in symbolic joint allegiance to the Fatherland. Wars thus often began with ecstatic displays of patriotism as people of different ethnicities, religions, classes, and regions rallied to the same flag. To be sure, not all civilians welcomed the start of wars, but the nearly unanimous public mood of support for national goals often served to muffle opposing voices and keep doubters from expressing their feelings openly. Denouncing government goals not only opened people up to charges of patriotism but also might bring official charges that could lead to jail time or the loss of one's job.

French reactions to the outbreak of the Franco-Prussian War in 1870 help to make this point. France had actually declared war first, after a fairly transparent manipulation of French public opinion by the Prussian chancellor Otto von Bismarck. The "Iron Chancellor" had reworded a telegram, known as the Ems Dispatch, to create the impression that Prussia had insulted France's ambassador over a diplomatic impasse connected to the succession to the Spanish throne. Bismarck's ruse achieved its desired effect, offending French pride and thereby creating widespread popular demand for war.

As the Ems Dispatch incident shows, in an age when individuals were increasingly likely to identify themselves in terms of national identity, wars and declarations of wars became national events. Moreover, mass communications made the national distribution of inflammatory documents like the Ems Dispatch possible, facilitating both national debate and the growth of a national consensus for war. Through these means, civilians could influence the course and pace of events in ways they never could before. Thus, in 1870 Napoleon III might well have avoided war if he had wanted to do so, but public sentiment in favor of war greatly complicated his decision making, just as Bismarck had guessed it would.

Bismarck had judged well, for the multitudes demonstrating in favor of war played on the minds of skeptical French politicians. Many of the latter, especially republicans who remembered Napoleon III's blundering attempt to create an empire in Mexico in the 1860s, suspected that the emperor was once again fabricating reasons for a war France was not prepared to fight. But those same politicians could not easily ignore the chanting crowds and their calls of "À Berlin," "Vive la France," and "À bas Guillaume" (Down with Kaiser Wilhelm). One hundred years earlier, politicians would not have needed to keep so careful an ear to the ground to listen for soundings of public opinion.

That same public opinion could be very fickle at times. Many of the French civilians who greeted the prospect of war with frivolous anticipation were among those who had opposed Napoleon III's ostentatious militarism. Indeed, the very phrase "militarism" dates from this period and has its origins in opponents of Napoleon III's overreliance on the army. The term came to mean the devotion of resources to the military far in excess of what was needed for national defense, as well as the pervasive negative influence of the military on civilian society. Notwithstanding domestic opposition, antimilitarist sentiment was noticeably absent in 1870 as the crisis with Prussia began to brew.

Thus, despite a thin pretext for war and a sense of foreboding from the French left, thousands of civilians greeted the outbreak of war with an almost giddy expectation of victory. A battlefield triumph would not only restore the wounded pride of their nation but also reassert to any doubters in Berlin (as well as in London, Vienna, and Moscow) France's position as the final arbiter of European diplomacy. Troops moving through Paris found civilians eager to buy them drinks or lighten their load by carrying their backpacks to their departure depots. Nor was enthusiasm limited to Paris; troops from the provinces saw civilians lined up at their departure stations to wish them well and thrust baskets of food or flasks of wine upon them.[20]

Of course, few nations become enthusiastic about wars that they expect to lose. Most French civilians expected their army to make short work of its Prussian rival, perhaps because of the efficiency they had seen from it on parade and in quelling domestic disturbances. The mood might have been different among those same civilians had they known of Napoleon III's massive shortcomings as a military commander, his name and lineage notwithstanding. French civilians also remained ignorant of major problems in the organization, equipment, leadership, and doctrine of the French Army itself. Slow to mobilize and even slower to plan for stopping a Prussian invasion, the French Army lost important time and momentum and had likely lost the war before the first shots were even fired.

The bliss that often accompanies ignorance allowed French civilians to celebrate even minor early victories as if they were truly decisive. The premature announcement of great French successes at Spicheren and Froeschwiller in the first weeks of the war sent a Parisian crowd into a flurry of patriotism. Anticipating a decisive war-winning victory along the lines of Napoleon I's great achievements at Austerlitz and Jena, citizens waved flags, clasped hands, and presumed that Spicheren and Froeschwiller were signs of more momentous triumphs to come. Those French civilians who had supported the war seemingly had the first confirmation of their faith in the glory of their cause, their army, and their nation. Unfortunately for France, the announcements were soon revealed as hoaxes perpetrated by two speculators who had hoped to make a quick fortune selling junk bonds on the Paris Bourse, which usually surged on good war news.[21]

Actual battlefield success (and even a few failures) often entered into national legend. The 1854 "charge of the Light Brigade" at Balaclava in the Crimean War remains one of the most famous such episodes. A poorly commanded and poorly planned charge by 637 British cavalrymen to recapture lost artillery pieces resulted in the death of more than 247 members of Lord Cardigan's Light Brigade. The well-known journalist W. H. Russell of *The Times* sent a report back describing the heroism displayed by the men under fire. A series of paintings and a famous poem by Lord Tennyson (discussed later) immortalized the battle. As news of command mistakes also filtered back to Britain, the charge came to be seen as an example of British heroism even amid incompetent military leadership, a theme that no doubt resonated with thousands of working- and middle-class Britons.

Battlefield victories were often occasions for lavish public commemoration. Schools and factories closed, and churches rang bells or sang Te Deums. In towns and cities, these victory parties sometimes took on the air of a public carnival. Patriotic speeches from veterans, soldiers, or local notables completed the air of triumph. Sometimes these celebrations were spontaneous outpourings of civilian enthusiasm. In other cases, they were carefully conceived and constructed products of governments attempting to fuel the public mood. In this way, they resembled the spectacles that helped build public support for the army in peacetime.

Governments, of course, rarely delivered news of military defeat by throwing a party. News of defeats often trickled down to civilians slowly and inconsistently. Pronouncements of battlefield reversals normally arrived couched in language designed to soften the blow or to leave hope for recovery. One French bulletin from August 1870 announced rather innocuously: "Marshal MacMahon has retreated to his second line. Everything will be reestablished there. . . . Our resources are immense. Fight on with firmness and France will be saved."[22] Only the last part of this message gives any hint as to the scale of the French defeat. The remainder makes it appear as if all is well. In fact, as the writers of the bulletin knew all too well, the French had suffered a terrible defeat from which it would be difficult to recover. Marshal MacMahon had needlessly sacrificed his cavalry in costly frontal assaults, lost more than 17,000 men, and left the approaches from the Vosges to Paris unguarded. The second line, to which he had supposedly retreated, did not in fact exist. Newspapers, subject as they were to deep censorship, were often no more informative than government headlines, providing either the briefest sketches of realities at the front or publishing outright falsehoods.

A series of even carefully crafted negative bulletins might begin to shake the confidence of civilians in ultimate victory. More tangible signs, such as the movement of bedraggled and wounded soldiers away from the front lines, soon followed. As news from the war fronts grew more and more negative, civilians often began to lose faith in the same government they had cheered months, or even weeks, earlier. The same crowds that had once loudly celebrated victories often began tearing symbols of the regime from public buildings and demanding political change. The enthusiasm that governments fomented at the start of wars thus often turned into disillusion and anger.

Rising nationalism, fueled by tales of stunning heroism, also led civilians to support wars of empire. Although the point remains controversial among historians, the best evidence suggests that imperialism drew wide support from all social classes in Europe. For some civilians, imperialism represented an extension of national power worldwide. Many people thus drew a degree of pride from what their nation had conquered. The exoticism of empire no doubt contributed to this sense of pride. Governments and wealthy civilians encouraged interest in empires by highlighting that exoticism, which in turn formed a central theme of romantic art and literature. From 1841 to 1885, the Royal Botanical Gardens at Kew, outside London, built two magnificent greenhouses to display tropical plants from Africa and India. The founding, in 1830, of the London Zoological Society allowed citizens to see animals from the empire, as well. Gardens, zoos, and exhibits added a foreign and exotic flair to the notion of military spectacle. Only through the work of the soldier-guardians of empire could such shows be possible.

Ironically, imperialism led to support for foreign wars from some of the same people who held intensely negative views of the army and of soldiers more generally. Antislavery societies saw in imperial ventures a means to put a final end to the slave trade and slavery itself in Africa and Asia. Britain had officially made it illegal for any British ship to carry slaves in 1807, but the trade still flourished outside British reach well into the nineteenth century. Many of the philanthropic and paternalistic members of these societies would quite likely have sympathized with workers who connected the army with the Peterloo Massacre, but in the empire they saw a chance to use the army and navy to fulfill higher missions. The movement of British soldiers into the interior of Africa, they hoped, would end the slave trade by cutting it off at its source. Similarly, evangelical Christians needed soldiers, whom they often degraded as alcoholics and hopeless sinners, in order to proselytize safely in foreign environments.

For French civilians, success in imperial ventures after 1871 helped to erase the ignominy of the defeat in the Franco-Prussian War. The projection of French power in far-flung places such as Indochina, Algeria, and Madagascar helped to reestablish the glory of France. As the French politician Jules Ferry, a firm advocate of imperialism, noted, in 1882, "Everywhere, in all matters where our interests and honor is engaged, it is our will and duty to obtain for France the standing she deserves."[23] Empires served a similar purpose for European nations who were minor players in continental affairs. Belgian, Portuguese, and Dutch civilians thus drew a large measure of pride from their nations' influence in places like the Congo, Mozambique, and the East Indies. Much more than pride was at stake; these colonial ventures often proved to be critical sources of income both for national treasuries and for individuals.

One noted scholar of the French Army argues that imperialism caught the attention of a wide variety of civilians in France. They included "Some Bordeaux and Marseilles merchants . . . , Christians looking for conversions, and discovery-hungry members of the French Geographical Society."[24] While some Frenchmen saw notions of a French "civilizing mission" with cynical eyes, others genuinely embraced it, as did the thousands of Britons who were inspired by Rudyard Kipling's call to take up the "White Man's Burden." Ending what European civilians saw as "native tyranny" gave imperial soldiers important missions and made imperialism seem to be something other than a blatant grab for power and money.

As a result of imperialism, armies that represented tyranny and oppression at home came to represent progress and civilization abroad. In Africa and Asia, military forces became progressive instruments capable of ending native practices that struck Europeans as barbaric, such as the Indian custom of burning widows, with or without their consent, on the funeral pyres of their husbands (a ritual known as *suttee*). The British outlawed this practice in 1829, although it continued in rural India for several decades. To many civilians, soldiers made possible the European dream of bringing the benefits of civilization to the most isolated corners of the globe. Thus could Winston Churchill celebrate Britain's 1898 victory at Omdurman, in modern Sudan, as "the most signal triumph ever gained by the arms of science over barbarism."[25] European imperialists like Churchill saw imperial war as the means not of subduing native peoples for the benefit of Europeans but of lifting them up to the heights of civilization.

Wars of empire captured the imaginations of civilians across the European continent. Some colonial soldiers became national heroes. In France, generals like Joseph Gallieni and Hubert Lyautey received the lion's share of the credit for "pacifying" areas like Morocco, Tunisia, Indochina, and, most important for the French, Algeria. Their prestige grew to such heights that "in confrontations with popular and successful colonial soldiers, politicians, even the most skilled, were never absolutely sure of finishing in the first place."[26] Paintings and newspaper stories about splendidly dressed soldiers pacifying savages in exotic locales appealed to civilian imaginations as a fantastic break from the drudgery of daily life.

Even in Britain, where the reputation of the soldier was as low as anywhere else in Europe, colonial soldiers became larger-than-life figures. Of course, most of the fame and prestige fell to senior officers from the upper class. Sir Garnet Wolseley achieved such a reputation for his exploits around the world (including putting down the Indian Sepoy mutiny of 1859) that the phrase "all Sir Garnet" became popular shorthand for efficiency. General Sir Frederick Roberts became so popular in Britain that virtually all Britons knew him simply as "Bobs." Similarly, Horatio Herbert Kitchener became one of Britain's most celebrated individuals of the nineteenth century. In 1898, already a national figure, he marched an army to the Sudan to avenge the death of another popular British general, Major General Sir Charles Gordon, whom the local Sudanese leader had beheaded. Kitchener routed the Mahdist forces, killing almost 11,000 of them while losing just 48 men. In grateful thanks, Britain awarded him a peerage and £30,000. Thereafter Kitchener practically became the personification of the British Army until his death in 1916; his face glared out from World War I recruitment posters over the words "You! Join Your Country's Army."

Civilians did not always embrace war; sometimes they tried to stop it. One of the largest such efforts began in Britain in response to Turkey's attempt to crush a rebellion in Bulgaria in 1876. London newspapers publicized Turkey's brutality, and, while estimates of the numbers of dead vary tremendously, it soon became clear to many Britons that only the influence of the great powers of Europe could stop the horrors. Initially the British government refused to take action. Benjamin Disraeli, the Conservative Prime Minister, dismissed reports of the Turkish atrocities in Bulgaria as "coffee house babble" and at one point crassly tried to make light of the situation by claiming that the testimonies of Bulgarian victims could not be true because Turks rarely left survivors behind.[27]

Britons sympathetic to Bulgarian suffering responded by forming an Eastern Question Association that kept the issue in the public eye.

Disraeli's arch-nemesis, William Gladstone, took up the issue in part out of sympathy for the Bulgarians and in part as a way to embarrass Disraeli for his inaction. The Ottoman Empire's use of Turkish irregulars to commit atrocities against Bulgarian Christians fed the flames and turned Britain's reaction to the "Bulgarian Horrors" crisis into a minor political scandal. In the end, the great powers of Europe did little to help the Bulgarians, whose insurrection died away in 1876, although public guilt did lead to British diplomatic involvement in the negotiation of the Treaty of San Stefano following the Russo-Turkish War of 1877–1878, which gave Bulgaria its formal independence.[28]

Civilians thus reacted to soldiers and war with an ambivalent mix of revulsion and fascination. They often condemned wars fought by other states while defending those fought by their own. In large part, this seeming schizophrenia is explained by the increasing hold that nationalism had over Europeans in the nineteenth century. Europeans could thus deride the use of soldiers as strikebreakers one week, then marvel at the spectacle of a military review the next. As the following section demonstrates, this odd hold of war on the European mind repeated itself in European culture, reinforcing idealized and stylized notions of war.

WAR AND EUROPEAN CULTURE

Although European civilians of this period experienced relatively few wars, war nevertheless formed an important source of inspiration and material for art. The historian Peter Paret explains this seeming contradiction by arguing that martial images in art served important political and cultural purposes for Europeans:

Two political and social forces, above all, put their stamp on this art: the growth of the nation-state and the expansion of political activity to broader groups of society. The thousands of paintings by contemporaries and near-contemporaries of battles from the 1790s to the wars of Italian and German unification and of the colonial campaigns in Africa and Asia became pictorial testimony to the violent course of state building and imperialism. Paintings of [military] subjects of the more remote past—whether chosen from antiquity, the Crusades, or, as the century progressed, the Napoleonic era—documented claims of political rights on the one hand, and the reality of the nation and the validity of its demands on the citizen on the other.[29]

In other words, depicting war helped to reflect two trends in European society in the nineteenth century. First, images of what Paret calls "imagined battles" legitimated the political rule of Restoration regimes by connecting their behavior to supposed glory from past eras. Second, it showed the importance of nationalism and mass support for new political regimes by emphasizing the shared communal experience of war.

The first of these themes emerges in Horace Vernet's "The Battle of Valmy, 1792," painted in 1826. The battle that the painting commemorates seems an odd choice of subject matter for a France then under the rule of the arch-conservative King Charles X (ruled 1824–1830). Charles's "ultra" movement attempted as far as possible to return France to the social and political conditions of the *ancien régime.* Charles had "governed in an almost inconceivably unpopular way" by restoring the palace at Versailles with public money, dissolving Parliament, indemnifying nobles who had lost property during the Revolution, and returning responsibility for French primary-school education to the Catholic Church.[30]

The Battle of Valmy, by contrast, represented one of the most important early achievements of the revolutionaries, when a largely amateur army had defeated a larger, more experienced professional army of Prussians and Austrians. In doing so, they might well have saved the Revolution itself from its conservative enemies. Vernet's painting was thus a political expression of opposition to Charles X as much as it was an historical representation, and its military subject matter lay at the heart of this symbolism. Valmy showed the power of the citizens to defeat the agents of repressive kings. Vernet's patron, the Duke of Orléans (the future King Louis-Philippe, who ruled 1830–1848), had other motives in mind, as well; he hoped to show the power of citizens united with enlightened monarchs. The future king had been at Valmy as a young man. In 1830, a nearly blood-less revolution deposed Charles X in favor of Louis-Philippe's "bourgeois monarchy," which, while far from perfectly democratic, was considerably more representative than Charles X's ultra system. Vernet's popularity thus "cut across class lines" as he captured a national mood in favor of political and social change.[31]

A second, and ultimately more important, military theme in nineteenth century art involved the extension of warfare from the preserve of kings and emperors to an event of national importance. By emphasizing the shared national suffering of soldiers and civilians, wars became for nineteenth-century artists moments of communal transcendence. Although portraits of Napoleon like the massive canvases painted by Jacques-Louis David remained popular, they became increasingly less relevant than paintings that showed the participation of common soldiers and the damage war wrought on noncombatants. Even images of Napoleon became less heroic, as evidenced in Ernest Meissonier's "1814: The Campaign in France," completed in 1864. In that painting, a frowning Napoleon leads an army away from battle across a muddy field under a gray sky, hardly the same triumphal representation of Napoleon that David would have painted.

Meissonier typifies and personifies the use of art for military purposes in the nineteenth century. He was far and away the most famous and best-regarded French painter at midcentury. He saw Napoleon as a transcendent subject for art and history as his most important source of inspiration. Nor was he alone. Only Christ appeared in more French canvases than Napoleon. According to Ross King, one Paris Salon had nine different canvases of the battle of Wagram, and another had 18 paintings depicting the battle of Austerlitz. Meissonier's subject matter fascinated (one might say obsessed) him, but he also knew that Napoleonic and military subjects paid extremely well. For "1814: The Campaign in France" Messonier received 85,000 francs from a wealthy banker, a sum King describes as "gargantuan."[32]

Francisco de Goya, whose 1814 painting "The Shootings of May Third 1808" vividly showed the execution of Spanish civilians by French soldiers, carried this theme even further. Unlike French artists who focused on the grandeur and missed opportunities of the Empire, Goya focused on how war devastated civilians. His "Disasters of War" series, drawn between 1809 and 1820, was belatedly released to European audiences in the 1860s, more than three decades after Goya's death. Fourteen of the 47 panels in the series depict women or children. In all of the panels, these noncombatants are depicted as the helpless victims of war. Panels show women being executed by firing squads, raped by soldiers, killed by random shell fire, and in flight with children from their burning homes. Another Vernet painting, "Scene of the French Campaign of 1814," painted in 1826, depicts a woman trying to save her young son and wounded husband from Cossacks.[33]

One of the nineteenth century's most celebrated paintings, Théodore Géricault's "Raft of the Medusa" (1819), at first glance might appear to have little connection to war. Géricault was inspired by the story of the ship *Medusa,* which crashed in 1818 "due to the ignorance and cowardice of its officers, who saved themselves at the expense of their crew and passengers."[34] The survivors made crude rafts out of the driftwood that had once been their ship. Only a few lived to tell the story of the shipwreck to an outraged public. The analogy of the incompetent ship's commanders to incompetent military officers is as transparent as the comparison of the suffering of the *Medusa*'s passengers to the suffering of civilians in wartime. It is no coincidence that Géricault also painted several military themes, including "Wounded Soldiers in a Cart" from 1818 and "The Wounded Cuirassier Leaving the Field of Battle" from 1812, both of which show the tragic consequences of war.

Other paintings showed less confrontational interactions between soldiers and civilians. The soldier's return home was a common theme. Most armies lacked provisions for regular leave for enlisted soldiers, and many soldiers served for long periods of time overseas. This combination meant that families spent years, or even decades, apart. Three paintings in the National Army Museum in Chelsea Barracks, in London, show the moment of this return in somewhat different ways. Henry Nelson O'Neill's 1860 painting "Home Again" shows exhausted soldiers returning from having put down the Sepoy Mutiny in India the previous year. Although bedraggled, the men carry medals and souvenirs showing off their heroic service. The mutiny, along with lurid tales of savageries inflicted upon British civilians by Indians, had received tremendous media attention in England. The men who suppressed it were thus greeted, as O'Neill depicted them, as heroes, although it is noteworthy that in this painting they appear less gallant than one might suppose. Instead, they seem simply tired and relieved to be home.

Another O'Neill painting, "The Soldier's Return," painted around 1861, shows a far more depressing side to military life. In this work, a tired and wounded veteran sits forlornly in a tattered uniform, perhaps because he cannot afford civilian clothes. The stripes on his coat indicate that he is a long-term veteran, but, even so, he might not have been eligible for any pension or medical care. His time in the army, moreover, would likely have placed him at a severe disadvantage in the civilian job market, making it all the harder for him to find a job. Two female figures, presumably his wife and his daughter, gaze at him with sympathetic looks. They are integral figures to the painting, not least because, in the absence of an army medical or pension system, they will be responsible for caring for him for the rest of his life. The painting thus highlights the difficulties women in military families faced.

Similarly, Charles Martin Hodges's "Home Sweet Home" indicates the pressures military service could place on marriage. O'Neill also explored this theme in "Home Again," a painting showing a Highlander receiving a "Dear John" letter. In "Home Sweet Home," painted in 1890, a seated soldier stares across a room at his wife. The scene shows few signs of domesticity; even the fireplace is cold. The title is thus ironic, suggesting perhaps that one or both partners has not been faithful during the husband's long-term service in Africa or Asia. As a set, these paintings suggest the ways that wars and military service affected the lives not just of men but of wives and children, as well.

Not all images were negative. Heroic interpretations of soldiers and war also appeared in nineteenth-century art. R. A. Hillingford's 1882 painting showing the departure of the elite Coldstream Guards regiment for Egypt depicts adoring crowds cheering on immaculately dressed soldiers, with the Houses of Parliament building in the background to remind the viewer of the connection between soldiers and patriotism. Richard Caton Woodville in 1881 and William Watson Race in 1879 both painted critically acclaimed works showing the courage of British soldiers in battle. The latter painting proved to be particularly poignant as it captured the final moments of the elimination of a British column by Zulu warriors at Isandhlwana in what was then one of the British Army's most tragic defeats.

A similar ambivalence appears in literary representations of wars and soldiers. As a group, soldiers are often vilified for their harsh and repressive treatment of soldiers. Javert, the police inspector, is the chief villain of Victor Hugo's 1862 masterpiece *Les Misérables,* but it is the soldiers of the national guard who destroy the barricades and kill Marius Pontmercy's friends. Writers such as Émile Zola, Honoré de Balzac, and Leo Tolstoy also wrote with war at the center of some of their most important works, and soldiers rarely appeared as heroes. More popular writers also used

Charles Martin Hodges's ironic "Home Sweet Home" hints at the often difficult returns families experience after prolonged periods of military service. Note the formal poses and the cold hearth, as well as the way that the gazes of the husband and wife never cross. Courtesy of the Council, National Army Museum.

soldiers and war as key themes, most notably Rudyard Kipling and Arthur Conan Doyle. The latter created a former army officer, Dr. Watson, to narrate his famous Sherlock Holmes stories. Notably, Watson was an army doctor, not a combat officer, although he used the knowledge he gained in the army to help Holmes solve several of his cases.

The most important literary work on war in nineteenth-century Europe, Leo Tolstoy's *War and Peace*, became a continental literary event upon its publication in 1869. The popularity of the work to contemporaries is related at least in part to its connection to the themes highlighted by Paret's discussion of art, mentioned earlier. Tolstoy's masterpiece tied war and the military to emergent senses of nationalism and to the role of common people in shaping national identity. Tolstoy saw war "as the great instrument of change" in European life, especially in Russia, where the war against Napoleon that forms the backdrop to *War and Peace* led to a "very strong feeling for Russia as a moral force."[35] The notion of war as a transformative and transcendent national experience was familiar across Europe, making the book much more than a Russian phenomenon.

Tolstoy's description of war itself came in for a great deal of criticism from contemporary historians and from survivors of the battles Tolstoy depicted. One critic derided Tolstoy's battlefield imagery as "all falsehood and chaos," while another described his treatment of historical subjects as "puppetry and charlatanism."[36] The success of the book therefore did not derive from realistic recountings of events such as the Battle of Austerlitz. Rather, Tolstoy touched a nerve because his understanding of history fit into a developing European ethos that transcended national borders. *War and Peace* rejected the popular idea of history as the product of notable individuals like Napoleon. As part of the philosophy that underpinned the book, Tolstoy "turned his back upon the romanticism of Alexandre Dumas and Walter Scott and proclaimed himself the enemy of all great men."[37] Thus, for Tolstoy, the Napoleonic wars became less the terrible work of one man than a moment for the collective moral power of the Russian nation to rise to defeat the invader. No doubt even French audiences could relate to this manner of thinking after their own sufferings in the Franco-Prussian War, which occurred shortly after the novel was published.

Thus, to Tolstoy, heroes become distinguished less for their actions on battlefields than for their understanding of the metaphysical link to their nation that they represent. In *War and Peace* Field Marshal Mikhail Kutusov receives a sympathetic treatment despite being the commander who loses numerous battles, including humiliating defeats at Austerlitz and Borodino. Even so, he is more heroic in Tolstoy's eyes than the more able Mikhail Barclay de Tolly, whom he replaces, because, according to one Tolstoy biographer, Kutusov "never loses touch" with the Russian people. Barclay de Tolly, being German by ancestry, cannot maintain an important moral link with his soldiers. Kutusov, by contrast, understands the nature of the Russian peasant soldier and, according to Tolstoy, is able thereby to develop the guerrilla strategy that forces the French out of Russia.[38]

Nationalism formed an important part of Tolstoy's worldview. Consequently, *War and Peace* focuses less attention on the nobility as it developed. By the book's end, the suffering of Russian soldiers and peasants takes center stage. Thus, the book is "[begun] as a novel of the aristocracy and completed as a national epic."[39] Although the national themes are in this case Russian, the notion of war as a nationalizing force had broad international appeal, as witnessed by the widespread continental acclaim for the novel and the author.

Of course, not all Europeans read literary works such as *War and Peace*. Nevertheless, the influence of certain pieces reached deeply across class lines. Alfred, Lord Tennyson's famous poem commemorating the charge of the Light Brigade at Balaclava in 1854 became nationally known. The poem appeared within a few months of the actual event and became standard reading for generations of British pupils:

Half a league, half a league,
Half a league onward,
All in the valley of Death

Rode the six hundred.
'Forward, the Light Brigade!
Charge for the guns!' he said:
Into the valley of Death
Rode the six hundred.
'Forward, the Light Brigade!'
Was there a man dismay'd?
Not tho' the soldier knew
Some one had blunder'd:
Theirs not to make reply,
Theirs not to reason why,
Theirs but to do and die:
Into the valley of Death
Rode the six hundred.
Cannon to right of them,
Cannon to left of them,
Cannon in front of them
Volley'd and thunder'd;
Storm'd at with shot and shell,
Boldly they rode and well,
Into the jaws of Death,
Into the mouth of Hell
Rode the six hundred.
Flash'd all their sabres bare,
Flash'd as they turn'd in air
Sabring the gunners there,
Charging an army, while
All the world wonder'd:
Plunged in the battery-smoke
Right thro' the line they broke;
Cossack and Russian
Reel'd from the sabre-stroke
Shatter'd and sunder'd.
Then they rode back, but not
Not the six hundred.
Cannon to right of them,
Cannon to left of them,
Cannon behind them
Volley'd and thunder'd;
Storm'd at with shot and shell,
While horse and hero fell,
They that had fought so well
Came thro' the jaws of Death,
Back from the mouth of Hell,
All that was left of them,
Left of six hundred.
When can their glory fade?
O the wild charge they made!
All the world wonder'd.

Honour the charge they made!
Honour the Light Brigade,
Noble six hundred!

To highlight the heroism of the men of the Light Brigade, Tennyson matched the rhythm of the poem to an older poem commemorating the British victory at Agincourt in 1415. But, in keeping with the ambivalence of nineteenth-century civilians toward war and soldiers, Tennyson saw something more than simple heroism in the charge. This version of the poem includes the line "Someone had blundered," which Tennyson added to emphasize the fruitless nature of the great sacrifice of the brigade. Most published versions in the nineteenth century did not include the line, which, according to legend, Tennyson took out at Queen Victoria's personal request. She evidently thought it detracted from the martial and heroic air she wanted the poem to project. The allegation of poor leadership could also have undermined Britons' faith in aristocratic leadership, which was noticeably poor in the Crimea.

Military images reached deeply into European society, going far beyond literature and painting. Popular theater played on military themes and used battles as centerpieces of their productions. One 1831 play in London featured 90 horses to recreate a battle scene; another used live elephants to create the same effect. In 1850, three major London theaters ran plays with military themes simultaneously. The popular playwright Philip Astley used his own experiences as a sergeant major in the British Army to craft many of these plays. His most popular play was, not surprisingly, *The Battle of Waterloo*. Scott Hughes Myerly even credits Astley's influence with creating the modern spectacle of the circus, complete with "military-style brass bands" and "ringmasters dressed like cavalry officers."[40]

Even philanthropy and evangelism adopted military tropes. In 1865, a London minister, William Booth, began an aggressive movement designed to bring the word of God to the world's poor and the homeless. In 1878, this movement adopted the telling name "The Salvation Army," and it consciously adopted military models in fighting its "war" against moral decadence. The Salvation Army developed a hierarchy, military-style marching bands, and parades. In both Germany and Britain, Lad's Brigades followed a similar route, culminating most famously in Robert Baden-Powell's scouting movement and the attendant creation of the Boy Scouts, in 1908.

Military influences also affected toys and games. One study of toys in late Victorian and Edwardian Britain argues that this period witnessed "something of a craze for toy soldiers," among children and even among "the leading literary and political figures of the day." Such toys "turned the current of my life," wrote Winston Churchill of his childhood. Churchill owned literally thousands of toy soldiers. The widespread militarization of play had become so worrisome to pacifists that Oscar Wilde's wife made a speech in 1888 to the International Arbitration and Peace Society in which she argued that such toys should be kept away from children altogether. Her efforts were in vain, especially after the 1893 invention of a hollowing method for making lead toy soldiers, which made the toys cheaper to manufacture and to ship. The new method brought sales of such toys to unprecedented levels. By 1900, British toy companies were marketing more than 100 different models of toy soldiers, most of them wearing British regimental uniforms.[41]

War affected children in other ways, as well. Stephen Heathorn argues that war was "a central theme in the books that taught them how to read."[42] Military drill was also a critical method for teaching physical fitness in the nineteenth century. Moreover, wars formed a main component of history lessons for the same reasons that some painters turned to military themes, namely the promotion of nationalism. Military themes grew more pervasive in education as the nineteenth century progressed. By 1894, one representative teacher's manual urged teachers to keep military influences in their curricula, arguing that they were both natural and healthy. To cite one other example, the leading author of French history textbooks noted that "If the pupil does not become a soldier who loves his gun, the teacher will have wasted his time."[43] Such influences appeared in the educations of both boys and girls. They served to remind students of a shared history and underscored the role of the military in forming patterns of citizenship.

The fascination with military subjects did not stop in the schools. Adolphe Thiers's *History of the Consulate and the Empire of France under Napoleon* evolved into a 20-volume series of extremely popular books published between 1845 and 1862. They were among the best-selling books in France. Only Alexandre Dumas's legendary *Three Musketeers* sold more, and that book, too, had a military theme, set as it was during France's religious wars with Spain. The return of Napoleon's body from St. Helena and its placement inside Les Invalides, in 1840, helped to revive popular interest in Napoleon. Cuttings from plants allegedly taken from St. Helena were popular items in French gardens, and relics associated with the great emperor quickly became expensive collection pieces for France's wealthiest citizens.[44]

War also influenced fashion. At various points in the nineteenth century, the aesthetic of military uniforms appeared in civilian clothing. Epaulets, brass buttons, and hat styles (including the knit mask known as a balaclava) are all cases in point. Specific examples include the navy's double-breasted reefer jacket, which buttoned on the side so that the rigging lines would not get caught in sailors' jackets when "reefing" (or rolling) sails. The design influenced the development of the men's blazer, the most popular color for which was, of course, navy blue. To emphasize the masculine and martial nature of the garment, the feminine version buttoned on the left side, not on the right as the reefer did. This convention remains standard today. The buttoned sweater favored by officers of Lord Cardigan's army in the Crimea retains the name of its creator, as does the raglan sleeve, designed by an officer in Lord Raglan's army to defend against the Russian cold. British soldiers returning from India also introduced and helped to popularize pajamas as a replacement for nightshirts. Cavalry twill, cummerbunds, and khakis, too, have military origins. To cite one final example, the wearing of plaids by civilians may have been influenced by the military uniforms of Scottish and Irish units in the British Army that civilians saw on parade or maneuvers.

THE CIVILIAN EXPERIENCE OF WAR

As we have already noted, civilians in this era were normally spared the horrors of war experienced by civilians in the preceding and following centuries. The downfall of Napoleon, in 1815, ended (at least for a time) the constant advance and retreat of armies across the European continent. By contrast, the wars of the nineteenth century were normally contained in small areas and limited to brief periods of time. While historians often consider the eighteenth century the period of "limited wars," this sobriquet applies equally to the nineteenth century after 1815. Even some of the period's most dramatic and important wars were of relatively short duration. The Austro-Prussian War of 1866 took less than seven weeks of operations in Bohemia to decide, and the main conventional actions of the Franco-Prussian War were over in approximately seven months.

Nor did the wars of the nineteenth century normally sink to the depths of barbarity of other periods. Most of the nineteenth century wars were what German military thinkers called "cabinet wars," fought for specific goals by professional armies. Although they could still be fought with intense hatred and cause widespread devastation, these wars were neither religious nor ethnic in their motivations. Thus, the atrocities of the Thirty Years' War (1618–1648), fueled in part by confessional passions, were generally absent in the nineteenth century. Moreover, while in their colonies or on frontiers western armies practiced what some scholars have called proto-genocidal policies, these practices did not appear on large scales in Europe itself until the hatred of the Balkan Wars (1912–1913) and the genocide perpetrated against the Armenians in 1915.[45] Turkish atrocities against Bulgarian civilians in 1875 and 1876 showed the direction in which Europe was headed, but they, too, stopped well short of genocide.

When wars struck, however, they did so with a fury that left civilians bewildered, impoverished, and often devastated. Most often this devastation was economic in nature. Armies on campaign needed more supplies than they could bring with them. In the best cases, organized army quartermasters arranged to buy food, fodder, and lodging from peasants and townspeople as they advanced. This method was expensive but kept all parties satisfied. Especially if the civilian merchants could arrange favorable terms, they might welcome wars as means to get rich quick. Foreign armies, of course, paid in foreign currency (they rarely paid in gold or silver), meaning that civilians often had a financial stake in the outcome of war. Sometimes armies paid in special military scrip, which was reimbursable for hard currency only if the side issuing the scrip actually won the war. Thus, a farmer or merchant might sell goods to an army, only to learn later that the compensation he had received was worthless.

Armies also needed places to stay. Selling lodging proved more problematic than selling supplies, because lodging meant the presence of soldiers (whether the enemy's or one's own) for days, weeks, or even months. Few communities wanted hungry and bored soldiers of any allegiance around their food, drink, and daughters. Consequently, many relatively wealthy towns paid poorer neighboring communities to house soldiers in a fashion similar to draftees buying substitutes. The relationship was not always confrontational, as many civilians struck up friendships with soldiers, many of whom sought to build good will by helping with harvests or plantings in exchange for money or food.

Such relationships between soldiers and civilians, while not always characterized by friction, were always unequal. Invading armies did not always pay for what they needed; they often just seized the goods they wanted as the contraband of war. Indeed, the rules of war permitted an invading force to requisition what it needed from local populations. Of course, many armies took much more than they needed. Towns that did not cooperate or offered resistance often received no mercy. Many such towns simply disappeared off the map.

The second phase of the Franco-Prussian War brought increased misery to civilian communities as a consequence of the changing nature of the war. The defeat of the main French field armies did not lead to the end of hostilities. Instead, groups of irregular French soldiers known as *franc-tireurs* continued the struggle, although at a much lower level of intensity. German soldiers developed a heightened fear of such partisan fighters, whom they did not see as members of a legitimate military system. Rather, the German army saw *francs-tireurs* as civilians and thus as criminals who had no legal right of recourse to military justice or international law. The German Army thus summarily executed *francs-tireurs* who fell into their grasp and tried to solve the *franc-tireur* menace by exacting punishment on towns that harbored irregulars. These punishments ranged from imposing fines on town councils to, in some extreme cases, burning entire towns. This method not only increased the suffering of civilians but also proved to be ineffective, except at the cathartic level.

Armies used their power and the protections afforded them by international law to extract complete surrenders from enemy towns. A common German practice during the Franco-Prussian War involved siting cannon 1,500 yards from a village or town's defensive walls (that is, just outside rifle range) and demanding either food or a high ransom to spare the town.[46] Sometimes, the besieger demanded that towns hand over mayors and other local notables to be kept as prisoners until the residents delivered the promised goods. In some cases, the Germans paid for the goods so acquired, but more often they took what they wanted and left behind notes obligating the French government to pay locals for goods seized. Many merchants, frustrated at the French Army's inability to protect them, inflated their charges many times over. In cases where invading armies could not or would not pay, troops simply took whatever they needed—or wanted.

An interesting observation on the damage a nineteenth-century army might cause to civilians comes from an American observer of the Franco-Prussian War, General Philip Sheridan. Sheridan knew a thing or two about inflicting damage on civilian communities from his experience as a cavalry commander for the Union in the American Civil War. Like his comrade William Tecumseh Sherman, Sheridan had made war on Confederate property, seizing or destroying everything he and his men could get their hands on as a means to force southern civilians to admit that the Confederacy could not win the war. Sheridan later turned this destructive power on the American Indians on the western frontier; he usually receives the "credit" for popularizing the phrase "the only good Indian is a dead Indian."

For all that he had seen and done in America, however, Sheridan was impressed by the behavior of German troops toward French civilians. Observing the war from German headquarters after the major victory at Sedan, Sheridan remarked with considerable professional admiration on the German strategy for turning a victory in that battle into a plan for winning for the war:

The proper [German] strategy consists in inflicting as [many] telling blows as possible on the enemy's army, and then in causing the inhabitants so much suffering that they must long for peace, and force the government to demand it. The people must be left nothing but their eyes to weep with over the war.[47]

This harshness notwithstanding, it is worth noting that the goal of the German brutality was to bring the enemy to peace, not to enact genocide. That goal the German soldiers of the nineteenth century left to the German soldiers who participated in genocide in World War II.

Thus, the presence of an enemy army might prove to be devastating, but, ironically, the presence of a friendly army might not be much better. Hungry, bedraggled, and anxious soldiers rarely hesitated to use harsh tactics on their own people, especially if they were far from their home regions. Needing food, shelter, or firewood, soldiers rarely drew fine distinctions of politics; more often, they simply took what they needed. They led away livestock, broke up furniture for fuel, and ransacked wine cellars. Friendly troops often rationalized their system for requisitioning supplies by arguing that local peasants had a responsibility to contribute to their own defense. Locals thus often saw little difference between being invaded by the enemy and being invaded by the soldiers of one's own army.

When retreating, armies could be even crueler. In an effort to deny supplies to a pursuing enemy, soldiers often scorched ground, leaving nothing in their path. Soldiers poisoned wells, slaughtered animals, and set fire to granaries and larders. The sight of a retreating army setting fire to the very villages they were unable to protect underscored the desperate plight of those civilians unfortunate enough to be caught in the middle. Left without homes, crops, or livestock, most peasants had little choice but to gather their few remaining belongings and begin walking away from the path of the enemy's troops in the hope of finding help somewhere. The sight of columns of helpless refugees walking with their meager possessions and no certain destination had the power to move the hearts of even the coldest commanders. Refugees often lost hope, plundered towns they passed through, and caused no end of problems for local officials who attempted to enforce the law.

In such cases, civilians suffered horribly from the voracious ability of armies to "requisition" supplies. One German officer noted, of the war in France in 1870, "I am shocked by the misery that war brings to peasants. . . . Every village in these parts [near Metz] has been eaten out by successive echelons, leaving the locals with nothing, yet ever more troops arrive needing food."[48] Even soldiers sympathetic to the plight of suffering civilians could do little to help. Nor did the end of war end the misery of the peasantry. With livestock slaughtered and driven off, crops burned, and stores ransacked, peasants struggled terribly to find enough food to meet immediate needs as well as seed crops for the next year's harvests. Like a hurricane or a tornado, a single day's experience with war could leave a community scarred (both physically and psychologically) for months or even years.

War thus often appeared to many civilians as a kind of natural disaster, descending quickly and leaving people powerless to help their neighbors, their relatives, or even themselves. Occasionally, however, civilians became proactive and did what they could to protect themselves and their possessions. Peasants became quite crafty in hiding supplies from men in both friendly and enemy armies. Indeed, it was just this ability that made soldiers so skeptical of peasant claims that they had no goods to share or to sell. Hearing a peasant in a relatively well-furnished house claim to have no food might drive a soldier to tear apart furnishings and homes in search of caches of sausages, wine, and other items normally found in peasant communities in all months of the year.

In a few notable cases, townspeople took active measures against their own army in order to save their communities. In early August 1870, during the Franco-Prussian War, the French 74th Regiment took refuge in the Alsatian border town of Wissembourg. Although the town sat on the French side of the border, its residents pleaded with regimental officers not to offer any futile resistance that might lead the Prussians to fire on the town. Residents also refused to feed French soldiers or even give them directions through the town's winding streets. When French soldiers decided to fight on and began firing at German forces outside the town, the locals ended the battle by raising a white flag and lowering the town's drawbridge, thus allowing German forces to come into the city and outflank the French soldiers.[49] Although this event is sometimes read as an example of French defeatism, it is more likely that the residents of Wissembourg believed that saving their town was more important than the strategic and political motivations that placed the town in the line of fire between French and German armies in the first place.

After the conclusion of battles and wars, civilians were often the ones responsible for dealing with the detritus of combat. Lacking an organized system of medical care capable of dealing with mass casualties, armies were not always prepared for caring for the medical needs of their soldiers. By midcentury, the Germans had devised Europe's most effective medical system, with each corps going to war in 1870 with 3 medical detachments, 21 doctors, 450 stretcher bearers, and 12 field hospitals capable of caring for 200 wounded men each.[50] Still, even this system might not be adequate in the wake of large-scale engagements or if the advance of an army left many wounded men behind.

Consequently, civilians were often left to care for wounded men who appeared in or around their towns. Few such people had any sustained medical training; most medical professionals would have likely been pressed into military service at the start of hostilities and long ago dispatched to the front with the local regiment. The courage of civilians who treated horrific military wounds and did what they could to ameliorate the suffering of unfamiliar soldiers should not be underestimated, even if the care these civilians provided often did as much harm as good.

More systematic attempts to improve military medicine also came as a result of the efforts of civilians. A Swiss businessman, Jean Henri Dunant, and an English nurse, Florence Nightingale, deserve much of the credit for modernizing and organizing medical care for wounded soldiers in the nineteenth century. Nightingale went to the Crimea with 38 other nurses determined to put in place contemporary notions of sanitation and emergency medical practices. In the Crimea, her methods helped to reduce the appalling seven-to-one ratio of deaths from disease to deaths in battle for British soldiers. Her success, combined with the truly harrowing tales of conditions in military hospitals telegraphed to London newspapers by field reporters, led to the professionalization of military nursing in most nations by the end of the century.

Nursing allowed women to become directly involved in the wars that men fought. Not all societies welcomed women coming even this close to an arena that had previously marked their near total exclusion. Postunification Germany, for example, trained only men for the jobs of military medic. Women were officially part of a voluntary auxiliary that focused primarily on midwifery and childcare. Still, even in Germany, women took on responsibilities such as feeding and caring for veterans and wounded soldiers, and, in the event of emergencies, military medics of both genders cared for those in need.[51]

Inspired by Nightingale and her comrades in the Crimea, Dunant worked to build an international system to help wounded soldiers from all nations. Horrified at the lack of care (or even the lack of planning for care) at the 1859 battle of Solferino, Dunant wrote a book detailing the suffering of the wounded men he had helped there. His efforts built upon widespread revulsion at the misery of wounded soldiers from the Crimea that Nightingale had helped bring to light. In 1863, Dunant's efforts paid off with the creation of the International Committee of the Red Cross. The following year, a dozen European nations signed a Geneva Convention detailing measures for the protection of wounded soldiers. Since then, the civilian-run Red Cross has dedicated its efforts to caring for the wounded, supervising conditions for prisoners, and ensuring proper burial for the dead, when possible. Over time, of course, the Red Cross has assumed a primary role in disaster relief, as well.

Soldiers were not the only ones to suffer from disease during wars. Wars not only cause a breakdown in the normal standards of local health care but also force large numbers of people together, thereby contributing to germ transmission. Illnesses thus spread more quickly at the same time that adequate medical care becomes more scarce. During the Franco-Prussian War, more than 200,000 French civilians died of smallpox alone, on top of the 23,400 French soldiers who died of the disease. These high mortality figures underscored France's failure to keep pace with scientific advancements in the fields of sanitation and public health. Although a Frenchman, Louis Pasteur, had first systematically advanced germ theory, the French government and army had been slow to make use of this theory. Prussia, which lost just 400 soldiers and a minimal number of civilians to smallpox, had been much more vigilant in adapting both Pasteur's theories and those of Joseph Lister, who advanced the concept of antiseptic surgery.

The war thus exposed a wide chasm in French and Prussian medical practices. Two-thirds of French soldiers who had amputations died of resulting infections, compared to just 1.5 percent of Prussian soldiers. These gaps underscored and played upon cultural stereotypes that projected images of Germans as naturally more clean than their Gallic neighbors. The large number of civilian deaths by disease also highlighted France's failure to enact a national program of obligatory vaccinations on the Prussian model. The French Public Health Law of 1902 brought public vaccinations to France, too late to save those who had died during the Franco-Prussian War.[52]

Defeat in war could also lead to moral and spiritual impacts, including intensive self-examination, even among civilians not directly affected by war. The bumbling and incompetence that characterized Napoleon III's handling of the run-up to the Franco-Prussian War and the prosecution of the war itself led to revolutionary changes in French governance. The fallout from the war not only ended Napoleon's Second Empire but also guaranteed that a Third Empire would never form. The new French system quickly moved toward intensive changes at the military and political levels, opening the doors to more middle-class officers and removing many privileges for aristocrats. It also represented an entirely new theory of French governance and political philosophy, with widespread impacts on the social and culture lives of French civilians.[53]

Major Russian reforms also came about in the wake of military defeat, most notably following the national humiliation of the Crimean War. Tsar Alexander II's royal proclamation announcing the end of the war promised reform to pull Russia out of its traditional backwardness. Shortly after concluding the final peace treaty, Alexander lifted the ban on foreign travel for Russians and vastly increased the number of students attending universities. Both of these measures aimed to make the Russian upper and middle classes more sophisticated and better educated.

Most important, Alexander also abolished, at least on paper, the traditional Russian system of serfdom. The war had brought home both the degraded physical condition of the serfs and their lack of any sustained attachment to Russia. Their lack of education, moreover, made military training all that more difficult. Serfs thus made awful soldiers, a condition exacerbated by the unwillingness of many Russian nobles to train their serfs in the use of weapons for fear of a serf rebellion. Talk of emancipation had been widespread even before the war, but the defeat on the battlefield starkly revealed the need for major reform. In 1861, Alexander II formally announced the end of serfdom, although the Russian aristocracy's desires not to move too fast combined with a lack of meaningful land reform to limit the actual freedom enjoyed by newly liberated Russians.

Spanish civilians, although thousands of miles from the theaters of the Spanish-American War of 1898, nevertheless saw their nation's humiliating defeat as the cause for "a flood of self-examination."[54] The "generation of 1898" blamed corruption and the inefficiency of the monarchy for the defeat, which cost Spain the Philippines and its Caribbean islands and, with them, its status as an international power. The result was a revived republican movement with two wings. Its more militant wing, led by Barcelona's Alejandro Leroux, argued that Spain's backwardness came from the arch-conservative nature of its monarchical institutions (including the army) and Catholic traditions.

Leroux's association of the church, the army, and the monarchy with Spanish decadence and decline had deadly results. In 1909, when Spanish women began handing crosses to soldiers headed for Morocco (note the symbolic links among gender, religion, and the military), Leroux's followers responded by attacking nuns and burning down convents.[55] What became known as Tragic Week resulted in the formation of a more conservative republican party and a furthering of the divisions of Spanish politics that eventually contributed to the outbreak of civil war in Spain in 1936.

Defeat also brought more immediate consequences. Most obviously, defeat could mean a region's transfer from one state to another. When redrawing political boundaries, of course, statesmen rarely took the needs and desires of locals into consideration. Major changes in political boundaries that occurred as a result of war included the seizure of Lombardy from Austria by the Kingdom of Sardinia-Piedmont, with French support, in 1859. Sardinia-Piedmont then compensated the French for their support by ceding to them Nice and Savoy. Seven years later, Sardinia-Piedmont took advantage of Austria's preoccupation in the Seven Weeks' War with Prussia to capture Venetia, thus laying the foundation for the unification of Italy. That war also led to Prussia's taking control of the provinces of Schleswig and Holstein, which had been under shared Prussian-Austrian domination since 1864. Residents there thus experienced three different governments in as many years.

The most important such territorial exchange occurred after the Franco-Prussian War of 1870–1871. The new nation of Germany annexed the valuable French provinces of Alsace and Lorraine from France. The French had attempted to offer Germany other compensation, including colonies and a portion of the French fleet, but the unequal position of the two states in 1871 sealed Alsace-Lorraine's fate and rendered empty pledges by French politicians not to cede "a clod of our earth." These losses stung France badly on many levels. Economically, the two regions contained much of France's industry; strategically, they left France's frontiers much more difficult to guard; politically, they transferred the important city of Strasbourg, which had been French since the time of Louis XIV, to Germany.

But the loss of Alsace-Lorraine stung France's pride most of all. The new French Third Republic responded by placing a black shroud over the statue representing Strasbourg in Paris's central Place de la Concorde, located between the Louvre and the Champs Élysées. It stood there under its funereal cover until the French recovered the two provinces, in 1918, as a daily reminder of a loss that the French politician Léon Gambetta told Frenchmen they should think of always but speak of never. French geographers continued to place the provinces inside French borders on their maps, often in dark colors designed to elicit feelings of mourning. French nationalists made the two "lost provinces" the central symbols of the "mutilation" of France.

Tens of thousands of Frenchmen and women left Alsace-Lorraine rather than live under German rule. They included the future French president Raymond Poincaré, who left his home with his family at the age of 11.

Poincaré carried the lasting memory of his home with him as he became a key feature in French nationalist politics. One of France's most aggressive generals from World War I, Charles Mangin, was also a native of the lost provinces and used his anger as motivation during the war. Rootless and dispossessed Alsatians and Lorrainers also moved in large numbers to the French colonies, most notably to Algeria, where they contributed to the growing population of poor Europeans known as the *pieds noirs.*

For the French residents who remained in Alsace and Lorraine, occupation meant major, long-term changes to daily life. The German government ordered clocks set to German time, virtually banned the use of both the French and the Alsatian languages in schools and official correspondence, and reoriented the local economy to suit the needs of German industry. Thousands of Germans moved into the regions and took many of the top jobs in government, the professions, and business. Massive changes in the arts and the presence of German military forces emphasized the transition from French control to German and underscored the totality of the change.

Not all French civilians cried over the losses of Alsace and Lorraine. Especially in the south and the west, the losses did not greatly affect daily life. But defeat in the war did cost the French people dearly, no matter where they lived. The war itself had led the French government to spend much of its metal reserves and to print more paper currency, which in turn led to runaway inflation that wiped out savings and ruined investments. To fight the war, France had amassed debts of more than 12 billion francs (approximately $36 billion today) that future governments would need to honor. Germany also imposed on France an indemnity of 5 billion francs (approximately $15 billion today) intended to, in the words of Otto von Bismarck, Germany's chancellor, "cripple France for thirty to fifty years." When French politicians complained that they could not possibly raise that much money, Bismarck threatened that Germany would occupy all of France "and *we* will see if we can get 5 billion from it."[56] The Germans underscored the humiliation of such harsh peace terms with a triumphal victory march through the heart of Paris.

Bismarck did not carry out his threat to occupy all of France, but he did order an occupation of northeastern France in order to guarantee prompt and complete payment of the indemnity. The Germans further exacerbated the humiliation of France by imposing local indemnities on top of the national one to pay for the costs of the occupation. Those indemnities added another billion francs (approximately $3 billion today) to the total bill. The French responded with an aggressive effort to pay the costs of the occupation as quickly as possible in order to hasten the departure of German soldiers. To the surprise of observers both in France and overseas, two national bond drives in 1871 and 1872 (assisted by an unusually bountiful harvest of export crops) raised enough money to end the occupation ahead of the schedule set by German authorities.

The first bond drive involved 331,906 individual subscribers, 88 percent of whom came from outside Paris. The second subscription was even larger, with more than 934,276 subscribers, of whom 85 percent came from outside Paris.[57] These figures indicate a popular groundswell in support of ending the occupation. The interest rates for the two subscriptions (6 percent and 7.88 percent, respectively) were reasonably generous, but not spectacular. They were insufficient to attract large numbers of overseas investors, who accounted for just 6.7 percent of subscribers in the first bond and 11.5 percent of subscribers in the more lucrative second bond.

Paying the indemnity off early allowed the French to end the occupation, but the costs of the war and the indemnity cut deeply into the French economy. The bond subscriptions raised to pay off the indemnity would themselves have to be paid over time, and with interest. The lack of funds available for government spending undercut a French economy that had been steadily growing in the years before the war. The end of that growth also meant the end of the large-scale public works projects that had characterized the Second Empire. These projects included the bridges and streets with which this essay began.

Having to pay indemnities for a lost war (and, worse still, for the cost of the enemy's occupation) was not the only humiliation suffered by civilians in war zones. Occupying soldiers took numerous liberties in the towns they held, pilfering food and souvenirs, propositioning women, and lodging in private homes. Ferdinand Foch, who had volunteered to fight in the Franco-Prussian War but did not see action, recalled as a young man studying for exams to enter the French officer corps in Metz in 1871 that the German occupiers played martial music and *Deutschland über Alles* through the streets on a regular basis. In nearby Nancy, the German occupation commander ordered his band to play "Retreat" at the end of every day to emphasize French humiliation. Foch did not forget these humiliations once the occupiers headed home. Forty-seven years later, as the commander of the allied force that defeated Germany in World War I, he ordered French military bands to accompany advancing French forces and to play French music in every town in Alsace and Lorraine.[58]

CONCLUSION

The 100 years from the downfall of Napoleon, in 1815, to the outbreak of World War I, in 1914, represent an unusually pacific period in European history. The three short, sharp wars of German unification from 1864 to 1871 stand out as exceptions that prove the rule. Prussia's wars with Denmark (1864) and Austria (1866) left few lasting impacts on civilians. The horrors of the Franco-Prussian War and the Paris Commune, by contrast, struck many Europeans as deriving less from the war itself than from France's unwillingness to accept the outcome.

EMBLÈMES PATRIOTIQUES

LE BALLON

LE CHEVAL	DEUX ANNEAUX
LA TORCHE	CROIX DE GENÈVE
L'OBUS	CROIX DE DEUIL
LE SABRE	LE PIGEON

Military symbolism dominates this illustration of "patriotic emblems" from the Franco-Prussian War of 1870–1871. Marianne, the female representation of the French Republic, stands with a dagger in one hand, with a still-burning Paris in the background. The "1870" shield reads "Don't Forget. Work. Wait."

Indeed, nineteenth-century Europeans prided themselves on the progress that their civilizations had made. Many theorists argued that Europe had become so interconnected and sophisticated that future wars, if they occurred at all, would be brief and limited, like the Wars of German Unification. Soldiers still planned for war and regularly updated their stocks of weapons, but even many of them had become convinced that large wars were a part of Europe's past, not its future. Civilians like Norman Angell agreed. His 1910 book *The Great Illusion* argued that nations understood the futility and basic unprofitability of war and would therefore avoid them in the future. A number of thinkers and writers, like the Polish banker Jan Bloch and the communist theorist Frederick Engels, predicted otherwise, but most Europeans felt safe in ignoring their dire warnings of the calamity to come. The shared consensus that Europeans need not fear a long, destructive war helps to account for much of the disillusion and psychological confusion of 1914–1918.

This chapter has shown the many ways that war did affect the daily lives of European civilians, but it is worth noting that, in many cases, the effects were stylized and idealized. Most of the wars European states fought occurred far from the continent in their colonial empires. Because Europeans rarely saw the horrors of war up close, they came to understand it through filters such as the media, poetry, and painting. Most important, wars served as conductors for nationalism and the growing linkages between men and women of all classes with their states. Wars were therefore as important for their strategic meanings as for what those wars meant within domestic contexts. As a result, a Parisian might well walk across the Pont de l'Alma with a certain sense of pride in his nation's martial prowess but without considering the horrors of war that the bridge represents.

Finally, although it is beyond the scope of this essay, it is worth considering how much these idealized representations of war affected the outbreak of the First World War. Having known only short wars and having believed that the horrors of the Napoleonic period could never recur in a more sophisticated and more civilized Europe, civilians and military leaders alike entered into war with no realistic idea of what they were unleashing. The result was four years of unimaginable suffering and a fundamental change in the ways that war and civilians interacted.

NOTES

1. Geoffrey Best, *War and Society in Revolutionary Europe, 1770–1870* (New York: St. Martin's Press, 1982), p. 191.

2. F. R. Bridge and Roger Bullen, *The Great Powers and the European States System,* 2nd ed. (London: Longman, 2005), p. 14.

3. Ute Frevert, *A Nation in Barracks: Modern Germany, Military Conscription, and Civil Society* (Oxford: Berg, 2004), pp. 84–85.

4. Marion Miliband, ed., *The Observer of the Nineteenth Century* (London: Longman, 1966), pp. 59–60.

5. These ideas are best represented in the work of the French socialist leader Jean Jaurès. His 1907 book, *L'Armée nouvelle,* is probably the best-articulated account in print. A recent edition is Jean Jaurès, *L'Armée nouvelle* (Paris: Editions Sociales, 1977).

6. Boulanger fled to Belgium after the government issued a warrant for his arrest. Support for his political efforts dwindled, and he died in 1891. For more, see William Irvine, *The Boulanger Affair Reconsidered: Royalism, Boulangism, and the Origins of the Radical Right in France* (Oxford: Oxford University Press, 1989), and Michael Burns, *Rural Society and French Politics: Boulangism and the Dreyfus Affair, 1886–1900* (Princeton: Princeton University Press, 1984).

7. France's right-wing newspaper *L'Action Française* kept a regular "Affaire Dreyfus" column until the outbreak of World War I. Stéphane Audoin-Rouzeau and Annette Becker, *14–18: Understanding the Great War* (New York: Hill and Wang, 2002), p. 118.

8. Douglas Porch, *The March to the Marne: The French Army 1871–1914* (Cambridge: Cambridge University Press, 1981), p. 60.

9. Michael S. Neiberg, *Soldiers' Lives through History*, vol. 4, *The Nineteenth Century* (Westport, CT: Greenwood, 2006) covers this subject in much greater detail.

10. Frevert, *A Nation in Barracks*, p. 155.

11. The anti-hero of Jaroslav Hašek's *The Good Soldier Schweik* (New York: Crowell, 1974) is an excellent case in point. Schweik is an ethnic Czech who, despite having served in the Austro-Hungarian Army, has virtually no attachment to it or to the empire it serves.

12. Frevert, *A Nation in Barracks*, p. 106.

13. Ibid., p. 155.

14. Scott Hughes Myerly, *British Military Spectacle from the Napoleonic Wars through the Crimea* (Cambridge, MA: Harvard University Press, 1996), p. 142.

15. Peter Burroughs, "An Unreformed Army? 1815–1868," in David Chandler and Ian Beckett, eds., *The Oxford Illustrated History of the British Army* (Oxford: Oxford University Press, 1994): 160–188. See the illustration and associated caption on p. 177.

16. Maurice Allem, *La Vie quotidienne sous le Second Empire* (Paris: Hachette, 1948), p. 134.

17. Frevert, *A Nation in Barracks*, p. 213.

18. Myerly, *British Military Spectacle*, p. 160.

19. See chapter 17 of Eugen Weber, *Peasants into Frenchmen: The Modernization of Rural France, 1870–1914* (Stanford: Stanford University Press, 1976).

20. Geoffrey Wawro, *The Franco-Prussian War* (Cambridge: Cambridge University Press, 2003), p. 65.

21. Ibid., pp. 138–139.

22. Quoted in ibid., p. 139.

23. Quoted in Jeremy D. Popkin, *A History of Modern France*, 2nd ed. (London: Prentice Hall, 2001), p. 145.

24. Porch, *The March to the Marne*, pp. 135–136.

25. Quoted in Edward Spiers, "The Late Victorian Army, 1868–1914," in Chandler and Beckett, eds., *The Oxford Illustrated History of the British Army*, 189–214, quotation on p. 210.

26. Porch, *March to the Marne*, pp. 149–150.

27. Mark Rathbone, "Gladstone, Disraeli, and the Bulgarian Horrors," *History Review* 50 (December 2004): 3–7, quotation at p. 3.

28. The literature on the Bulgarian Horrors is thin, but see Harold Temperley, *The Bulgarian and Other Atrocities, 1875–8 in the Light of Historical Criticism* (London:

British Academy, 1931), and David Harris, *Britain and the Bulgarian Horrors of 1876* (Chicago: University of Chicago Press, 1939).

29. Peter Paret, *Imagined Battles: Reflections of War in European Art* (Chapel Hill: University of North Carolina Press, 1997), p. 65.

30. Geoffrey Wawro, *Warfare and Society in Europe, 1792–1914* (London: Routledge, 2000), p. 35.

31. Paret, *Imagined Battles*, p. 81.

32. Ross King, *The Judgment of Paris: The Revolutionary Decade That Gave the World Impressionism* (New York: Walker, 2006), p. 10.

33. Paret, *Imagined Battles*, pp. 72–74, 79.

34. Sister Wendy Beckett, *Sister Wendy Beckett's 1000 Masterpieces* (New York: DK Publishing, 1999), p. 169.

35. Henry Gifford, *Tolstoy* (Oxford: Oxford University Press, 1982), p. 28.

36. Henri Troyat, *Tolstoy* (Garden City, NY: Doubleday, 1967), pp. 299–300.

37. Ibid., p. 312.

38. Gifford, *Tolstoy*, p. 28.

39. Troyat, *Tolstoy*, p. 313.

40. Myerly, *British Military Spectacle*, pp. 145–146.

41. Kenneth D. Brown, "Modelling for War? Toy Soldiers in Late Victorian and Edwardian Britain," *Journal of Social History* 24, 2 (Winter 1990): 237–254. Quotations from pp. 241 and 243.

42. Stephen Heathorn, "Representations of War and Martial Heroes in English Elementary School Reading and Rituals, 1885–1914," in James Martin, ed., *Children and War: A Historical Anthology* (New York: New York University Press, 2002), pp. 103–115. Quotation from p. 103.

43. Quoted in Roger Magraw, *France, 1800–1914: A Social History* (London: Longman, 2002), p. 201.

44. King, *Judgment of Paris*, pp. 9–11.

45. On the drift to total war by European and American armed forces in nineteenth-century colonies and on the frontier, see two essays from Manfred Boemeke, Roger Chickering, and Stig Förster, eds., *Anticipating Total War: The German and American Experiences, 1871–1914* (Cambridge: Cambridge University Press, 1999). The essays are Robert Utley, "Total War on the American Indian Frontier," on pp. 399–414, and Trutz von Trotha, "'The Fellows Can Just Starve': On Wars of 'Pacification' in the African Colonies of Imperial Germany and the Concept of 'Total War,'" on pp. 415–436. The British creation of concentration camps for Boer civilians is also a case in point.

46. Wawro, *The Franco-Prussian War*, p. 263.

47. Quoted in Michael Howard, *The Franco-Prussian War* (London: Routledge, 1961), p. 380.

48. Quoted in Wawro, *The Franco-Prussian War*, p. 145.

49. Ibid., pp. 101–102.

50. Dennis Showalter, *The Wars of German Unification* (London: Arnold, 2004), p. 293.

51. Jean H. Quataert, "Mobilizing Philanthropy in the Service of War: The Female Rituals of Care in the New Germany, 1871–1914," in Boemeke, Chickering, and Förster, eds. *Anticipating Total War*, pp. 217–238.

52. Andrew R. Aisenberg, *Contagion: Disease, Government, and the "Social Question" in Nineteenth Century France* (Stanford: Stanford University Press, 1999), p. 130.

53. See, among others, Eugen Weben, *France: Fin de siècle* (Cambridge, MA: Belknap Press of Harvard University, 1986), and R. D. Anderson, *France 1870–1914: Politics and Society* (London: Routledge, 1977).

54. Raymond Carr, "Liberalism and Reaction," in Raymond Carr, ed., *Spain: A History* (Oxford: Oxford University Press, 2000), pp. 205–242, quotation at 224.

55. Carr, "Liberalism and Reaction," pp. 230–238.

56. Wawro, *The Franco-Prussian War*, pp. 303–310.

57. Allan Mitchell, *The German Influence in France after 1870: The Formation of the French Republic* (Chapel Hill: University of North Carolina Press, 1979), pp. 26 and 39. See also Charles P. Kindleberger, *A Financial History of Western Europe* (Hemel Hempstead: George Allen and Unwin, 1984), pp. 239–251.

58. Michael S. Neiberg, *Foch: Supreme Allied Commander in the Great War* (Dulles, VA: Brassey's, 2003), p. 5.

FURTHER READING

The literature on this subject is remarkably thin, mostly because of the limited nature of war in this period. Good general surveys of war in nineteenth-century Europe include Geoffrey Best, *War and Society in Revolutionary Europe, 1770–1870* (New York: St. Martin's Press, 1982); Geoffrey Wawro, *Warfare and Society in Europe, 1792–1914* (London: Routledge, 2000); Brian Bond, *War and Society in Europe, 1870–1970* (Guernsey: Sutton, 1984); Jeremy Black, *Western Warfare, 1775–1882* (Bloomington: Indiana University Press, 2001); Jeremy Black, *Warfare in the Western World, 1882–1975* (Bloomington: Indiana University Press, 2002); the dated but still useful Byron Farwell, *Queen Victoria's Little Wars* (New York: Harper and Row, 1972); and Bruce Vandervort, *Wars of Imperial Conquest in Africa* (London: Routledge, 1998). See also the essays in Manfred Boemeke, Roger Chickering, and Stig Förster, eds., *Anticipating Total War: The German and American Experiences, 1871–1914* (Cambridge: Cambridge University Press, 1999).

Nation-specific case studies include Ute Frevert, *A Nation in Barracks: Modern Germany, Military Conscription, and Civil Society* (Oxford: Berg, 2004); Douglas Porch, *The March to the Marne: The French Army 1871–1914* (Cambridge: Cambridge University Press, 1981); Hollis Clayson, *Paris in Despair: Art and Everyday Life under the Siege* (Chicago: University of Chicago Press, 2005); and David Chandler and Ian Beckett, eds., *The Oxford Illustrated History of the British Army* (Oxford: Oxford University Press, 1994). The Franco-Prussian War has been the subject of two excellent studies: Michael Howard, *The Franco-Prussian War* (London: Routledge, 1961), and Geoffrey Wawro, *The Franco-Prussian War* (Cambridge: Cambridge University Press, 2003). Wawro is also the author of the most complete study of the Austro-Prussian War. See his *The Austro-Prussian War: Austria's War with Prussia and Italy in 1866* (Cambridge: Cambridge University Press, 1996). Dennis Showalter, *The Wars of German Unification* (London: Arnold, 2004) deftly treats these three wars a whole.

Some of the best works on the cultural component of war in nineteenth-century Europe include Scott Hughes Myerly, *British Military Spectacle from the Napoleonic Wars through the Crimea* (Cambridge, MA: Harvard University Press, 1996); Peter Paret, *Imagined Battles: Reflections of War in European Art* (Chapel Hill: University of North Carolina Press, 1997); Kenneth D. Brown, "Modelling for

War? Toy Soldiers in Late Victorian and Edwardian Britain," *Journal of Social History* 24, 2 (Winter 1990): 237–254; and Stephen Heathorn, "Representations of War and Martial Heroes in English Elementary School Reading and Rituals, 1885–1914" in James Martin, ed., *Children and War: A Historical Anthology* (New York: New York University Press, 2002), pp. 103–115.

Index

About the Contributors

Michael Broers became a fellow of Lady Margaret Hall and a member of the history faculty of Oxford University in 2004, after a career in several universities in the United States and the United Kingdom. Broers was a senior Leverhulme Research Fellow, 2002–2003, and in 2003 was a visiting member at the Institute for Advanced Study, Princeton.

He is the author of five books: *Europe under Napoleon* and *Europe after Napoleon* (both 1996); *Napoleonic Imperialism and the Savoyard Monarchy* (1990; won the prize of the International Napoleonic Society); *The Politics of Religion in Napoleonic Italy, 1801–1814* (2002); and, most recently, *The Napoleonic Empire in Italy. Cultural Imperialism in a European Context?* (2005), winner of the Prix Napoléon, 2006, awarded by the Fondation Napoléon, in Paris. He has also published in *The American Historical Review, Past & Present, The Historical Journal,* and the *English Historical Review,* as well as in publications in France and Italy. His third book, *Napoleonic Imperialism and the Savoyard Monarchy* (1997), won the prize of the International Napoleonic Association. He is currently writing a book provisionally entitled *Napoleonic Civilization: A Regime and Its Agendas.*

Linda S. Frey and Marsha L. Frey are professors of history at the University of Montana and Kansas State University, respectively. After receiving PhDs from The Ohio State University, they have written in tandem *Frederick I, the Man and His Time; A Question of Empire: Leopold I and the War of the Spanish Succession, 1701–1705; The History of Diplomatic Immunity;* and *The French*

Revolution and have edited *The Treaties of the War of the Spanish Succession,* among other works.

Both have held visiting professorships at the U.S. Military Academy, West Point.

Fellowships from the National Endowment for the Humanities (NEH), the Earhart Foundation, the American Council of Learned Societies (ACLS), the U.S. Department of Education, the American Philosophical Society, and the International Center for Jefferson Studies have funded their research on early modern Europe and the development of international law.

Tryntje Helfferich's research focuses on the imperial German state of Hesse-Cassel during the Thirty Years' War, and especially on the period of the reign of the Hessian landgravine Amalia Elisabeth. She received her master's degree at the University of New Mexico, Albuquerque, and her PhD at the University of California, Santa Barbara. She is currently writing a source book, *A Documentary History of the Thirty Years War,* and is completing a political biography of Amalia Elisabeth titled *"The Scepter Rests Well in the Hands of a Woman": Faith, Politics, and the Thirty Years War.*

Michael S. Neiberg is professor of history and co-director of the Center for the Study of War and Society at the University of Southern Mississippi. He is the author or editor of nine books and numerous articles and specializes in World War I and the global dimensions of the history of warfare. His most recent books include *Fighting the Great War: A Global History* and *Soldiers' Daily Lives: The Nineteenth Century* (Praeger). He is currently at work on a study of the Second Battle of the Marne and a larger project on the interrelationship of war and peace since 1756.

At Southern Miss, Dr. Neiberg regularly teaches undergraduate and graduate courses in French history, the history of the two world wars, and the history of war and peace more generally. He is currently serving as the department of history's director of graduate studies and the head of Southern Miss's USM in Paris program. Before coming to Southern Miss, Dr. Neiberg taught at the U.S. Air Force Academy and at Carnegie Mellon University.

Michael Rowe is lecturer in modern European history at King's College London and fellow of the Royal Historical Society. Previously, he held a lectureship in Queen's University Belfast (1999–2004) and a research fellowship in Nuffield College Oxford (1996–1999). He was awarded his doctorate from Cambridge University in 1996 and his BA from the University of London in 1992.

Rowe's research interests are focused on Continental Europe in the era spanning the French Revolution and Napoleon, with particular focus on the German-speaking lands. Thematically, he has ranged widely, looking in particular at modernization and state and nation building and at matters associated with these broad processes: administrative structures, propaganda, the formation of identities, concepts of citizenship, center-periphery conflicts, and the role of military conscription in integrating new populations, to name some of the more important. Publications include the award-winning book *From Reich to State: The Rhineland in the Revolutionary Age, 1780–1830* and the edited volume *Collaboration and Resistance in Napoleonic Europe. State-Formation in an Age of Upheaval, c. 1800–1815* (2003), as well as numerous chapters and articles devoted to the Napoleonic period.

Dennis Showalter is professor of history at Colorado College, past president of the Society for Military History, and joint editor of *War in History.* His primary academic interest is establishing the operational effectiveness of military cultures in the context of the societies to which those cultures belong.

Professor Showalter is the author or editor of 20 books and more than 100 articles, essays, and contributions to anthologies. His major relevant publications include *The Wars of Frederick the Great* (1996); "The Prussian Military State" (2004); and "Hubertusburg to Auerstaedt: The Prussian Army in Decline?" (1994).

Paul Sonnino is professor of history at the University of California, Santa Barbara, and specializes in the seventeenth century. He received his BA, MA, and PhD from UCLA and has written, in addition to a number of articles, several books, including *Louis XIV's View of the Papacy, 1661–1667* (1996), *Louis XIV: Mémoires for the Instruction of the Dauphin* (1970), and *The Refutation of Machiavelli's Prince: Anti-Machiavel* (1981), among others. Professor Sonnino is currently writing a book on the Treaty of Westphalia, "combining sadomasochist sex with court intrigue, war, diplomacy, and a hundred million Europeans." He is also just one document short of revealing the identity of the Man in the Iron Mask.

Recent Titles in the
Greenwood Press "Daily Lives of Civilians during Wartime" Series

Daily Lives of Civilians in Wartime Africa: From Slavery Days to the Rwandan Genocide
John Laband, editor

Daily Lives of Civilians in Wartime Early America: From the Colonial Era to the Civil War
David S. Heidler and Jeanne T. Heidler, editors

Daily Lives of Civilians in Wartime Modern America: From the Indian Wars to the Vietnam War
David S. Heidler and Jeanne T. Heidler, editors

Daily Lives of Civilians in Wartime Asia: From the Taiping Rebellion to the Vietnam War
Stewart Lone, editor